Loeb Classical Monographs

In Memory of James C. Loeb

Chance and Intelligence in Thucydides

Lowell Edmunds

Harvard University Press

Cambridge, Massachusetts

1975

The Loeb Classical Monographs are published with assistance
from the Loeb Classical Library Foundation

3-2-76

Library of Congress Catalog Card Number 74–75311

ISBN 0–674–10740–3

Printed in the United States of America

To John H. Finley, Jr.

Preface

This monograph, a rewritten Ph.D. thesis, was not altogether an individual effort but received encouragement and furtherance from the beginning. I studied the antithesis of chance and intelligence first in the later Euripides with Professor Cedric H. Whitman. My thesis adviser was Professor John H. Finley, Jr. In the course of research and writing, conversations on Thucydides with fellow students Douglas Frame, Leonard Muellner, and Rolly Phillips were a help and a pleasure. I am especially indebted to Professor Robert Renehan of Boston College for counsel and instruction.

The penultimate draft was carefully read by Dr. Daniel P. Tompkins, who saved me from many an error. I am grateful also to an anonymous referee for his or her detailed criticisms. Miss Margaret Barton and Mrs. Louise DeGiacomo typed the manuscript accurately and with despatch.

Final revisions and additions were made during a stay of several months in Munich. The helpfulness of Herr Miklos Farkas, the supervisor of the classical library in Ludwig-Maximilians-Universität, and the hospitality of Dr. Siegmar Döpp and Professor Uvo Hölscher were a blessing.

L. E.

Contents

Contents

Chance and Intelligence in Thucydides

Abbreviations

AC	*L'Antiquité Classique*
AJP	*American Journal of Philology*
BICS	*Bulletin of the Institute of Classical Studies of the University of London*
CJ	*Classical Journal*
CP	*Classical Philology*
CQ	*Classical Quarterly*
CR	*Classical Review*
CW	*Classical World*
D.-K.	H. Diels, W. Kranz, *Die Fragmente der Vorsokratiker*[11]. Zurich and Berlin, 1964.
Gomme, I	A. W. Gomme, *A Historical Commentary on Thucydides,* vol. I. Oxford: Oxford University Press, 1950.
Gomme, II	———*A Historical Commentary on Thucydides,* vol. II. Oxford: Oxford University Press, 1956
Gomme, III	———*A Historical Commentary on Thucydides,* vol. III. Oxford: Oxford University Press, 1956.
Gomme, IV	A. W. Gomme, A. Andrewes, K. J. Dover, *A Historical Commentary on Thucydides,* vol. IV. Oxford: Oxford University Press, 1970.
Gymn.	*Gymnasium*
HSCP	*Harvard Studies in Classical Philology*
JHS	*Journal of Hellenic Studies*
LSJ	Liddell and Scott, *Greek-English Lexicon,* 9th ed., rev. H. Stuart Jones, 1925–1940.
MH	*Museum Helveticum*
OCD[2]	*The Oxford Classical Dictionary*[2]. Oxford, 1970.
Philol.	*Philologus*
RE	A. Pauly, G. Wissowa, and W. Kroll, *Real-Encyclopädie d. Klassischen Altertums Wissenschaft,* 1893–
REA	*Revue des Etudes Anciennes*
REG	*Revue des Etudes Grecques*
Rev. de Phil.	*Revue de Philologie de Litterature et d'Histoire Anciennes*
RFIC	*Rivista di Filologia e d'Istruzione Classica*
RM	*Rheinisches Museum*
TAPA	*Transactions and Proceedings of the American Philological Association*
YCS	*Yale Classical Studies*
YFS	*Yale French Studies*
ZPE	*Zeitschrift für Papyrologie und Epigraphik*

Introduction

"Intelligence" in the title of this study is an intention-
ally general rubric for the complex of notions implied by
techne (τέχνη) and *gnome* (γνώμη)—perception, foresight,
planning, technical competence, and the like. "Chance"
is a translation of *tyche* (τύχη).

The techne-tyche and gnome-tyche antitheses, the
germs of which are to be found even in Homer, were
commonplace in Thucydides' time.[1] The sophists intended to better man's lot through the arts of life.[2] The
Hippocratics saw medicine as the conqueror of tyche.

1. See the analysis in Chap. II, sec. c.2.b, of certain details in the
Funeral Games, *Il.* 23. The word tyche does not occur in the *Il.* and
Od. but in the Homeric Hymns (11.5) and as a proper name in the
Hymn to Demeter (420).
2. F. Heinimann, "Ein vorplatonische Theorie der τέχνη," *MH* 18
(1961), 108. Schmid-Stählin, *Geschichte der griechischen Literatur* I.3
(Munich, 1940), 79. In n. 13 on this page, Schmid states that the
techne-tyche antithesis is unknown to Herodotus. Although
Herodotus does not use these very terms, the antithesis is known to
him, as one would expect: . . . Λίχης . . . συντυχίη χρησάμενος καὶ σοφίη
(1.68.1); ἐπιτεχνᾶται ·. . . ἐπιτυχόντων (2.2.2). Cf. the antithesis between
τύχη and σοφίη in Democritus, fr. B 197.

1

Chance and Intelligence in Thucydides

The author of the *De Arte* (for which a fifth-century date is likely) defends medicine as a techne against detractors who attribute its success to tyche (*De Arte* 1ff.; cf. *VM* 1, 12; *Loc. hom.* 46).[3] What could be more fitting for the epitaph of Hippocrates than the statement that he won his great reputation οὐ τύχαι, ἀλλὰ τέχναι (not by chance, but by skill)?[4] Euripides uses the techne-tyche antithesis as if it were *au courant* (*Alc.* 785ff.; *IT* 89), and indeed the wit of Agathon's τέχνη τύχην ἔστερξε καὶ τύχη τέχνην (skill loves chance, and chance loves skill) (fr. 6N) presupposes familiarity with techne and tyche as opposite terms.

The kindred antithesis of gnome and tyche appears in Aeschylus (fr. 389N[3]), Andocides (*De Myst.* 1.140), Gorgias (D.-K. II.295.12), and Lysias (34.2), and may have figured in Socrates' thought (Xen. *Mem.* 1.4.1; cf. 1.4.4, 9).[5]

The present study deals with the broad function of these antitheses in Thucydides' *History*. The antithesis of gnome-tyche occurs more often in Thucydides than in any other fifth-century writer, and the concepts are at work even in places in which the verbal antithesis is not stated.[6] As Cornford said, "in Thucydides γνώμη, man's foresight and decision, and Τύχη share the world be-

3. Heinimann, *MH* 18 (1961), 112, n. 32.
4. *Greek Poems on Stones*, I (Epitaphs), ed. G. Pfohl (Leiden, 1967), 144 (= *AP* VII, 135).
5. In the same spirit, Sophocles contrasts τύχη and πρόνοια (*OT* 977–978); cf. Eur. *IA* 864. The many occurrences of these various related antitheses in the fourth century and later cannot be discussed here.
6. Gnome-tyche in 1.144.4; 2.87.3; 4.64.1; 4.86.6; 5.75.3; 6.78.3; cf. 1.120.5 (γνωσθέντα-τυχόντα). This antithesis is drawn less sharply in 2.62.5 and 4.55.3–4 (cf. 5.75.3), and is implied in 2.62.4 and 7.63.4. An antithesis between τέχνη and τυγχάνω occurs in 1.142.9.

2

tween them."[7] It is fitting to make mention of Cornford's *Thucydides Mythistoricus* at the beginning of a study so much concerned with tyche, since Cornford if anyone was determined to give tyche a place of honor in Thucydides' thought. But Cornford's preconceptions about Thucydides' limitations led him to extravagant conclusions.[8] To take but a single example, Cornford cites as expressions of the same point of view statements by Hermocrates and Pericles which are in fact opposite in meaning.[9] Cornford regarded tyche in the *History* as an indication of Thucydides' religious beliefs. It is the finding of the present study that tyche, and the concepts antithetical to it, techne and gnome, are descriptive and analytical in the *History*.

Thucydides uses these concepts to describe the contrasting outlooks of Athens and Sparta and of various individuals. The first chapter of this study shows how Thucydides consistently characterizes Pericles in terms of gnome and of the gnome-tyche antithesis. The second chapter shows how the Spartans and Nicias are characterized by their deference to tyche.

Thucydides might have described the cities and individuals in the *History* as conceiving of themselves in terms of these antitheses while himself stating or implying that, for example, social and economic forces were the real

7. F. Cornford, *From Religion to Philosophy* (London, 1912), p. 120, n. 1. Cf. A. Parry, "Thucydides' Use of Abstract Language," *Yale French Studies* No. 45 (1970), 20: "The central problem of history is, How, and when, can man impose his *gnome* on things outside himself?"

8. For these preconceptions, see *Thucydides Mythistoricus* (London, 1965), pp. 106ff.

9. Cornford, *Thucydides Mythistoricus*, p. 107.

determinants. But Thucydides clearly regarded gnome, techne, and tyche as historical forces and saw events in these terms among others. The question arises, then, where Thucydides himself stood on these matters. My third chapter investigates this question, especially apropos of Thucydides' statements about his method and his use of τύχη and τυγχάνω.

In this book I seek to distinguish as carefully as possible between views of tyche, techne, and gnome voiced by actors in the *History*, or views attributed to them by Thucydides, and Thucydides' own view, which is not assumed to be identical to any of the former. Nor, it is concluded, can any such simple identification be supported.

A study of Thucydides' statements about his historiographical method suggests that his own stance with respect to tyche, techne, and gnome is quite different from that of anyone in the *History* except Pericles, whom Thucydides resembles intellectually, but only resembles. Indeed, it is just this difference between the actor in history, facing the unknown future, and the historian, looking back on the better-known past, on which the *History* is constructed. Thucydides remains true to both perspectives by narrating events from the actors' point of view, which is often articulated in speeches, while expressing his own point of view in the design of the narrative and in the relation of narrative and speeches.

Thus there may be two truths, that of the actor and that of the historian. The actor may, for example, fear, attempt to forestall, and then fall prey to what he believes is chance; and his belief is correct, in that he could not, with his limitations, have done other than he did. The

4

historian, however, sees that in this case chance had no absolute power—at least in retrospect, another outcome was possible. But these two truths present themselves, for the most part, as one. Every speech in the *History* is a combination of an ideal speech and the real one (see Chap. III. sec. A.5). The narrative is both empirical and artistic. Here and there Thucydides stands apart and makes a judgment or a comment, and yet all the statements of this sort do not add up to an interpretation of the Peloponnesian War or a philosophy of history. The conflated truths of history and of historian remain to be distinguished, but cannot be distinguished while one is taken for the other. As regards tyche, techne, and gnome, each of which has already received a good deal of attention,[10] no advance

10. For gnome in Thucydides and in general, see the items cited below, Chap. I, nn. 2, 3, 5, 6, 11. For gnome and tyche in Thucydides, see J. Steup, in Classen-Steup, *Thukydides*, I⁵ (Berlin, 1919), lxii-lxv. For general studies of tyche, see A. A. Buriks, Περὶ τύχης: *De ontwikkeling van het begrip tyche tot ann de Romeinse tijd, hoofdzakelijk in de philosophie* (Leiden, n.d.); H. Herter, *Glück und Verhängnis. Über die altgriechische Tyche, Hellas* (Bonn) IV, 1–2 (1963), 1–16; G. Herzog-Hauser, "Tyche," in *RE* 14, cols. 1643–89; P. Joos, τύχη φύσις τέχνη *Studien zur Thematik frühgriechischen Lebensbetrachtung* (Zurich, 1955); N. Robertson, "Tyche," in *OCD*² (Oxford, 1970), pp. 1100–01; L. Ruhl, "Tyche," in W. H. Roscher, *Ausführliches Lexikon der griechischen und römischen Mythologie* (Leipzig, 1916–1924), V, 1309–57; L. Deubner, ibid., III, 2142–45 (personified Tyche); Wilamowitz, *Der Glaube der Hellenen* (Basel, 1956), II, 294–305. For the fourth century and after: M. Nilsson, *Geschichte der griechischen Religion*² (Munich, 1961), II, 200–221; O. Kern, *Die Religion der Griechen*, III (Berlin, 1938), 74–79. On tyche in Thucydides: Schmid-Stählin, *Geschichte der griechischen Literatur*, I.5, 30–33; H. Herter, "Freiheit und Gebundenheit des Staatsmannes bei Thukydides," *RM* 93 (1950), 133–153, repr. in *Thukydides* (Darmstadt, 1968), pp. 260–281; W. Müri, "Beit-

Chance and Intelligence in Thucydides

can be made beyond prevailing interpretations of their roles in Thucydides so long as they are treated as isolated concepts and so long as it is assumed that Thucydides' thought can be reduced to one such concept or another and that his mood is unambiguous, either pessimism or optimism. On the contrary, the complexity just adumbrated will mean that Thucydides is both detached and compassionate, that his work is both rational and tragic.

A useful convention permits students of Thucydides to speak of his work as the *History*.[11] The present study uses this convention.

rag zum Verständnis des Thukydides," *MH* 4 (1947), 253–255. In Pindar: H. Strohm, *Zur Schicksalsauffassung bei Pindar und den frühgriechischen Dichtern* (Stuttgart, 1944). In Democritus and Leucippus: L. Edmunds, "Necessity, Chance, and Freedom in the Early Atomists," *Phoenix* 26 (1972), 342–357. In Herodotus, H. Bischoff, *Der Warner bei Herodot* (Marburg, 1932), pp. 20–25. In Euripides, G. Busch, *Untersuchungen zum Wesen der τύχη in den Tragödien des Euripides* (Heidelberg, 1937). In Plato, A. Zimmerman, *Tyche bei Platon* (Bonn, 1966). In Aristotle, H. Weiss, *Kausalität und Zufall in der Philosophie des Aristoteles* (Basel, 1942).

For techne, see R. Schaerer, ἐπιστήμη et τέχνη: *Etude sur les notions de connaissance et d'art d'Homère à Platon* (Lausanne, 1930); L. Camerer, *Praktische Klugheit bei Herodot: Untersuchungen zu den Begriffen μηχανή, τέχνη, σοφία* (Cologne, 1965); Heinimann, *MH* 18 (1961), 105–130.

11. J. H. Finley, Jr., *Thucydides* (Cambridge, Mass., 1942), p. 3.

I

Pericles and Gnome

A. The first speech of Pericles (1.140–144)

Since the prooemium to the first speech of Pericles contains the gist of Thucydides' characterization of Pericles as statesman and as political thinker, one must begin here:

'Τῆς μὲν γνώμης, ὦ Ἀθηναῖοι, αἰεὶ τῆς αὐτῆς ἔχομαι, μὴ εἴκειν Πελοποννησίοις, καίπερ εἰδὼς τοὺς ἀνθρώπους οὐ τῇ αὐτῇ ὀργῇ ἀναπειθομένους τε πολεμεῖν καὶ ἐν τῷ ἔργῳ πράσσοντας, πρὸς δὲ τὰς ξυμφορὰς καὶ τὰς γνώμας τρεπομένους. ὁρῶ δὲ καὶ νῦν ὁμοῖα καὶ παραπλήσια ξυμβουλευτέα μοι ὄντα, καὶ τοὺς ἀναπειθομένους ὑμῶν δικαιῶ τοῖς κοινῇ δόξασιν, ἢν ἄρα τι καὶ σφαλλώμεθα, βοηθεῖν, ἢ μηδὲ κατορθοῦντας τῆς ξυνέσεως μεταποιεῖσθαι. ἐνδέχεται γὰρ τὰς ξυμφορὰς τῶν πραγμάτων οὐχ ἧσσον ἀμαθῶς χωρῆσαι ἢ καὶ τὰς διανοίας τοῦ ἀνθρώπου· δι' ὅπερ καὶ τὴν τύχην, ὅσα ἂν παρὰ λόγον ξυμβῇ, εἰώθαμεν αἰτιᾶσθαι.

Athenians, I am ever of the same mind, that we must not yield to the Peloponnesians, though I know that men do not act in war with the same mettle with which they persuade themselves to go to war, but change their policies in accordance with their fortunes. I see that now again I must give you similar counsel, and I think it just that those of you who are persuaded come to the rescue of our common resolutions, if, as it turns out, we meet a setback, or, if we succeed, that you not claim a share in our sagacity. For it is possible for the circumstances of

7

our affairs to take as blundering a course as mortal plans do, too. For this very reason we are accustomed to blame chance for whatever turns out contrary to expectation.[1]

Not only the stylistic excellence of this prooemium, its conciseness, balance, and austerity, which Rose Zahn has so well analyzed,[2] but also its conceptual generality and complexity invite detailed attention. These last traits arouse the expectation that Pericles' statements apply to more than the specific recommendations of policy which he will make. In fact, the emphatic first noun of the prooemium, gnome, proves to be a leitmotiv of Pericles in the *History*, and the concept of gnome proves to be the basis of Pericles' policy.[3] Along with *chremata*, gnome is the basis of Pericles' military strategy (2.13), and although this word occurs only twice in the Funeral Oration, it is clear that Pericles regards gnome as the guiding principle of Athenian life, since he speaks of the Athenian holidays as "rest for the gnome" (2.38.1). Gnome is the standard to which he recalls the Athenians in the third speech, at the time of the plague.

When Pericles uses gnome of himself in the first sentence of the prooemium, the term has two main connotations, that of intelligent policy and that of will. As for the first of these, when Pericles speaks of his gnome he of course means his opinion of what should be done, his

1. Thuc. 1.140.1. Certain points in the translation will be argued for in the following discussion.
2. Rose Zahn, *Die erste Periklesrede (Thukydides I 140–144): Interpretation und Versuch einer Einordnung in den Zusammenhang des Werkes* (Borna-Leipzig, 1934), pp. 10–14.
3. Similarly, γιγνώσκειν is used by Pericles to characterize himself (2.60.5; cf. 2.22.1). Cf. P. Huart, *Le Vocabulaire de l'analyse psychologique dans l'oeuvre de Thucydide* (Paris, 1968), p. 297.

policy. But in contrasting his consistent policy with the policies of the general run of men, which are swayed by emotion (ὀργῇ), he shows that, for him, gnome is a matter of reason.[4] In this way gnome, as Pericles uses the word of himself, comes to mean not simply "policy" but to have the normative sense, too, of "policy based on reason." This sense will become apparent in the discussion of the last speech of Pericles, especially 2.62.4–5. Pericles could not maintain that wars are generally won by gnome and money unless he meant by gnome not simply policy but intelligent policy.[5]

The association of gnome with *xynesis* illustrates the normative sense of gnome. Since Pericles' policy is rational, those who support it can, in the event of success, lay claim to xynesis (1.140.1). Xynesis may be the expression of gnome: so Thucydides describes Pericles, by implication, as γνώμη μὴ ἀξύνετος (2.34.6). Xynesis relies on gnome (2.62.5; cf. 1.75.1). Xynesis, as its definition emerges from the description of Themistocles (1.138.2–3), is an innate, unlearned talent, especially associated with foresight.[6] This talent is said to originate in

4. Compare Thucydides' use of this antithesis in explaining why Pericles did not call an assembly after the first invasion of Attica: τοῦ μὴ ὀργῇ τι μᾶλλον ἢ γνώμῃ ξυνελθόντας ἁμαρτεῖν (2.22.1). The same antithesis can be found in Soph. *OT* 524; Antiphon 5.69.

5. This normative connotation of gnome was noticed by Harald Patzer, *Das Problem der Geschichtsschreibung des Thukydides und die thukydideische Frage* (Berlin, 1937), p. 45: "γνώμη heisst bei Thukydides nichts anderes als sonst im Griechischen, nämlich 'Erkenntnis', diese nach den drei Seiten des *Vermögens*, *Vollzuges*, und *Ergebnisses* aufgespalten. Damit ist immer ein Anspruch auf *Wahrheit* ursprünglich mit dem Wort mitgegeben."

6. See Zahn, *Die erste Periklesrede*, pp. 76–77. Bruno Snell, *Die Ausdrücke für den Begriff des Wissens in der vorplatonischen Philosophie* (Berlin, 1924), p. 58, n. 1, says that the meaning of xynesis in

gnome because one of the meanings of gnome is "intelligence." In Snell's formulation, as "intelligence," gnome designates the organ by which we perceive, as "opinion," the result of the perception.[7]

That gnome, as the faculty of perception or intelligence, can be the grounds of xynesis also shows why the term gnome can retain the normative connotation of "intelligence" or "reason" as opposed to unreasoning passion (cf. again ὀργῇ . . . μᾶλλον ἢ γνώμῃ 2.22.1). At the same time, when gnome in the sense of *result* of perception, namely, "opinion," has established itself, it is possible to speak of gnome as based on the passions which are the opposite of gnome in the former sense.[8] When gnome comes to mean simply "opinion" or "state of mind," then gnome can be the locus of will and suspicion (1.90.2), even of memory (2.43.3).

Thus in the prooemium to the first speech, Pericles is apprehensive of a change in the Athenians' gnomai which might result from a change in their feelings. This distinction between gnome in the sense of "policy based on intelligence or insight" and gnome in the sense of "(potentially fickle) state of mind" points to the second main connotation of gnome as Pericles uses the term of himself in the first sentence, the connotation of "will."

Thucydides is "(angeborenes) Verständnis," "Intelligenz." In 2.62.5, Snell (p. 58) thinks that gnome grows out of xynesis; but in fact Pericles says that xynesis "trusts less to hope . . . and rather to gnome based on present circumstances, of which the foresight is more secure."

7. B. Snell, *Die Ausdrücke*, p. 32: "als 'Intelligenz' würde γνώμη das Organ bezeichnen, durch das wir erkennen, als 'Meinung' aber das Resultat der Erkenntnis." This bifurcation of meanings issues from the original sense of γιγνώσκειν, "to perceive."

8. See Zahn, *Die erste Periklesrede*, p. 75, n. 20.

Pericles and Gnome

Pericles says τῆς μὲν γνώμης, ὦ Ἀθηναῖοι, αἰεὶ τῆς αὐτῆς ἔχομαι. The tone and sense of his words can be shown by comparison with a passage of Theognis (319–322) with which they have something in common:

Κύρν᾽ ἀγαθὸς μὲν ἀνὴρ γνώμην ἔχει ἔμπεδον αἰεί,
τολμᾷ δ᾽ ἔν τε κακοῖς κείμενος ἔν τ᾽ ἀγαθοῖς.
εἰ δὲ θεὸς κακῷ ἀνδρὶ βίον καὶ πλοῦτον ὀπάσσῃ
ἀφραίνων κακίην οὐ δύναται κατέχειν.

Cyrnus, the noble man is always of steadfast gnome. He keeps his strength both in adversity and in prosperity. But the base man, if a god grants him livelihood and wealth, loses his head and cannot restrain his bad nature.

The verbal similarity of the first of these lines to Pericles' opening words should be obvious, even if there is insufficient evidence for imitation. The two places have in common the words αἰεί, γνώμη, and ἔχω. A fuller discussion of the idiom may be postponed to a more appropriate place.[9] For present purposes, it is enough to see that Pericles attributes to himself that constancy which the aristocrat, Theognis, says belongs to the agathos, the aristocrat, and which the kakos, the man of the people, can never possess.[10]

Gnome, then, as Pericles uses the word of himself, connotes both reason as opposed to passion and also

9. See Chap. III, sec. A.4.

10. Cf. Snell, *Die Ausdrücke*, p. 35, and D. Kagan, *The Great Dialogue* (New York, 1965), pp. 41–42. The aristocratic side of Pericles will be discussed more fully in connection with certain parts of the Funeral Oration. Cf. the Odyssean constancy (*Od.* 13.330): αἰεί τοι τοιοῦτον ἐνὶ στήθεσσι νόημα. It is misleading, however, to speak of "the" gnome-tyche antithesis, as if it meant the same thing to everyone in the *History;* on the contrary, thanks to the ambiguity of gnome, the antithesis takes on a very different meaning when the Spartans use it (see Chap. II below).

steadfast conviction, or will, as regards what is to be done.[11] Gnome in the two main senses in which Pericles

11. Snell, *Die Ausdrücke*, p. 35, states "Diese Bedeutung [i.e., (adlige) "Gesinnung"] liegt offenbar auf derselben Seite wie die Bedeutung Intelligenz, nur dass sie in das Praktische hineinragt, und so ist γνώμη oft geradezu der Wille, dem dann allerdings nichts Triebhaftes eigen ist, der vielmehr intellektuel beherrscht ist." There is, in fact, a consensus of scholars on the strict ambiguity of gnome. Zahn, *Die erste Periklesrede*, p. 75, states: "Zwei Komponenten sind in dem Begriff γνώμη vereinigt, eine erkenntnismässige und eine willensmässige." The same point is made by E. Schwartz, *Gnomon* 2 (1926), 69, in a review of F. Taeger, *Thukydides* (Stuttgart, 1925). J. Stenzel, *Göttingische gelehrte Anzeigen* 7–8 (1926), 200–201, in a review of the same work, following Schwartz, stresses the unity of what are to us different meanings: "Bedenkt man, dass Bedeutungen sich nicht aus den zufälligen Komponenten zusammenaddieren lassen, in die notgedrungen ein Lexicon auf dem Grunde einer fremden Bedeutungsgliederung sie zerfällen muss, so sieht man mit einem Blicke, dass mit γνώμη genau der geistige Sachverhalt bezeichnet ist, der dem sokratischplatonischen Tugendwissen zu Grunde liegt; wir sehen, dass wir vielleicht an vielen anderen Stellen des gr. Bedeutungsytems jenen unmittelbar mitgemeinten Zug auf Verwirklichung des als wahr Erkannten immer mitverstehen müssen, dass Wissen, Erkennen, Können (τέχνη!) und Wollen für gr. Denken in einem anderen Weise verbunden sind, als für uns heutige Menschen." The exclamation point is Stenzel's. Patzer also saw that techne is implicit in gnome: see below, n. 24. Patzer, *Das Problem*, pp. 44–51, maintains that "perception" is the key to the meaning of gnome in Thucydides, that the word almost always means "Erkenntnis des zu Tuenden" (p. 45). Patzer's method is unusual in that he seeks not an original sense from which the plurality of meanings manifested in the *History* might have developed but a central meaning with which they can all be coordinated. Yet Patzer is really in fundamental agreement with the interpretation of gnome which I have just sketched (cf. p. 46 with his paraphrase of Zahn's interpretation of gnome, p. 44, n. 104). For a survey of meanings of gnome, see Huart, *Le Vocabulaire*, pp. 304–313. Huart stresses the realism of the kind of thinking designated by gnome. Cf. Patzer's definition of gnome. For gnome as both intellectual and moral, see W. S. Barrett, *Euripides: Hippolytus* (Oxford, 1964), p. 228. Cf. 2.62.3, where the construction (zeugma) brings out both these senses of gnome.

uses the word of himself contrasts with the sense of gnome as he uses it of "mortals" (cf. Archil. fr. 68) and, by implication, of Athenians. It is in terms of this contrast that Thucydides presents Pericles in relation to the Athenians. Pericles was γνώμη μὴ ἀξύνετος (2.34.6) and led the Athenians because he was δυνατός . . . τῇ γνώμῃ (2.65.8; cf. 1.139.4 ἀνὴρ κατ' ἐκεῖνον τὸν χρόνον πρῶτος Ἀθηναίων, λέγειν τε καὶ πράττειν δυνατώτατος). Thucydides corroborates the statements made by Pericles in the prooemium to the first speech. Pericles shows the strength of his will. After the first invasion of Attica, the Athenians were angry with Pericles. They remembered nothing of his previous counsel and blamed him for cowardice in not resisting the Lacedaemonians. They considered him the cause of all they were suffering. But Pericles πιστεύων . . . ὀρθῶς γιγνώσκειν περὶ τοῦ μὴ ἐπεξιέναι (2.22.1) does not call an assembly, lest the Athenians come together ὀργῇ . . . μᾶλλον ἢ γνώμῃ (2.22.1). In the second year of the war, echoing Pericles' words in the prooemium, Thucydides says that Pericles περὶ . . . τοῦ μὴ ἐπεξιέναι . . . τὴν αὐτὴν γνώμην εἶχεν (2.55.2; cf. 1.140.1). But the Athenians, because of the second invasion and the plague, ἠλλοίωντο τὰς γνώμας (2.59.1; cf. 1.140.1 τὰς γνώμας τραπόμενοι, 140.5). They were ἄποροι τῇ γνώμῃ (2.59.2), and thus Pericles attempted to restore τὸ ὀργιζόμενον τῆς γνώμης to a calmer and less fearful state (2.59.3). The same antithesis between ὀργή and γνώμη which appears first in the prooemium to the first speech reappears in Thucydides' summary of the last speech of Pericles (2.65.1):

τοιαῦτα ὁ Περικλῆς λέγων ἐπειρᾶτο τοὺς Ἀθηναίους τῆς τε ἐς αὐτὸν ὀργῆς παραλύειν καὶ ἀπὸ τῶν παρόντων δεινῶν ἀπάγειν τὴν γνώμην.

13

With such words Pericles attempted to free the Athenians of their anger against him and to turn their minds from present afflictions.

Thucydides conceives of the statesmanship of Pericles in terms of gnome, the intelligence and the strategy of Pericles himself, on the one hand, and, on the other, the changing gnomai, the states of mind, of the Athenians, which for the most part Pericles was able to control.

In this respect Pericles has achieved one of the goals of sophistic rhetoric, the ability to sway the passions of the mob from one state to its opposite. Plato says of Thrasymachus, who was the sophist par excellence,[12] ὀργίσαι τε αὖ πολλοὺς ἅμα δεινὸς ἀνὴρ γέγονε, καὶ πάλιν ὠργισμένους ἐπᾴδων κηλεῖν, ὡς ἔφη (As he said, he was a man skilled both at provoking anger in the many and also at charming and soothing them when they were angry) (*Phaedr.* 267c9–d1 = D.−K. B6). Thucydides attributes the same sort of ability to Pericles (2.65.9):

ὁπότε γοῦν αἴσθοιτό τι αὐτοὺς παρὰ καιρὸν ὕβρει θαρσοῦντας, λέγων κατέπλησσεν ἐπὶ τὸ φοβεῖσθαι, καὶ δεδιότας αὖ ἀλόγως ἀντικαθίστη πάλιν ἐπὶ τὸ θαρσεῖν.

Whenever he saw them inopportunely carried away with arrogance, he inspired fear in them with his words, and again, when they were unreasonably afraid, he restored them to boldness.

Here, in this point of resemblance between Pericles and Thrasymachus, is an indication, for which further evidence will not be wanting, of how Thucydides portrays Pericles as a representative of intellectual trends of the

12. W. K. C. Guthrie, *A History of Greek Philosophy* (Cambridge, 1969), III, 295.

second half of the fifth century. In fact, the uses of gnome already discussed would so portray him.[13]

But Pericles, as we learn from the prooemium to the first speech, understood gnome in terms of an antithesis, namely, the gnome-tyche antithesis.[14] The Periclean understanding of this antithesis is the conceptual framework of the prooemium, and the antithesis is implicit in the other speeches of Pericles, too. Now, since Thucydides' account of Pericles' career preserves so carefully the term gnome, one may suppose that the gnome-tyche antithesis is also the conceptual framework of Thucydides' understanding of the historical meaning of Pericles' career. Analysis of pertinent sections of the other speeches of Pericles will support this point.

To return to the gnome-tyche antithesis in the prooemium to the first speech, it is remarkable, first of all, that Pericles should even mention tyche. The *topos* of the *incerta belli* was, according to the rhetorician Anaximenes, to be used in dissuading an audience from war.[15] Archidamus so uses this topos in attempting to dissuade the Lacedaemonians from going to war with Athens (1.84.3). In fact, Pericles' prooemium is, rhetorically, pessimistic in tone: to look forward to possible reversals of expectations surely does nothing to inspire martial ardor. While the hypothesis of the prooemium, with its rationalism as regards tyche, is optimistic, the rhetorical pessimism persists. In the second sentence of the

13. B. M. W. Knox, *Oedipus at Thebes* (London and New Haven, 1957), pp. 124ff.

14. Zahn, *Die erste Periklesrede,* pp. 12–13.

15. διεξιτέον δὲ τὰς μεταβολὰς τὰς ἐν τῷ πολέμῳ ὡς πολλαὶ καὶ παράλογοι γίνονται (1425b2–3 = 2,30 Fuhrmann [Teubner edition, Berlin, 1966]). Cited by Zahn, *Die erste Periklesrede,* pp. 73–74.

prooemium Pericles admits the possibility of the Athenians' being "tripped up." In the third sentence he explains why he has admitted this possibility. Let us first examine the first clause of the third sentence (1.140.1):

ἐνδέχεται γὰρ τὰς ξυμφορὰς τῶν πραγμάτων οὐχ ἧσσον ἀμαθῶς χωρῆσαι ἢ καὶ τὰς διανοίας τοῦ ἀνθρώπου.

The problematic word here is ἀμαθῶς. It is active in sense.[16] Though an English translation of the adverb which will fit both subjects of the infinitive is difficult to find, "blundering" may be ventured: "It is possible for the circumstances of our affairs to take as blundering a course as men's plans."[17]

Events may fail us as much as we are capable of failing ourselves through bad planning. The simile implicit in

16. Zahn, *Die erste Periklesrede*, pp. 76, 79. LSJ cite only this place in Thucydides and Euripides, *Ion* 916, for a passive sense of ἀμαθής. The *Supplement* (1968) recognizes that in both these places the sense may be active. I have adopted the translation suggested in the *Supplement*. Cf. Sir Ronald Syme, *Thucydides, Transactions of the British Academy*, vol. 48 (Oxford, 1960), 56: " . . . ἀμαθῶς . . . has not a passive meaning (that you cannot learn about events) but an active meaning. Pericles is speaking ironically, as befits an intellectual and one of the men of understanding whom Thucydides admired. You cannot teach events. They are stubborn, but reason is all we have."

17. For the sense of *dianoia*, which is here akin to that of *doxanta* in the second sentence of the prooemium and gnomai in the first sentence, see Zahn, *Die erste Periklesrede*, p. 75. Gomme is undoubtedly right in finding irony here, but his paraphrase ("the turn of events may prove as unwise as the plans of men," "fortune may support the wrong side") perhaps misses the point of the irony (Gomme, I, 453). Pericles is not making an ironic comment on the fickleness of fortune, but, as the last clause of the prooemium shows, on the general tendency of mankind to blame tyche for their bad luck, when they should, Pericles implies, blame themselves.

ἀμαθῶς (namely, events *are like* plans *with respect to* ignorance or senselessness) masterfully understates the disparaging view of tyche which then emerges with a climactic sharpness in the last clause of the prooemium. To put the case in this way is to make planning primary: through the use of this simile, Pericles describes adversity *in terms of* human planning, which thus becomes the criterion. Adverse luck is then understood as that which was unplanned, badly planned, or contrary to plan. This orientation is epitomized in the phrase ὅσα . . . παρὰ λόγον in the next clause: that which is contrary to calculation. In this way Pericles trivializes chance, while yet admitting its existence. Chance is not an objective force impervious to human reason as in Archidamus' view (1.84.3), but, through the implications of Pericles' simile, is reduced to the same status as human error, that is, to the subjective. So the disdainful conclusion: δι' ὅπερ καὶ τὴν τύχην, ὅσα ἂν παρὰ λόγον ξυμβῇ, εἰώθαμεν αἰτιᾶσθαι ([Since events may be as senseless as our plans,] for this very reason we are accustomed to blame chance for whatever turns out contrary to calculation). The self-confidence of Pericles is in marked contrast with the humbler view of Hermocrates (4.64.1), who considers it foolishness to believe τῆς τε οἰκείας γνώμης ὁμοίως αὐτοκράτωρ εἶναι καὶ ἧς οὐκ ἄρχω τύχης (that I am complete master equally of my own mind and of chance, which I do not rule).

The unpredictability of the outcome is proverbial with speakers in the *History*, especially as regards war (1.78.2, 82.6, 122.1; 2.11.4). Though Athenians may voice this sentiment, it is more characteristic of Peloponnesians. Thus the Corinthians, at the conference of the allies in Sparta, state (1.120.5):

πολλὰ γὰρ κακῶς γνωσθέντα ἀβουλοτέρων τῶν ἐναντίων τυχόντα κατωρθώθη, καὶ ἔτι πλείω καλῶς δοκοῦντα βουλευθῆναι ἐς τοὐναντίον αἰσχρῶς περιέστη· ἐνθυμεῖται γὰρ οὐδεὶς ὁμοῖα τῇ πίστει καὶ ἔργῳ ἐπεξέρχεται, ἀλλὰ μετ᾽ ἀσφαλείας μὲν δοξάζομεν, μετὰ δέους δὲ ἐν τῷ ἔργῳ ἐλλείπομεν.

Many plans succeed though ill-conceived, if they have the luck to find worse-counseled enemies, and still more plans that seemed good meet with a disgraceful reversal. For no one goes into action with the same assurance with which he deliberates; rather we form our speculations in security, but in action our fear causes us to fall short of them.[18]

Their statement bears a certain similarity to the prooemium of the first speech of Pericles: gnome and tyche, the different moods of planning and of fighting, and the consequent reversals of expectations. Yet the Corinthians regard this state of affairs as incontrovertible: planning and the course of events are fundamentally at odds.[19] Their view is in the tradition of the archaic pessimism and *amechania* (cf. Solon 1.65–70D³; Theog.

18. I have translated τυχόντα (CG Stob.). In his note on this passage (1.120.5), Steup, *Thukydides* (Berlin, 1919), vol. I, read τυχόντων (cett.) on the grounds that it was more Thucydidean, but granted that either reading could seem *difficilior*. It would not, however, be un-Thucydidean to say that bad plans found a worse-counseled enemy. This notion is simply a variation of the topos by which a speaker attributes his opponent's success to luck rather than to his ability: cf. the Corinthians' use of this topos in 1.69.5. The choice between ὅμοια and ὁμοίᾳ does not alter the meaning appreciably: see Gomme on this passage (1.120.5). By either reading, the Corinthians assert an inevitable disproportion between plans and actions.

Since τυγχάνω with the genitive can have the connotation of chance (see Chap. III, sec. B.4), there is an implied opposition between γνωσθέντα and τυχόντα—i.e., between γνώμη and τύχη.

19. On the theme of counsel and action in Herodotus, see H. R. Immerwahr, *Form and Thought in Herodotus* (Cleveland, 1966), pp. 73ff. and 73, n. 76, for references to scholarship on this subject.

161–164, 639–640, 1075–78, etc.; Hdt. 7.49), which is religious in origin (Theog. 133–142). In the prooemium to the first speech of Pericles, Thucydides characterizes him as scornful of this tradition.

It is fitting to compare Pericles' statement with Democritus B 119:

ἄνθρωποι τύχης εἴδωλον ἐπλάσαντο πρόφασιν ἰδίης ἀβουλίης. βαιὰ γὰρ φρονήσει τύχη μάχεται, τὰ δὲ πλεῖστα ἐν βίῳ εὐξύνετος ὀξυδερκείη κατιθύνει.

Men have moulded an image of chance as an excuse for their own ill-advisedness. For seldom does chance contend with prudence. A quick sharp-sightedness sets right most of life's affairs.[20]

The same disdain of tyche appears here in Democritus, the same human, subjective orientation, and the same opposition of planning to tyche (n.b. ἀβουλίης; cf. in the prooemium ξυμβουλευτέα).[21]

20. All references to the pre-Socratics are to H. Diels and W. Kranz, *Die Fragmente der Vorsokratiker*[11] (Zürich and Berlin, 1964). Where B fragments are cited, usually only B and the number will be given. In other cases, the abbreviation D.-K. will be used, followed by the volume number (I or II), followed by the page number in Arabic numerals.

21. Helen North, *Sophrosyne: Self-Knowledge and Self-Restraint in Greek Literature* (Ithaca, N.Y., 1966), pp. 104–105, notes Thucydides' reluctance to use *sophrosyne* of Athens in the Athenian ambassadors' speech in Sparta and in three speeches of Pericles. The ambassadors "choose to call by the name *euboulia* what Archidamus describes as *sophrosyne* in his remarks about the danger of relying on *tyche* and *elpis.*"

On the basis of my interpretation of the prooemium I disagree with Zahn's comparison of the Democritus fragment with Pericles' strictures on tyche. She thinks that whereas Democritus is polemical and gives a definition of tyche, Pericles is not polemical and gives no definition, and furthermore, unlike Democritus, Pericles recognizes tyche as a reality. "Ohne besondere persönliche Stellungnahme

Whether Democritus' words have reference to political matters is not clear, but in Herodotus the same antithesis between tyche and planning occurs in the context of Xerxes' deliberations over the invasion of Greece, when Artabanus says (7.10.δ):

τὸ γὰρ εὖ βουλεύεσθαι κέρδος μέγιστον εὑρίσκω ἐόν· εἰ γὰρ καὶ ἐναντιωθῆναί τι θέλει, βεβούλευται μὲν οὐδὲν ἧσσον εὖ, ἕσσωται δὲ ὑπὸ τῆς τύχης τὸ βούλευμα· ὁ δὲ βουλευσάμενος αἰσχρῶς, εἴ οἱ ἡ τύχη ἐπίσποιτο, εὕρημα εὕρηκε, ἧσσον δὲ οὐδέν οἱ κακῶς βεβούλευται.

I find that a well-conceived plan is the greatest gain. For even if it meets some obstacle, the plan is just as good but is overcome by chance. But he who has planned badly, if chance favors him, comes upon a windfall but his plan is nonetheless bad.

The similarities between this passage and Pericles' prooemium are remarkable, although again it would be wrong to argue for imitation. Planning is primary for Artabanus as for Pericles. The excellence of the plan is unimpaired even if the plan is defeated by tyche. But the good luck of a bad plan is nothing but good luck, which is thus inferior, Artabanus implies, both to the good plan followed by good luck and also to the good plan followed by bad luck. Good planning is thus primary, in that it is the criterion by which Artabanus distinguishes between mere good luck and the good luck which attends a good

schliesst er sich in das allgemeine menschliche Denken ein" (*Die erste Periklesrede,* p. 81). On the contrary, Pericles takes an ironic, critical view of general human thought concerning tyche. More to the point is Hans Herter, "Zur ersten Periklesrede des Thukydides," in *Studies Presented to David Moore Robinson,* ed. G. E. Mylonas and Doris Raymond, II, 622: "Gewiss hat Perikles wie alle Welt von der τύχη reden können, aber gerade in der Hochschätzung der γνώμη ihr gegenüber fassen wir ein Moment, das für Thukydides' ganze Anschauung grundlegend ist."

plan. To this extent Artabanus is in fundamental agreement with Pericles.

But there is an equally fundamental disagreement between Artabanus and Pericles.[22] Artabanus' strictures on good planning are set in a context of traditional religious belief. Artabanus intends to dissuade Xerxes from invading Greece, whereas Pericles is attempting to incite the Athenians to war with the Lacedaemonians. Artabanus argues that the best plan is not to invade Greece, since to invade Greece would be to incur divine envy. Good planning proves to mean the traditional moderation. So Artabanus, with dramatic asyndeton, follows the words quoted above with (7.10.ε):

ὁρᾷς τὰ ὑπερέχοντα ζῷα ὡς κεραυνοῖ ὁ θεὸς οὐδὲ ἐᾷ φαντάζεσθαι, τὰ δὲ σμικρὰ οὐδέν μιν κνίζει· ὁρᾷς δὲ ὡς ἐς οἰκήματα τὰ μέγιστα αἰεὶ καὶ δένδρεα τὰ τοιαῦτα ἀποσκήπτει τὰ βέλεα. φιλέει γὰρ ὁ θεὸς τὰ ὑπερέχοντα πάντα κολούειν. οὕτω δὲ καὶ στρατὸς πολλὸς ὑπὸ ὀλίγου διαφθείρεται κατὰ τοιόνδε· ἐπεάν σφι ὁ θεὸς φθονήσας φόβον ἐμβάλῃ ἢ βροντήν, δι' ὧν ἐφθάρησαν ἀναξίως ἑωυτῶν. οὐ γὰρ ἐᾷ φρονέειν μέγα ὁ θεὸς ἄλλον ἢ ἑωυτόν.

You see how the god strikes with thunder the most exalted creatures and does not let them make a show, while small creatures do not vex him. You see how his missiles always fall on the largest buildings and trees. For the god is wont to abase everything exalted. And so it is that a great army is destroyed by a small one in this way: whenever the god from jealousy sends thunder or panic, by which they are unworthily destroyed. For he does not permit pride in any but himself.

In fact, Artabanus is far from Periclean. He is a latter-day Solon (cf. Hdt. 7.46 with 1.31.3).

22. Zahn, *Die erste Periklesrede*, p. 80, discusses the Herodotean passage and its similarities to the prooemium, but, in neglecting the context of this passage, fails to notice the differences, which show more about Pericles than the similarities.

To conclude, the prooemium to the first speech is a concise and subtle adumbration of the political philosophy of Pericles. This prooemium introduces not only the first speech but also the other speeches, which are fundamentally consistent in theme with the first. Furthermore, the main terms of the prooemium appear again in important places in which Thucydides explains the actions of Pericles. The conceptual framework of the prooemium, and thus, by implication, of the thought of Pericles in general, is a gnome-tyche antithesis. Pericles opposes a normative understanding of gnome as he uses the term of himself to a neutral sense of the term as he uses it of the Athenians ("state of mind"). There lies behind Pericles' self-description in terms of a steadfast gnome an old aristocratic principle; but Pericles, abandoning this gnome as a mark of social class, presents it as a standard to the democratic assembly. In the conclusion of his speech, he makes gnome the tradition of the democracy when he states that the ancestors defeated the Mede and raised Athens to its present height more by gnome than by tyche (1.144.4).

He seems to go beyond the polemicism of Democritus B 119 in maintaining a political application of Democritus' point: since bad luck is possible, Pericles asks the Athenians to abide by the common resolutions (cf. Pseudo-Xen. *Ath. Pol.* 2.17). As the last speech of Pericles shows more clearly, he conceived of the willing unity of the citizens in support of policy determined in common as the strongest resistance to the misfortunes of the city. This theme of the "whole city"[23] is intimated here in this

23. John H. Finley, Jr., *Thucydides* (Cambridge, Mass., 1942), p. 162.

prooemium. In implying the sufficiency of gnome, Pericles frees the antithesis between tyche and planning from its subordination to a theological outlook, as it appeared in the speech of Artabanus to Xerxes. The prooemium to the first speech is a document of the humanism and rationalism of Pericles.

But after all it is still a prooemium to a speech which contains a specific recommendation of policy, namely, reliance on capital and on the navy. The relationship of the thought of the prooemium to the specific recommendation lies in Pericles' notion that political power can be built on the consistent application of intelligence to matters of policy. In this way gnome comes to mean techne, in some respects, as the discussion of the main points of Pericles' policy will show.[24] This consistent reliance on gnome and techne is in marked contrast with the notion of Archidamus. Pericles, for his part, tends to think of the Spartans as stupid (1.142.8–9) and of the Athenians as intelligent (the Funeral Oration passim). The Spartan point of view, however, is that men are generally equal in understanding (Archidamus 1.84.3; cf. Theog. 221–224). The Periclean policy is an expression of the difference between the Athenian, or Periclean, and the Spartan points of view, but the Spartans have a single, simple policy which they would presumably always apply against any enemy (Archidamus 1.84.4), and which follows from their view of the general equality

24. Patzer, *Das Problem*, p. 45, remarks on the technical implications of gnome: "So ist sie [*gnome*] auch bei Thukydides fast ausnahmslos 'Erkenntnis des zu Tuenden'. Und dieses wiederum ist nicht *sittlich*, auf letzte allgemeine Anweisungen ausgerichtet, verstanden, sondern *technisch;* so ist die γνώμη nicht so sehr auf τὰ τέλη gerichtet als auf τὰ πρὸς τὰ τέλη."

of men in respect to intelligence (consider also the speech of the Spartans in Athens after the Pylos episode: 4.18.2). The Periclean policy, however, is specific, because it is based on an analysis of the difference between Athens and Sparta.

This policy, as it is stated in the first speech, contains two main points: reliance on capital, in which the Athenians so excel the Spartans that the Spartans will eventually have to quit, since they have no means of support except private income; and reliance on the navy. The first of these points will be discussed in connection with the Periclean speech in *oratio obliqua* (2.13). What should be noted in Pericles' statement on the navy is the technological emphasis (1.142.9):

τὸ δὲ ναυτικὸν τέχνης ἐστίν, ὥσπερ καὶ ἄλλο τι, καὶ οὐκ ἐνδέχεται, ὅταν τύχῃ, ἐκ παρέργου μελετᾶσθαι, ἀλλὰ μᾶλλον μηδὲν ἐκείνῳ πάρεργον ἄλλο γίγνεσθαι.

The use of ships is a branch of technology, not less than other things, and it is not possible to get naval training whenever you happen to do so, on the side. . . .[25]

Pericles' gnome relies, then, in one main point of policy, on techne.

What lies behind Pericles' technological confidence is a theory concerning the relation of practice and experience to techne:

We have more experience (ἐμπειρίας) of warfare conducted on land from the fleet as a base than they have of naval operations from their land-base. It will not come easily to them to learn the

25. On ὅταν τύχῃ see W. S. Barrett, *Euripides: Hippolytus*, p. 237: this phrase is used of things which a person does "casually or unpredictably." On the connection of techne and shipbuilding, cf. Hom. *Il.* 5.59–62, 15.410–412.

sea. For neither have you, though you have been practicing (μελετῶντες) straight from the time of the Persian War, yet reached an end. How might men who are farmers, not seafarers, and, furthermore, not even allowed to practice (μελετῆσαι), through your continual blockading them with many ships, accomplish anything notable? Even if, emboldening their ignorance with numbers, they should risk an attack against a few of the blockading ships, prevented by many they will keep their peace and they will be less skilled through their want of practice (ἐν τῷ μὴ μελετῶντι) and for that reason also more reluctant (1.142.5–8).[26]

Pericles' point concerning Athenian naval experience is confirmed by other speakers in the *History*. Archidamus calls the Athenians θαλάσσης ἐμπειρότατοι (1.80.3). The Lacedaemonians did not remember this fact, and, in their astonishment at their defeat in their first sea-battle, suspected their sailors of cowardice, οὐκ ἀντιτιθέντες τὴν Ἀθηναίων ἐκ πολλοῦ ἐμπειρίαν τῆς σφετέρας δι᾿ ὀλίγου μελέτης (not comparing the Athenians' long experience with their own short practice) (2.85.2). Addressing the Syracusans after their defeat in the harbor (autumn 415), Hermocrates consoles his people by reminding them (6.72.3):

οὐ μέντοι τοσοῦτόν γε λειφθῆναι ὅσον εἰκὸς εἶναι, ἄλλως τε καὶ τοῖς πρώτοις τῶν Ἑλλήνων ἐμπειρίᾳ ἰδιώτας ὡς εἰπεῖν χειροτέχναις ἀνταγωνισαμένους.

Their defeat was not so great as might have been expected, especially since they had fought against the most experienced of the Greeks—unskilled workers, as it were, against craftsmen.

Hermocrates stresses practice and experience in his plans for rebuilding the Syracusan forces (6.72.4).

26. I have followed Gomme in the first part of this translation.

The concept of techne which Thucydides attributes to Pericles must be understood in the context of fifth-century theories concerning the origin and development of human society. For what Pericles maintains of the Athenian navy, in particular its development out of practice and experience, is identical with theories of broader application which can be traced to Democritus and Protagoras.[27] Democritus said that "in general, *use* itself taught man everything, leading the way to knowledge of each thing in a manner befitting a stout creature who possessed hands to help him with everything and reason and presence of mind" (D.-K. II.136.12–15). Galen, in Περὶ τῆς ἰατρικῆς ἐμπειρίας, preserves the same tradition: " . . . we find that of the bulk of mankind each individual by making use of his frequent observations gains knowledge not attained by another; for as Democritus says, *experience* and vicissitudes have taught men this, and it is from their wealth of *experience* that men have learned to perform the things they do."[28]

This trend in fifth-century thought comes closer to Pericles in the possibility that his friend Anaxagoras also

27. Heinimann, *MH* 18 (1961), 105–130, argues that a unified theory of techne preserved or reflected in the Hippocratic writings, in the *Dissoi Logoi,* and in Plato and Isocrates must go back to a sophistic origin, most probably Protagoras. *Empeiria* is integral to this theory of techne (115–116).

28. D.-K. II.423.17–22. This is the translation by R. Walzer (Oxford 1944, repr. 1946/7), p. 99, of the Arabic version. *Usus* and *experientia* occur in four (Lucretius, Vitruvius, Diodorus, Tzetzes) of the five ancient histories of technology discussed by Thomas Cole in the first two chapters of *Democritus and the Sources of Greek Anthropology* (1967), pp. 40–41. Cole traces these related histories back to a common origin in Democritus.

maintained the connection of *empeiria* and techne. Plutarch preserves this testimonium (D.-K. II.43.19ff.):

ἀλλ' ἐν πᾶσι τούτοις ἀτυχέστεροι τῶν θηρίων ἐσμέν, ἐμπειρίαι δὲ καὶ μνήμηι καὶ σοφίαι καὶ τέχνηι κατὰ Ἀναξαγόραν † σφῶν τε αὐτῶν χρώμεθα καὶ βλίττομεν καὶ ἀμέλγομεν καὶ φέρομεν καὶ ἄγομεν συλλαμβάνοντες.²⁹

In all these respects [speed and strength] we are inferior to the beasts but we use our characteristic [?] experience, memory, wisdom, and skill, and we take their honey and their milk and, subjecting them to us, we take what they have as our booty.

Although tyche has favored the beasts in many ways, we have an advantage over them through accumulated experience and the resulting *sophia* and techne.

But, no matter what the particular philosophic background of Pericles' concept of naval technology may be, there is good evidence that Pericles' concept had become current perhaps a decade or more before the time of the first speech in the *History*. For the unphilosophic Old Oligarch, in *The Constitution of the Athenians*, for which a *terminus ante* of 443 to 441 has been proposed,³⁰ could already say of Athenian naval excellence (1.20): καὶ κυβερνῆται ἀγαθοὶ γίγνονται δι' ἐμπειρίαν τε τῶν πλόων καὶ

29. In Plato's *Gorgias*, Socrates mentions a treatise by Polus in which Polus called *empeiria* the source of techne (462b11–c1), a theory which Polus expounds in this dialogue (448c4–7). Socrates, addressing Polus, refers to Polus' knowledge of Anaxagoras' philosophy with the pointed σὺ γὰρ τούτων ἔμπειρος (465d4–5). Considering the subject of the dialogue and considering also Socrates' characteristic irony, it is difficult to believe that his use of *empeiros* does not implicitly associate Polus' theory with Anaxagoras.

30. G. W. Bowersock, *Pseudo-Xenophon: Constitution of the Athenians* (Cambridge, Mass. and London, 1968), p. 465. The controversy over the date cannot be pursued here.

διὰ μελέτην (and they become good helmsmen through experience of voyages and through practice). And this is hardly the only similarity between the Old Oligarch's discussion of Athens as a naval power and the first speech of Pericles, although the similar matters of concern receive quite different treatment.[31]

Pericles' gnome rests, then, on naval techne, which has arisen out of empeiria. The Periclean policy is thus, as Thucydides presents it, consciously humanistic and historical. It is humanistic in that, in finding the source of Athenian naval strength in experience and practice, it implicitly aligns itself with the humanistic theory of techne according to which the arts are not the gift of the gods, as they were traditionally held to be (Hom. *Od.* 6.232–4; *Hymn to Aphrodite* 12–15; Pl. *Menex.* 238b1–5; *Pol.* 274b5; Hdt. 2.53.2), but man's own creation. It is historical in that it regards techne as a development in time, proceeding from cause (empeiria) to effect (technical competence). As regards naval technology in particular, Thucydides represents Pericles as acting upon the basis of the same historical consciousness shown by Thucydides himself in the Archaeology, where Thucydides traces the development of shipbuilding and sailing in the context of the progressive achievement of power and wealth from the earliest times in political history about which one could make safe guesses. Thucydides presents Pericles as the only statesman of Pericles' time capable of thinking historically. Pericles sees that there is a new basis of power, the navy and the

31. Bowersock, ibid. For a detailed examination of the differences between Pericles and the Old Oligarch, see J. de Romilly, *Rev. de Phil.* 36 (1962), 225–241.

capital accruing to Athens from the maritime empire. The navy means the rowers, and the rowers mean democracy. Pericles' technological strategy and his democratic innovations in the Athenian constitution are of a piece (though Thucydides is silent about these innovations). While Pericles is alive and his policies are intact, his insight is vastly successful, so much so that even the Sicilian disaster does not finally deplete the Athenian resources. But after the death of Pericles Athens begins to move out of its greatest period, as another city, Syracuse, reaps the fruit of the same sort of experience which gave the Athenians their technical competence and consequent power. Thucydides presents a Hermocrates who is aware that the Syracusans' day has come, that they are the Athenians of their day: the Syracusans will acquire naval experience because of Athens just as the Athenians, not born with their ability, were forced to do by the Mede (7.21.3).

The political implications of the Periclean strategy deserve discussion. This strategy was technological and followed from a humanistic and historical concept of *techne*. As regards the Athenian constitution, it meant the bringing into eminence of the class of artisans. In short, the importance of technology meant the importance of the technological class, the artisans. The fleet and the crafts or trades emerged together (Isoc. *Panath.* 115–116; Pseudo-Xen. *Ath. Pol.* 1.12).[32] But in raising the

32. The same phenomenon of seafaring as an impetus to the crafts and sciences also had its modern form. Norbert Wiener, *The Human Use of Human Beings: Cybernetics and Society* (New York, 1967), p. 189, states: "We must . . . consider navigation and the instruments necessary for it as the locus of an industrial revolution before the main industrial revolution."

artisans to the rank of warriors, Pericles opposes the traditional Greek concept of warfare, according to which there is a strict distinction between these two classes. In discussing the Egyptian caste system, Herodotus points out that neither of the two subdivisions of the Egyptian military caste practices the arts (2.165–166). He observes: "Whether the Greeks learned this custom from the Egyptians I cannot judge with certainty, seeing that the Thracians, Scythians, Persians, Lydians and practically all the barbarians consider those who learn the arts (technas) and their offspring less honorable, *but believe those who are freed of handicraft to be noble, and especially those dedicated to war. At any rate,*[33] *all the Greeks and especially the Lacedaemonians have conceived this opinion . . ."* (2.167).

It is noteworthy that Herodotus speaks of this belief as

---

33. W. W. How and J. Wells, *A Commentary on Herodotus* (Oxford, 1928), I, 250: "The only thing he is sure of is (δ' ὦν 'at any rate') that the Greek prejudice is general." Cf. Hdt. 1.155.4, where engaging in trade is the opposite of manliness and the use of weapons. The strength of this prejudice persists through the *kallipolis* of Plato's *Republic* and the ideal constitution of Aristotle. Aristotle preserves exactly the same outlook known to Herodotus: "Even if one must judge [the state] with regard to the size of its population, one should not do so on the basis of an undifferentiated mass of people, but on the basis of those who are a part of the city, that is, the proper parts of which the city consists. For superiority in the number of these parts is the sign of a great city; the city from which many artisans (βάναυσοι) and few hoplites go forth to war—this city cannot be great" (*Pol.* 1326a17–24).

The distinction between the warrior and the banausic classes is heightened by Herodotus' use of ἀνίημι, a metaphor of the religious sense (LSJ s.v. II.6), to describe the freedom of the warriors (ἀνέωνται 2.165; ἀνειμένους 2.167). For the extreme antiquity of a class consisting of "those dedicated to war," see G. Dumézil, *L'Idéologie tripartite des Indo-Européens* (Brussels, 1958), Chap. 1, "Les Trois Functions Sociales et Cosmiques," and E. Benveniste, *Le Vocabulaire des institutions Indo-Européens* (Paris, 1969), Bk. 3, Chap. 1, "La Tripartition des if it were contemporary. To us it seems obvious that the Athenians should have relied on their navy; but to the Athenians, and especially to the more conservative element, perhaps it was not so obvious. This would be the reason why Thucydides represents Pericles as stressing an apparently obvious point: in both the first and last speeches, Pericles emphasizes the navy, and in the speech in indirect discourse (2.13) the navy appears as one of the cardinal points of Pericles' policy, which he was wont to reiterate (2.13.2, 9; cf. 2.62.1). Why would he have stressed the policy repeatedly unless there was resistance to it, or at least a failure, in Pericles' judgment, on the part of the Athenians to see where their real strength lay? "It is remarkable that at Athens the navy did not enjoy greater social prestige; that though the rich were ready enough to be admirals and trierarchs, no one was especially proud of being a κυβερνήτης or a subordinate officer, still less of being a rower."[34]

Functions."

Herodotus' own view of the matter was perhaps closer to Pericles'. In comparing Aeschylus' treatment of the battle of Salamis in the *Persae* with Herodotus', H. R. Immerwahr, *Form and Thought*, p. 256, observes: "Herodotus, in stressing the sea against the land, thereby stresses the progressive forces of the Athenian democracy, despite his great sympathy for certain aspects of Spartan conservatism; a direct line thus leads from his view of Athenian politics and life to the picture developed by Thucydides."

34. Gomme, I, 460. Cf. Thuc. 3.16. The old oligarchic typifies the state of mind which would have been impervious to the merits of the naval strategy. Cf. J. de Romilly, "Le Pseudo-Xénophon et Thucydide," *Rev. de Phil.* 36 (1962), 232: "Le Pseudo-Xénophon, en effet, n'arrive pas à penser les choses autrement qu'en fonction de combats de terre . . ."; 240: "il n'est pas impossible d'admettre que, parmi les milieux antidémocratiques auxquels appartenait le Pseudo-Xénophon, on pouvait vivre dans un monde si fermé à toute réalité contemporaine."

The Periclean concept of techne as originating in empeiria—a concept which we associate with fifth-century humanism—was necessarily historical. Techne represented change and progress. In the case of the Athenian navy, the development of the techne also meant a change in the political constitution, by which the practitioners of the new techne came in for a share of the wealth and power which they had helped to create. Furthermore, the predominance of the navy in Pericles' strategy meant a change in the traditional concept of warfare, according to which the "best" defended the city—a change which was bound to encounter resistance. Indeed, the aristocratic tradition never forgave Pericles for his innovations.[35] But Thucydides presents Pericles as aware that his period of dominance in Athens marks both the achievement by Athens of a new and unprecedented power on a new basis and also, at the same time, a brief period of glory, the end of which is imminent. This awareness was already intimated in the prooemium to the first speech. Pericles was in fact aware of the dangers of the historical, technological viewpoint, as the following reflections will suggest.

Pericles' assertion that the use of ships is a branch of technology "not less than other things" implies a consistently technological outlook.[36] Here Pericles perhaps reflects the Anaxagorean view that man's superiority to the other animals rests on his intelligence and his use of the arts (Anax. B 21b). If everything is a matter of techne, then so is politics—Democritus extolled politics

35. Pl. *Gorg.* 515e; Arist. *Ath. Pol.* 29.3; Isoc. 7.20ff.; Cic. *de Rep.* 1.27.
36. The translation is by Gomme, I, 459.

as the highest techne—and Pericles would agree with the Corinthians when they say (1.71.3):

ἀνάγκη δὲ ὥσπερ τέχνης αἰεὶ τὰ ἐπιγιγνόμενα κρατεῖν· καὶ
ἡσυχαζούσῃ μὲν πόλει τὰ ἀκίνητα νόμιμα ἄριστα, πρὸς πολλὰ δὲ
ἀναγκαζομένοις ἰέναι πολλῆς καὶ τῆς ἐπιτεχνήσεως δεῖ. δι᾽ ὅπερ
καὶ τὰ τῶν Ἀθηναίων ἀπὸ τῆς πολυπειρίας ἐπὶ πλέον ὑμῶν
κεκαίνωται.

Your habits are old-fashioned compared with theirs; but, of necessity, as in technology, the new developments always prevail, and for a city at peace unchanged customs are best, but for a city compelled to face many tests, there is need of much technological innovation, too. For this very reason the Athenians' customs, as the result of their great experience, have progressed more than yours.

The Athenians' innovations appear in the Corinthian account as the result of experience, as they do in Pericles' account of Athenian naval superiority. But what is most striking in the Corinthians' statement is the mode of their argument. They argue on the analogy of techne for changes in the customs of the polis; and they illustrate their recommendation to the Spartans by the example of the Athenians, who have in fact displayed the spirit of technological innovation in the political realm. Pericles is undeniably the foremost spokesman in the *History* of the Athens described by the Corinthians, and Pericles' own technological views, suggested apropos of the navy, can be set in the broader context of the Corinthian statement.

But there emerges a contradiction in Pericles' thought. On the one hand, the concept of politics as a techne requires constant change and innovation in the city; on the other, the city must not be changed to such a degree that its fundamental character is subverted. The consistently technological view of the city would involve Pericles in the demand at once for change and innovation and for the preservation of that which is changing. Pericles himself acknowledges this dilemma in the prooemium of the Funeral Oration, in which he dispraises the innovation by which the *epitaphios* (funeral oration) was added to the city's institutions. He does so on the basis of the *logos-ergon* antithesis: it should be sufficient to honor by deeds men who were brave in deeds. Pericles disparages mere words. But in the course of the speech it appears not only that Pericles himself is a consummate master of words—and indeed he appears in the *History* mainly as a speaker, not an actor—but also that the traditional *logos-ergon* distinction has in Athens been resolved: words are no hindrance to deeds here, and in this Athens is exceptional (2.40.3). Pericles does not then really have the grounds for his repudiation of the epitaphios as an innovation. In fact, Thucydides represents Pericles as carrying this innovation a step forward by neglecting conventional parts of the epitaphios.[37] He represents him as recognizing the dilemma implicit in the technological outlook but choosing the side of innovation rather than of preservation. Recognizing the riskiness of this choice, Pericles looks beyond its practical outcome, beyond success or failure. Thus he speaks in the same breath of "immortal memorials of victories and defeats" (2.41.5) and, at the time of the plague, gives the Athenians consolation before the fact: "the memory of our power, the greatest ever acquired up until now, even if we now give way a little—for all things are born to be

37. Johannes Kakridis, *Der thukydideische Epitaphios: ein stilistischer Kommentar, Zetemata* 26 (Munich, 1961), p. 14.

diminished—is bequeathed forever to future genera-
tions" (2.64.3).

The two passages just cited put one in mind of the
apparent rhetorical ineptitude noted in the prooemium
to the first speech. Similarly, in the Funeral Oration,
Pericles, in praising the city, alludes to its defeats
(2.41.5),[38] and in his last speech in the *History*, at the time
of the plague, he looks ahead to the extinction of the city
(2.64.3). But the statesman must, of course, maintain that
the city is immortal: ἡμετέρα . . . πόλις . . . οὔποτ' ὀλεῖται
(Our city will never die).[39] These passages show that the
speeches of Pericles have a double nature. On the one
hand, they arise from particular occasions and make
points bearing on particular, concrete situations; on the
other hand, they reflect a transpolitical perspective. The
gnome of Pericles is not limited to its expression in the
concepts of techne, the navy, and democracy as they
apply to Athens in his own day; this gnome has also a
transpolitical, historical dimension. It is because of this
dimension of his thought that he can speak of Athens as
monumental. Since Athens is herself a work of art, she
needs no Homer (2.41.4). Pericles' perspective on

38. It is possible, however, to interpret Pericles' words (μνημεῖα
κακῶν τε κἀγαθῶν ἀίδια ξυγκατοικίσαντες) as meaning Athenian benefits
conferred upon, and injuries inflicted upon, others. J. Classen (but
not Steup) so interpreted the phrase, and so did Nietzsche, *The
Genealogy of Morals*, trans. F. Golffing (New York, 1956), p.
175=*Werke*, II, ed. K. Schlechta (Munich, 1966), 786.

39. Solon fr. 3.1D. Cf. Cic. *de Rep.* 3.23: debet enim sic esse civitas ut
aeterna sit. itaque nullus interitus est rei publicae naturalis ut
hominis, in quo mors non modo necessaria est, verum etiam optanda
persaepe. civitas autem cum tollitur, deletur, extinguitur, simile est
quodam modo, ut parva magnis conferamus, ac si omnis hic mundus
intereat et concidat.

Athens is thus in one respect the same as Thucydides' own. Though Thucydides describes events from the point of view of the actors—a method that is especially apparent in his use of speeches—he nevertheless has a concept of the war as a whole, from its beginning to its end. As a whole, the war has a monumental character (1.1, 21.2). Thus the historical work that is the literary embodiment of this experience may have the same character and may challenge the work of poets (1.22.4).[40] In the same way that poetry preserves the memory of the κλέα ἀνδρῶν (glorious deeds of men) (Hom. *Il.* 9.189; cf. 6.358) historiography is the monument of historical greatness. Though Athens does not need Homer, she needs Thucydides.

B. *The speech in* oratio obliqua (2.13)

The prooemium to the first speech provided evidence of a demotion of tyche from its powerful position in the archaic tradition and in the contemporary Spartan view, and also of a reliance on intelligence and, in particular, on naval technology. The brief speech in *oratio obliqua* simply reiterates the points of policy that follow from these views, the same policy that Pericles often recommended to the Athenians (2.13.2 and 9; cf. 2.62.1): they should bring in their belongings from the countryside; should not go out from the city into battle on land, but should stay inside the walls and guard the city; should maintain their naval superiority and keep their allies in

40. See H. R. Immerwahr, "*Ergon:* History as Monument in Herodotus and Thucydides,"*AJP* 81 (1960), 261–290, esp. 281ff.

hand. For the strength of Athens lay in the income from the empire, and wars for the most part are won by superiority in capital resources (cf. 1.141.5 [αἱ περιουσίαι] and Archidamos' implicit agreement with Pericles: 1.83.2) and by intelligence (γνώμη).

As for the first point, superiority in capital, if this was correct, then Pericles had only to give the Athenians a catalogue of their wealth, and this he does (2.13.3–6). This catalogue in itself would have had an effect on Pericles' audience and on Thucydides' ancient Greek readers which we can hardly appreciate.[41] By comparison with other Greek cities, Athens was incredibly rich. Herein she had utterly controverted the principle of Demaratus, who held that the σύντροφος πενίη (habitual poverty) of the Greeks was the source of their *arete* (Hdt. 7.102.1), and also the widely held opinion that poverty was next to piety.[42] Arete, or success, now had a new foundation.

In this catalogue, one item is of special interest to the present study: the mention of the statue of Athena and its removable gold plate, which could be converted into cash. The time of the speech in indirect discourse is the summer of 431. The statue had been dedicated in 438/7. In the meantime, Phidias, the sculptor, had been tried for peculation and acquitted (Plut. *Per.* 31). Mention of the statue would surely have called the trial to mind,[43]

41. See K. J. Dover's remark on πολλὰ τάλαντα (6.31.5) in A. W. Gomme, A. Andrewes, and K. J. Dover, *A Historical Commentary on Thucydides* (Oxford, 1970), vol. IV.

42. On Greek notions of poverty, see G. Meyer, *Laudes Inopiae* (Göttingen, 1915), who, however, omits discussion of the important passage in Herodotus.

43. Cf. B. M. W. Knox, *Oedipus at Thebes*, p. 104.

and perhaps Aspasia, too, who was charged with impiety at about the same time (Plut. *Per.* 32). The trials of Phidias and Aspasia are often mentioned as examples of "omissions" in Thucydides. But is there not a Thucydidean comment implicit in the casual manner in which Pericles lists the statue as part of the disposable wealth of Athens? The scandals surrounding the friends of Pericles were trivial, Thucydides seems to say. In 431, Pericles did not have to feel any qualms about mentioning the statue of Athena before the people, even though it had been the cause of the charge against his friend.

But in another way mention of the statue and the suggestion of its use characterize Pericles as planning for the war on the basis of concepts that the people would not have shared. Here we are forced to argue from the subsequent history of the statue in order to establish the difference between Pericles' and the people's views. "So far as we know, and in this case our ignorance is practically decisive, the Athenians did not make use of this considerable gold reserve, even in the closing stage of the war, nor, when one might think it would be an even greater temptation, in the first difficult years of peace: neither the Thirty nor the restored democracy proposed it."[44] One is reminded of the Ionians' rejection, unexplained by Herodotus because it did not need to be explained, of Hecataeus' proposal that they use Croesus'

44. Gomme, II, on 2.13.5. Cf. W. S. Ferguson, *The Treasurers of Athena* (Cambridge, Mass., 1932), pp. 85ff., not cited by Gomme, though Ferguson is still more certain than Gomme that the statue was untouched. Ferguson's study makes it clear that less important objects could be converted into cash. Scrupulousness as regards the treasure of a sanctuary could have propaganda value: see Diod. 10.28, cited by K. J. Dover in Gomme, IV, on Thuc. 6.71.1.

votive offerings to Apollo Didymaeus for the construction of a fleet (Hdt. 5.36.3–4). Popular piety is at work in this reluctance to disturb the contents of temples. This piety would also explain the Athenians' displeasure at Phidias' representing himself and Pericles in ornamental carving on the Parthenon.[45] In his proposal concerning the statue of Athena Pericles again appears as the humanist and the rationalist.[46]

Sacred things may be converted to human use: in 2.13.5, note χρήματα, χρήσεσθαι, χρησαμένους. The translation of *chremata* by "capital" obscures Pericles' meaning, because we mean by capital a stock of money employed to earn more money. For us capital is something fixed, earning income or growing, whereas for Pericles chremata means "objects for use." For Pericles χρῆσθαι is implicit in chremata. As he says in the Funeral Oration, πλούτῳ τε ἔργου μᾶλλον καιρῷ ἢ λόγου κόμπῳ χρώμεθα (we use wealth as the occasion for deeds, not for vaunting words) (2.40.1). Since techne is implied in gnome and since *chresthai* is implied in techne,[47] there is no antithesis between gnome and chremata in Pericles' mind. In this, Pericles differs from the Peloponnesians, who contrast gnome with παρασκευή (preparation).[48]

45. For another interpretation, see F. Schachermeyer, *Religionspolitik und Religiosität bei Perikles* (Vienna, 1968), p. 36. This study illustrates the difficulty of showing any religiosity on the part of Pericles.

46. On Pericles the rationalist, see the remarks by V. Ehrenberg, *Sophocles and Pericles* (Oxford, 1954), pp. 91–98.

47. According to the anthropological account, the arts originate in *chreia,* "the utilitarian principle," as Cole says, *Democritus,* p. 41.

48. The Corinthians (1.71.1); Archidamus (2.11.5); cf. the same antithesis in Herodotus' description of Phanes: καὶ γνώμην ἱκανὸς καὶ τὰ πολέμια ἄλκιμος (3.4.1). No doubt the antithesis is a particular expression of the traditional *logos - ergon* antithesis. One recalls that Pericles

He differs also from the tradition epitomized in the proverb χρήματα χρήματ᾽ ἀνήρ (money makes the man) (Pind. *Isthm.* 2.11; cf. Alc. fr. 360),[49] and in the gloomy saying of Hesiod: χρήματα γὰρ πέλεται δειλοῖσι βροτοῖσιν (for wretched mortals, their goods are their life) (*Op.* 686). Pericles bids the Athenians lament not the loss of dwellings and land but of persons (τῶν σωμάτων), since these possessions do not acquire men (ἄνδρας), but men (ἄνδρες) acquire them (1.143.5). Pericles draws a line between σώματα and ἄνδρες on the one hand and chremata on the other, contrary to Pindar's proverb and the saying of Hesiod. Wars are won γνώμῃ καὶ χρημάτων περιουσίᾳ (2.13.2). The Lacedaemonians, on the contrary, are readier to use their own persons (σώμασι) than material resources (χρήμασι 1.141.5). The Lacedaemonians must follow this strategy since they lack chremata (1.141.3). Pericles' analysis of the Lacedaemonians' position squares exactly with Archidamus' (1.80.4) and with the Corinthians', who describe the *dynamis* of the Peloponnesians and their allies as τοῖς σώμασι τὸ πλέον ἰσχύουσα ἢ τοῖς χρήμασι (strong in able bodies rather than in money) (1.121.4). The Athenians, with their intelligent, technological outlook, are "users" of chremata; money and goods are instruments of strategy for them,

---

thought that in matters of policymaking the two sides of the traditional antithesis were not antithetical for the Athenians (2.40.3). Pericles himself, however, is fond of this antithesis. It is common in the Epitaphios. Furthermore, Pericles perhaps has in mind a gnome - *soma* antithesis in 2.38; and in 2.43.3 he uses a gnome - *ergon* antithesis, where *ergon* is thought by some to mean "monument."

49. Cf. Petr. LXXVII: assem habeas, assem valeas: habes, habeberis.

while the Peloponnesians "work for themselves"—they are αὐτουργοί (1.141.3 and 5).

As in the case of gnome and techne, here again in the case of chremata we see that Pericles' thought fits into an historical pattern already adumbrated by Thucydides himself. In the Archaeology, Thucydides traced the development of wealth and power from the earliest times in Hellas, which were characterized by achrematia (1.11.1–2). It was partly through the want of any surplus of goods that the conditions of life were unfixed in the earliest times (περιουσίαν χρημάτων οὐκ ἔχοντες 1.2.2). The acquisition of wealth marked a new stage in the history of Hellas (περιουσίαν μᾶλλον ἔχοντες χρημάτων 1.7.1; cf. Pericles 1.141.5). Like techne, the concept of chremata is also connected with the navy, because sailing was the source of wealth and power (1.7.1, 13.1, 15.1), and the Athenian Empire was based on chremata and the fleet (1.19, 96.1, 99.3, 101.3, 117.3). In comparing Sparta with Athens, Archidamus speaks in the same breath of Sparta's lack of a fleet and of her lack of chremata (1.82.1), and Sthenelaidas must agree in the same terms (1.86.1), though he disagrees with Archidamus' policy. Thus Thucydides presents Pericles as the statesman whose policy and military strategy follow from historical insight.[50]

50. D. Rokeah, *"Periousia chrematon:* Thucydides and Pericles," *RFIC* 91 (1963), 282ff. attempts to show that Pericles' policy influenced Thucydides' understanding of history. Rokeah's argument stands or falls on his assumption that "the speeches in Thucydides are essentially authentic" (p. 282). If so, similarities between the speeches of Pericles and statements by Thucydides show the influence of the former on the latter. But few would agree that the speeches are "essentially authentic." Cf. M. Chambers, "Studies on

The implicit connections of "use," techne, and the navy appear in Pericles' view of the sea as something "for use" (2.62.2). According to an earlier view, the sea is only potentially useful since it is so troubled by winds (Hdt. 7.16.1):[51]

τὴν πάντων χρησιμώτατον ἀνθρώποισι θάλασσαν πνεύματά φασι ἀνέμων ἐμπίπτοντα οὐ περιορᾶν φύσι τῇ ἑωυτῆς χρᾶσθαι

They say that blasts of wind falling upon the sea, which is the most useful of all things to men, do not permit it to follow its natural bent.

The Athenian techne of sailing, however, converts the sea to usefulness. In order to appreciate the revolutionary character of Pericles' concept of "use" and naval techne one must recall that in Pericles' time it was not long since it had required innovational daring on the part of an Athenian statesman to recommend that the Athenians "cleave to the sea" (1.93.4), since seafaring would be a source of political power. The Athenians were late-comers to sailing (1.14.3), and the distinction between Athens as a naval power and Sparta as a land power could be dated to the Persian Wars (1.18.2). In the fourth century it could still be debated whether the Greek victory over Xerxes was due to the land or the sea battles (Pl. *Laws* 707b–c; cf. Socrates' disinclination to seafaring, *Gorg.* 467d3–4). The usefulness of the sea would still have appeared rather dubious to the

_____

Thucydides," *CW* 62 (1969), 254. (Authenticity of style, so brilliantly argued by Finley in "The Origins of Thucydides' Style," *HSCP* 50 (1939), 35–84, included in *Three Essays on Thucydides*, pp. 55–117, and an authenticity consisting of *ipsissima verba* are, of course, two different things.)

51. For the many parallels to this notion, see Diehl[3] on Solon, fr. 11.

Marathonomachae, who no doubt shared Hesiod's feeling about the sea (*Op.* e.g., 618, 646, 689–691). They would no more base the whole Athenian policy on the navy than they would put all their possessions on a ship.[52]

In sum, the same subjective orientation, the same humanism and historical sense appear in Pericles' concept of chremata as in his concept of techne and gnome and his disdain of tyche. Pericles has used chremata and chresthai in their central meanings. The preceding remarks on Pericles' use of these words find corroboration in G. Redard, *Recherches sur* χρή, χρῆσθαι. The relation between subject and object designated by chresthai is one of appropriation of the latter by the former according to occasion.[53] Appropriation is in fact at the heart of Pericles' policy, since gnome and techne appropriate what they may for the ends of policy, even the whole sea, one half of the earth. Thus chresthai is an essentially human verb, expressing a process which sees things from the sphere of the subject.[54] Chrema is the object in which the fact of chresthai is realized.[55]

52. The earlier Greek feeling about the sea is described by A. Lesky, *Thalatta* (Vienna, 1947), Chap. 1. Lesky takes Hesiod's advice to Perses as epitomizing this feeling (p. 37). Cf. Aristotle Socrates Onassis, quoted in Willi Frischauer, *Onassis* (New York, 1968), p. 71: "'A Greek, particularly, if he has a blade of grass or a tree on his native island, does not want to go to sea. If he has only just enough to eat and a place to sleep he hates to be parted from his father and his mother, from his uncles and his brothers, from his girl friend. But if he is desperately poor, to sea he goes.'"

53. G. Redard, *Recherches sur* χρή, χρῆσθαι: *Etude Semantique* (Paris, 1953), p. 44.

54. Ibid.

55. Redard, *Recherches sur* χρή, χρῆσθαι, p. 89.

Chance and Intelligence in Thucydides

Turning from chremata to the other main point of policy in this speech (2.13), namely, intelligence, gnome, we find that nothing is said about intelligence. The reason is that the use of capital is itself an expression of intelligence. Gnome and chremata are coordinate because, for Pericles, gnome is a normative principle. It is intelligence. Since intelligence demands the use of chremata in warfare, there is no antithesis between one's inner disposition and one's practical conduct. The Athenian general, Phormio, maintains the Periclean strategy when he scorns the Lacedaemonians because τῇ δυνάμει πλέον πίσυνοι ἢ τῇ γνώμῃ ἐπέρχονται (they attack trusting in their strength rather than their intelligence) (2.89.6). For Athenians there is no such distinction, since their strength comes from gnome.[56]

C. The Funeral Oration (2.35–46)

The Funeral Oration is both an expression in itself of the exuberance of Athenian rationality and a celebration of the rational freedom which Pericles regards as the prime characteristic of the Athenian character. In the Funeral Oration the contrast between Athens and Sparta which Thucydides has developed in various ways throughout the first book of the *History* and the beginning of the second is perfected. The Athenian citizen makes a conscious choice of the city's ends, based on

56. Cf. Sall. *Cat.* 1: Sed diu magnum inter mortales certamen fuit vine corporis an virtute animi res militaris magis procederet. Nam et prius quam incipias consulto ... opus est. Etc. According to a scholium on *Od.* 8.76, Odysseus and Achilles quarreled about whether Troy should be taken by force or by guile.

knowledge of the alternatives (2.40.3). In other words, Pericles understands Athenian democracy as a subjective phenomenon. The city is the expression of individual will, of an aggregate of individual wills, which produces a more powerful unity than the compulsory dedication to the state experienced by the Spartans. For example, when Pericles first mentions the Spartans (though the contrast between Sparta and Athens has been implicit all along), apropos of the Athenian way of preparing for war, he says in effect that it is the inner disposition of the Athenians, not objective preparations, which makes them so successful (2.39.1–2. N.b. τῷ ἀφ' ἡμῶν αὐτῶν . . . εὐψύχῳ; cf. 1.123.1). In general in the Funeral Oration Pericles emphasizes the quality (οἴας . . . οἴας . . . οἴων 2.36.4) of the Athenian constitution and character, and this means the spirit of the institutions and of the citizens. It may be for this reason that Pericles does not mention the Parthenon or any other material achievement, not even the great wealth of Athens which was the theme of his exhortations concerning policy. He alludes to such matters only in terms of their psychological effect (2.38, 43.1).

But the Athenians, in using a constitution (χρώμεθα . . . πολιτείᾳ 2.37.1) of this sort, in which rational freedom comes into play, have innovated. They have opposed the traditional form of the city, in which the laws are felt as objectively posited and the individual, far from exercising rational freedom, is "conscious of his honor and sufficiency only in the consciousness of working for the State."[57] Democracy is then an episode in the "humanis-

57. G. W. F. Hegel, *Lectures on the History of Philosophy*, trans. E. S. Haldane (London, 1892), I, 323.

tic revolution"[58] of the fifth century, and the fact that
Pericles says nothing of the gods in the Funeral Oration is
an indication of his humanism. In the traditional form of
the state, however, of which Sparta is the exemplar in the
History, laws and customs are sacrosanct, and since they
have been given by the gods (Tyrt., fr. 2.1–2; Solon fr.
24.8D³), they cannot be changed by mortals. But the
restless innovating Athenians take a different view of
things. Pericles has simply carried a step further the view
of Aeschylus in the *Eumenides,* symbolized in Athene's
relation to the court of dicasts, that the gods would will-
ingly give up to humans—at least to Athenians!
—freedom of decision in human affairs; and the view
embodied in the *Prometheus* that the arts freed mortals
from an abject subjugation to the gods. In the Periclean
account of Athens the gods have disappeared altogether,
and the strength of the city now appears as originating in
human will, specifically, in Athens, in individual rational
freedom.

In this way, Athens opposes the traditional form of the
state; but while opposing it, Athens loses nothing of what
was valuable in that form. Athens is rather a synthesis of
the best of the old with her own innovations. For this
reason, the Athenian character—and it is this character,
the city as expression of subjectivity, which is the real
theme of the Funeral Oration—appears as a combination
of opposite qualities: as Kakridis has made so abundantly
clear, the Athenian citizen incorporates a series of contradictory traits.[59] The style of the Funeral Oration is

58. Cf. W. K. C. Guthrie, *A History,* II (1965), 346–347.
59. J. T. Kakridis, *Der thuk. Epitaphios,* p. 31: "der athenische
Bürger eine Reihe von sich widersprechenden Eigenschaften
verkörpert."

thus characterized by a certain density of antithesis and by a mood of paradox. The Athenian constitution is a wonder (2.39.4), and wonders are composed of extensive μέν's and δέ's, as one sees (to compare great things with small) in Herodotus' description of the hippopotamus (2.71).

Antithesis and paradox are also characteristic of Pericles' description of the Athenian constitution in 2.37.1, a passage which will be found to reflect Pericles' concept of tyche. If one considers the tripartite division of the subject announced in 2.36.4 (ἐπιτήδευσις, πολιτεία, τρόποι), it is curious how little Pericles says about the *politeia* as a system of laws and how much, by comparison, about the practices and habits of the citizens. One might venture to say that the second sentence of 2.37.1 comprises Pericles' analysis of the workings of the Athenian constitution. On the basis of the Funeral Oration it would be impossible to give even a vague description of this constitution. Pericles does not praise the structure of the constitution or the institutions but rather the spirit of Athenian life. For this reason, his lone statement on certain political institutions becomes all the more important and warrants the detailed analyses that it has received.

The sentence in question is 2.37.1:

Χρώμεθα γὰρ πολιτείᾳ οὐ ζηλούσῃ τοὺς τῶν πέλας νόμους, παράδειγμα δὲ μᾶλλον αὐτοὶ ὄντες τισὶν ἢ μιμούμενοι ἑτέρους. καὶ ὄνομα μὲν διὰ τὸ μὴ ἐς ὀλίγους ἀλλ' ἐς πλείονας οἰκεῖν δημοκρατία κέκληται· μέτεστι δὲ κατὰ μὲν τοὺς νόμους πρὸς τὰ ἴδια διάφορα πᾶσι τὸ ἴσον, κατὰ δὲ τὴν ἀξίωσιν, ὡς ἕκαστος ἔν τῳ εὐδοκιμεῖ, οὐκ ἀπὸ μέρους τὸ πλέον ἐς τὰ κοινὰ ἢ ἀπ' ἀρετῆς προτιμᾶται, οὐδ' αὖ κατὰ πενίαν, ἔχων γέ τι ἀγαθὸν δρᾶσαι τὴν πόλιν, ἀξιώματος ἀφανείᾳ κεκώλυται.

We enjoy a constitution that does not copy the laws of our neighbors; rather, we ourselves are a model for others, not imitators. In name it is called a democracy because it is governed in the interest not of the few but the many. By the laws, all have equal justice in private differences; by merit, each man, according as his particular ability is recognized, is advanced in public life—not by lot but by arete. Nor again is a man held back by poverty and obscurity of rank, if he is able to benefit the city.

The whole sentence is built on a μέν-δέ antithesis between what the Athenian constitution is called and what it is in fact. It is necessary to keep this main antithesis in mind if one is to understand the meaning of *demokratia* in the μέν clause. The meaning of demokratia is not rule by the whole people but rule by the many as opposed to the few (perhaps the "well-born"). Thus, in the first of the two main parts of the antithetical δέ clause, Pericles says that the laws give equality to *all*. There is an antithesis between demokratia in the sense of rule by one party and in the sense of rule by all the citizens.[60]

This equality of all the citizens, which is antithetical to demokratia in the narrower sense, is true of private differences. This is legal equality. In the second part of the δέ clause, which itself consists of another μέν-δέ antithesis, Pericles opposes to legal equality in private affairs an

60. Since *demos* can mean either the whole people or the many as opposed to the few, two senses of *demokratia,* a word which had appeared only in the mid-fifth century, have been argued for. I have followed Johannes Kakridis, *Der thuk. Epitaphios,* p. 25. Gomme, II, 109, and Helmuth Vretska, "Perikles und die Herrschaft des Würdigsten," *RM* NS 109 (1966), 110, disagree with Kakridis. Their observations on the meanings of *demos* and *demokratia* are right, as far as they go, but they do not see that the meaning of *demokratia* in this context has to be determined finally by the main μέν-δέ antithesis on which the whole sentence is built. For the two senses of *demos,* see Finley, *Thucydides,* p. 162.

aristocratic principle in advancement to public office. Arete would have had an aristocratic ring.[61] There is now general agreement that the phrase ἀπὸ μέρους does not refer to election on a class basis and thus does not refer to Sparta, but to sortition: as Gomme paraphrased, "We do not use the lot for election to important offices."[62] Thus another reality of Athenian democracy as against the name, demokratia, is that arete is more important than the lot in election to public office. This observation is coordinated with another (οὐκ . . . οὐδ᾽ αὖ), along the same lines. No one is held back by poverty, just as no one is advanced by the lot rather than by arete. The second observation thus seems to erase any possible connotations of social-economic class that arete might have had.[63]

61. Kakridis, *Der thuk. Epitaphios,* p. 26. Cf. Gomme, "Thucydides Notes," *CQ* 42 (1948) 10, who cites Arist. *Pol.* 1294a9: δοκεῖ δὲ ἀριστοκρατία μὲν εἶναι μάλιστα τὸ τὰς τιμὰς νενεμῆσθαι κατ᾽ ἀρετήν.

62. Gomme, II, 108; H. Flashar, *Der Epitaphios des Perikles: Seine Funktion in Geschichtswerk des Thukydides* (Heidelberg, 1969), p. 18; Vretska, *RM* NS 109 (1966), 112–114; cf. Kakridis, *Der thuk. Epitaphios,* pp. 26–27. For a view opposed to these, see Gregory Vlastos, " Ἰσονομία πολιτική," in J. Mau and E. G. Schmidt, eds., *Isonomia: Studien zur Gleichheitsvorstellung im griechischen Denken* (Berlin, 1964), p. 29, n. 2. Vlastos' main contention is that "it would be contrary to the strategy of this address (which is . . . an encomium first and foremost) to contradict explicitly the cherished formula that in a democracy the demos 'rules in turn' . . . " But Vlastos overlooks the obvious point that Pericles does in fact intend to contradict a certain understanding of what is meant by the word "democracy." Vlastos was led astray perhaps by his belief, which is merely asserted, that κατὰ δὲ τὴν ἀξίωσιν is the "real opposition" to δημοκρατία κέκληται. On the contrary, everyone would feel the antithesis between ὄνομα μὲν and μέτεστι δὲ. See the analysis by Kakridis, *Der thuk. Epitaphios,* pp. 24ff.

63. Kakridis, *Der thuk. Epitaphios,* p. 28.

It is especially these last two observations on democracy (κατὰ δὲ τὴν ἀξίωσιν through the end of the sentence) that are of interest to the present study, since they exemplify so well the paradoxical character of Athens in Pericles' account and since they both have a bearing on the Periclean concept of tyche.

As for paradox, probably nothing would have been more unexpected than the attribution of the cardinal aristocratic value to the citizens of a democracy, since it must have been the common view that ἔστι . . . πάσῃ γῇ τὸ βέλτιστον ἐναντίον τῇ δημοκρατίᾳ (everywhere the aristocracy is opposed to democracy) (Pseudo-Xen. *Ath. Pol.* 1.5, cf. 3.10; cf. Hdt. 3.80). Similarly, opponents of democracy would damn its insensitivity to *ta kala* (Hdt. 3.80), but Pericles says that the Athenians love beauty (2.40.1).

If anything could have been more paradoxical than the attribution of arete to democracy, it would have been the suggestion that public offices were filled on the basis of arete rather than by sortition. Even if some important offices were elective in Athens, the fact remains that democracy could be defined as the type of constitution in which offices were assigned by lot (Arist. *Rhet.* 1365b31; *Pol.* 1294b7–8; Eur. *Supp.* 406–407; cf. Hdt. 3.80.6). Most offices in Athens were in fact filled by lot. Now the lot was after all "the child of chance" (Eur. fr. 989N; cf. Pl. *Rep.* 619d7), and an opponent of sortition would argue against it on the analogy of the technai, implicitly basing himself on the techne-tyche antithesis.[64] What Pericles opposes to sortition is arete. One recalls the fact

64. The author of the *Dissoi Logoi*, a work dating from the end of the fifth century (D.-K. II.405), argues against the proponents of sortition as follows: "Some of the leaders of the people say that the offices

that Pericles' opening words in the *History,* with their echo of Theognis or of an aristocratic slogan, tended to characterize Pericles as a steadfast aristocrat attempting to stabilize the fickle passions of the mob. Such a recollection would not be misleading, since Pericles' observation on Athenian democracy in 2.37.1 points to the arete of Pericles himself. When Pericles himself is speaking, what other office than that of *strategos,* which he held so constantly, would one think of in connection with the contrast between arete and sortition? In fact, the office of strategos has been thought of as a sort of antidote to the potentially ill effects of sortition.[65]

---

should be determined by lot, but their beliefs are not the best. For if one should ask the man who maintains this position, 'Why don't you assign your servants their tasks by lot, so that the carter, if he draws the lot of cook, may cook, and the cook may be carter, and the other occupations after the same fashion? And why don't we assemble the blacksmiths, the cobblers, the carpenters, and the goldsmiths and distinguish them by lot and force each one to pursue the art he receives by lot and not the one he understands?' [What could he say in reply?] And it would be the same thing in musical competitions to choose the contestants by lot and for each to compete in the mode assigned by lot. The flautist will play the lyre if it so happens and the lyre-player the flute; and in war the archer and the hoplite will be cavalrymen and the cavalryman will be an archer, so that all will do what they do not understand and are incapable of. The proponents of sortition say that it is good and very much to the people's advantage. But I utterly disbelieve that it is to the people's advantage. For there are in the cities men who hate the people, and if the lot so decides, they will destroy the democracy. No, the democracy itself should choose those whom it observes to be well disposed to itself, and those who are best suited should be general, and others should be guardians of the laws and so forth" (D.-K. II.414.27–415.14). For Socrates' objection to sortition, see *Gorg.* 458e3–459c5. E. R. Dodds cites Xen. *Mem.* 1.2.9; Arist. *Rhet.* 1393b4–9.

65. Vretska, *RM* NS 109 (1966), 117. Vretska deserves the credit for seeing that 2.37.1 must apply to Pericles. He argues the matter somewhat differently than I do. Vretska observes that Pericles' de-

Pericles' description of Athenian democracy appropriately finds an echo in Thucydides' description of Pericles' relation to that democracy: ἐγίγετό τε λόγῳ μὲν δημοκρατία, ἔργῳ δὲ ὑπὸ τοῦ πρώτου ἀνδρὸς ἀρχή (in name it was a democracy but in fact it was rule by the first man) (2.65.9). The echo is unmistakable. As in 2.37.1, it is said that Athens is only nominally a democracy. What this means comes into the open in 2.65.9, however, where Thucydides explains that the true character of the constitution was rule by the "first man." If this is the truth about Athens in Pericles' time, then Pericles' praise of Athens is really, at least to some degree, self-praise, or, to put it another way, Pericles' praise of Athens is Thucydides' praise of Pericles. Pericles represents Thucydides' formulation of an ideal which Pericles did

---

scription of Athenian democracy in 2.37.1 does not correspond to historical realities. This fact is to be explained by Thucydides' dislike of democracy and his admiration of Pericles. Thucydides could praise Athens only by praising Pericles. Vretska's main evidence for this point is the use by Thucydides in describing Pericles (2.34.6, 65.8) of two key terms (ἀξίωμα; ἀξίωσις) which also occur in 2.37.1. Vretska's point holds good, I think; but his discussion is somewhat vitiated by his failure to see that these two terms have different meanings. I shall discuss this matter below. The arguments of Flashar, *Der Epitaphios*, p. 18, against Vretska are not strong. Flashar thinks that 2.37.1 does not apply specifically to Pericles, for two reasons. First, ὡς ἕκαστος ἕν τῳ εὐδοκιμεῖ shows that not Pericles alone is meant. But these words are easily explained as hyperbole. There is also the matter of rhetorical variation and contrast. Second, Flashar points out that Thucydides does not say that in political life offices are filled *only* on the principle of arete and not by lot, but that only in cases of special merit is sortition obviated. Flashar adds: for example, in the case of *strategos* or funeral orator. But this point brings Flashar right back to Vretska's position, for the office of *strategos* and the occasional (cf. 2.34.7) elections of a funeral orator were extremely important matters. Pericles, who is both funeral orator and *strategos*, personifies the arete which he says the Athenians value.

in fact realize but which the other Athenians did not approach.[66] In particular, Pericles realized the potentiality of the office of strategos as a means to the control of tyche. The office itself stood outside the chances of the lot, and, in that office, Pericles guided Athens in a policy based on the supremacy of gnome over tyche.

There remains for discussion Pericles' observation that "neither is anyone held back by poverty when he has it in him to benefit the city in some way, on account of the obscurity of his position" (ἀξιώματος ἀφανείᾳ). The scholiast commented on ἀξιώματος: ἀντὶ τοῦ τύχης (ABFc2). The interpretation is correct, since prosperity and the opposite are "the chances of life" (ἡ μὲν πενία ... ἡ δ' ἐξουσία ... αἱ δ' ἄλλαι ξυντυχίαι 3.45.4).[67] The notion that the Athenian constitution thwarts the chances of life is just what one would expect from Pericles. Again Pericles' words are paradoxical. As Aristotle says (*Ath. Pol.* 28.1), Pericles was the last of the popular leaders who belonged to an aristocratic family. Pericles looks back on a tradition in which the people had nearly always gone to the aristocratic families for their leaders. Pericles' suggestion that the scope of arete was unlimited by poverty and that thus the chances of life were overcome by the Athenian constitution is surely hyperbolic. When Pericles says that men are advanced by arete he refers to the people's choice of aristocratic leaders. Only in this way did arete prevail over chance!

The meaning of *axioma* in 2.37.1 is "rank in society based on wealth," as is clear from the fact that ἀξιώματος

66. Flashar, *Der Epitaphios*, pp. 22–23.

67. For the connection of ἀξίωμα and τύχη cf. Thuc. 4.86.6: ἀπάτῃ γὰρ εὐπρεπεῖ αἴσχιον τοῖς γε ἐν ἀξιώματι πλεονεκτῆσαι ἢ βίᾳ ἐμφανεῖ· τὸ μὲν γὰρ ἰσχύος δικαιώσει, ἣν ἡ τύχη ἔδωκεν, ἐπέρχεται. Cf. Arist. *Phys.* 197b4–5, and Sestus 423: Sors et patrimonium significat.

ἀφανείᾳ is in apposition to κατὰ πενίαν. Thus axioma has a different meaning from *axiosis,* which is further specified by ὡς ἕκαστος ἕν τῳ εὐδοκιμεῖ. The meaning of axiosis is "position in society based on good reputation in some activity." The difference between axiosis and axioma corresponds to the usual difference between pairs of -σις and -μα nouns from the same verb: "Là ou -σις et -μα coexistent, ce qui est fréquent, le premier exprime l'idée d'une puissance occulte, mais active efficace, le second est moins abstrait et plus matériel."[68]

Thucydides uses axiosis and axioma of Pericles in the meanings just given. In 2.34.6 of the choice of a funeral orator, there occurs the phrase: ὃς ἂν γνώμῃ τε δοκῇ μὴ ἀξύνετος εἶναι καὶ ἀξιώσει προήκῃ (whoever has the reputation of intelligence and is preeminent in merit). Here there is an implied contrast between gnome and axiosis, perhaps a variation of the *logos-ergon* antithesis so common in the *History.* Axiosis refers to Pericles' reputation as a public figure, a man of action. But in 2.65.8 the context makes it clear that axioma refers to the fact that Pericles was a man of means. Thucydides contrasts the venality of Pericles' successors with Pericles' incorruptibility: δυνατὸς ὢν τῷ τε ἀξιώματι καὶ τῇ γνώμῃ χρημάτων τε διαφανῶς ἀδωρότατος (being influential because of his means and his intelligence and obviously uncorruptible). Pericles says in the Funeral Oration that no Athenian is held back in public life ἀξιώματος ἀφανείᾳ, but he himself led the Athe-

68. A. Meillet and J. Vendryes, *Traité de Grammaire Comparée des Langues Classiques* (Paris, 1963), p. 416. Gomme asserted but did not prove that *axiosis* and *axioma* meant the same thing (II, 110) and in this he was followed by Kakridis, *Der thuk. Epitaphios,* p. 27, n. 2, and Vretska, *RM* NS 109 (1966), 117, n. 21.

nians because he was δυνατὸς ἀξιώματι. If the Athenian constitution thwarts the chances of life, as Pericles implies in 2.37.1, it is again not because of the structure of the constitution as such but because the Athenians have looked to aristocratic leaders who were unhindered ἀξιώματος ἀφανείᾳ, in particular to Pericles himself.

This conclusion would seem to contradict the remarks concerning freedom which prefaced the discussion of the Funeral Oration. The Athenians are only apparently free; in reality they are ruled by an aristocrat. In fact, Aristotle speaks of στρατηγία διὰ βίου, which Pericles' repeated tenures of this office resemble, as a kind of kingship (*Pol.* 1285a15), and the Old Oligarch points out that the Athenian people leave magistracies which affect the safety of the whole city—he mentions, of course, the στρατηγία—to the δυνατώτατοι (1.3). Thucydides describes Pericles as δυνατός in the phrase quoted in the preceding paragraph; the context, however, will show why the rule of the leading citizen was not, in Pericles' case, contrary to democratic freedom:

αἴτιον δ' ἦν ὅτι ἐκεῖνος μὲν δυνατὸς ὢν τῷ τε ἀξιώματι καὶ τῇ γνώμῃ χρημάτων τε διαφανῶς ἀδωρότατος γενόμενος κατεῖχε τὸ πλῆθος ἐλευθέρως, καὶ οὐκ ἤγετο μᾶλλον ὑπ' αὐτοῦ ἢ αὐτὸς ἦγε, διὰ τὸ μὴ κτώμενος ἐξ οὐ προσηκόντων τὴν δύναμιν πρὸς ἡδονήν τι λέγειν, ἀλλ' ἔχων ἐπ' ἀξιώσει καὶ πρὸς ὀργήν τι ἀντειπεῖν.

That man [unlike his successors], being influential because of his means and his intelligence and being obviously unvenal, used to control the people in a spirit of freedom and they did not lead him but he led them, since he did not flatter them in order to acquire power dishonestly but could even, thanks to his reputation, angrily oppose them.

55

This description of Pericles, taken with the results of the discussion of 2.37.1 in the Funeral Oration, seems to yield the paradox that the Athenians were free because Pericles controlled them. But the paradox is diminished by the nature of the control, by "the spirit of freedom" (ἐλευθέρως).[69] Pericles' control was not that of a tyrant or a king over a subject population but was rather exerted by persuasion. The discussion of the prooemium to the first speech has already shown how Pericles conceived of his policy in terms of the relation of his gnome to the gnomai of the citizens and how he exhorted them to the same constancy which he himself maintained. He asked them to abide by and support the city's policy arrived at in common. Thus Pericles saw the city's actions as reflecting a unity of will and policy based on intelligence as opposed to chance. Pericles can be said to have led the Athenians in a spirit of freedom because he conducted himself as a statesman on the principle of gnome, according to which the city is not a forced nexus of conflicting interests in which those who seek to acquire power do so for personal gain and those who lack power are inferior in every way to their betters, but a harmonious expression of a unified, rational will. We cannot pause here to compare the Thucydidean Pericles' principle with that of the Old Oligarch or with any earlier thought, but we can see immediately that Pericles has left behind an earlier view of the city which sees only classes and conflicts (cf., in the *History*, Athenagoras: 6.35–41).

69. See H. Diller, "Freiheit bei Thukydides als Schlagwort und als Wirklichkeit," *Gymn.*69 (1962), 201–202; K. von Fritz, *Die Griechische Geschichtsschreibung*, Ia (Berlin, 1967), 677, whose discussion supports my point. In general, however, von Fritz' discussion, arising

Pericles thus regards the city from the point of view of the individual, in particular, of the individual's subjective conviction concerning the worth of the city and of political life. This concept of Athens, already adumbrated in the prooemium of the first speech, emerges from a famous passage of the Funeral Oration:

ἐλευθέρως δὲ τά τε πρὸς τὸ κοινὸν πολιτεύομεν καὶ ἐς τὴν πρὸς ἀλλήλους τῶν καθ᾽ ἡμέραν ἐπιτηδευμάτων ὑποψίαν, οὐ δι᾽ ὀργῆς τὸν πέλας, εἰ καθ᾽ ἡδονήν τι δρᾷ, ἔχοντες, οὐδὲ ἀζημίους μέν, λυπηρὰς δὲ τῇ ὄψει ἀχθηδόνας προστιθέμενοι. ἀνεπαχθῶς δὲ τὰ ἴδια προσομιλοῦντες τὰ δημόσια διὰ δέος μάλιστα οὐ παρανομοῦμεν, τῶν τε αἰεὶ ἐν ἀρχῇ ὄντων ἀκροάσει καὶ τῶν νόμων, καὶ μάλιστα αὐτῶν ὅσοι τε ἐπ᾽ ὠφελίᾳ τῶν ἀδικουμένων κεῖνται καὶ ὅσοι ἄγραφοι ὄντες αἰσχύνην ὁμολογουμένην φέρουσιν.

We conduct our political life in a spirit of freedom both as regards the public realm and as regards suspicion of one

---

out of the engrossing question of Thucydidean scholarship in the last two decades, namely, the question of the nature of the Athenian empire, is directed to the kind of freedom to be found in Athens and Sparta respectively. He describes the paradox of the Athenian democratic freedom of the polis as against its tyrannical empire and the tyrannical character of Spartan statism as against the comparative freedom of its allies; and argues that on the basis of this paradox can be understood the "tension," as regards Athenian empire and freedom, between the Epitaphios and the last speech of Pericles (pp. 670–675).

For the controversy concerning the Athenian empire, see esp. A. H. M. Jones, "Athenian Democracy and its Critics," *The Cambridge Historical Journal* II (1953), 1–26; G. E. M. Ste-Croix, "The Character of the Athenian Empire," *Historia* 3 (1954–5), 1–41; D. W. Bradeen, "The Popularity of the Athenian Empire," *Historia* 9 (1960), 257–269; J. Quinn, "Thucydides and the Unpopularity of the Athenian Empire," *Historia* 13 (1964), 257–260. All these are commented upon by von Fritz, *Griech. Geschichtsschreibung*, Ib, 298, n. 4. Finally, on this subject, see J. de Romilly, *Thucydides and the Athenian Empire*, trans. P. Thody (Oxford, 1963).

another in daily affairs, without anger against our neighbor if he does as he likes, and without casting glances which, though harmless, are painful annoyances. Associating with one another unvexatiously in private, we do not break the laws, especially because of proper fear, through obedience to those in office at any given time and to the laws, and especially those laws which have been made for the help of the injured and those which, though unwritten, bring an acknowledged shame upon the transgressor (2.37.2–3).

The "spirit of freedom" in the public realm refers to the statement, already discussed in detail, in which Pericles rather obliquely describes the aristocratic element in the democratic constitution. This is the freedom of excellence to display itself for the good of the city; and Pericles embodies this freedom (2.65.8). He now goes on to describe this spirit in terms of the daily relations of the citizens in private life; and then, returning to the public realm, he maintains that the Athenians abide by the laws out of "proper fear."[70] The grounds of this constitution, as it has been described, and of daily intercourse are the laws, and the grounds of the laws are "proper fear." Both sorts of law that Pericles mentions as especially illustrating Athenian obedience would involve subjective conviction on the part of the citizen. One sort of law is that which has been made to protect the injured. Aristotle (*Ath. Pol.* 9.4) and Plutarch (*Sol.* 18.3–8) show that it was a provision of the Solonian constitution that anyone, not only a kinsman, could prosecute on behalf of the injured party.[71] In other words, the system of justice is to be

70. So Gomme, II, 112, translates *deos*. For *deos* as *bonne crainte*, see J. de Romilly, "La Crainte dans l'oeuvre de Thucydide," *Classica et mediaevalia* 17 (1956), 119–127.

71. These places are cited and discussed by Gomme, II.

supported by mutual concern on the part of the citizens. This is the ideal to which Pericles alludes. The other sort of law is the unwritten law. In the same way that the first sort presupposes mutual concern on the part of the citizens, their own determination to maintain the laws, so the unwritten laws bear an "acknowledged shame." They are like the funerary inscriptions written not on *stelai* but in men's minds (τῆς γνώμης 2.43.3). Unlike the famous unwritten laws of Sophocles' *Antigone* (450–461; cf. *OT* 863–870), Pericles' unwritten laws are not sanctioned by the gods but rather by an inner sense of shame at breaking them.[72] The same humanism that could be detected in Pericles' policy in his first speech in the *History* is all the clearer in his concept of Athenian policy life.

He associates fear (*deos*) with obedience, and obedience, in the case of the unwritten laws, with shame (*aischyne*). Fear of breaking the law thus has its source in the citizens themselves and not in external coercion. Pericles' notion evidently invites comparison with the speech of Athena in Aeschylus' *Eumenides* in which she ordains the court of the Areopagus (681ff.), because Athena stresses fear as a sanction of justice. Although her speech should surely not be treated as a legal document, one may be justified in finding a distinction between φόβος συγγενής, which would approximate Pericles' sense of deos, and σέβας, which is an externally imposed obligation of reverence (*Eum.* 690–691). But hardly anything else in this speech suggests such a distinction, and in fact Athena seems to regard the Areopagus as an object of fear (698–700). Furthermore, her language obviously

72. V. Ehrenberg, *Sophocles and Pericles*, pp. 37–44; cf. Gomme, II, 113–114, for criticism of some of Ehrenberg's points.

resembles that of the Erinyes in 517ff.,[73] where the Erinyes defend fear of punishment as necessary to Zeus' governance of the universe. Their language in turn resembles that of the Hymn to Zeus in the parodos of the *Agamemnon,* where it is said that men learn by suffering,[74] and there is no sense that men can guide themselves by their own lights. In sharp contrast, Pericles, with his humanistic notion of justice, sees the lawfulness of the Athenians as originating not in fear externally imposed but in an inner sense of shame.

The prooemium to the first speech was based on an antithesis of gnome and tyche. The same antithesis is implicit in that part of the Funeral Oration in which Pericles describes the bravery of the soldiers in whose honor he is speaking. Here he says: "in the briefest moment they were, at the height of their glory, released from chance rather than from proper fear" (2.42.4).[75] The same "proper fear" (*deos*) which preserves the city in the relations of the citizens to one another also preserves the city against its enemies. The fallen soldiers' deos is the same deos of which Pericles had spoken in 2.37.3. Since these soldiers are also said to have acted in the knowledge of their duty (γιγνώσκοντες τὰ δέοντα 2.43.1; cf. 2.40.3)—and analysis of the context will show how Pericles emphasizes the fact of the soldiers' conscious choice of their death—the notion of gnome is here associated with deos, not unexpectedly, since we have already seen that gnome embraces both the intellectual and the moral.

73. Cf. especially 696–697 with 526–528; 698 with 517–519; 699 with 522–525.

74. *Agam.* 177, 180–183; cf. the Erinyes in *Eum.* 520–521.

75. This interpretation of the passage is argued at length in the Appendix.

The soldiers γιγνώσκοντες τὰ δέοντα displayed at the level of action the same quality of which Pericles boasted when he said that he was second to none in his ability γνῶναι τὰ δέοντα (2.60.5). Thus the fallen soldiers were released from chance in the same way that Pericles' gnome aimed at protecting the city as a whole from tyche.

It might be objected that the notion of a release from tyche is un-Greek or meaningless. But in an earlier Greek view of things, chance is all. Since chance gives everything, one can only pray for good luck (Theog. 129–130; cf. Archil. fr. *8D³). Man is an essentially casual being: πᾶν ἐστι ἄνθρωπος συμφορή (Hdt. 1.32.4; cf. Pind. *Ol.* 12). Thus, when Pericles says that the fallen soldiers were released from chance, he means that they were released from the *amechania* that the earlier tradition held to be the human condition. The notion of such a release is not un-Greek. It can be found in the Hippocratic *De Arte* (4):

τῇ τέχνῃ ἐπέτρεψαν αὐτούς, ὥστε τῆς μὲν ἐς τὴν τύχην ἀναφορῆς ἀπηλλαγμένοι εἰσί, τῆς μέντοι ἐς τὴν τέχνην οὐκ ἀπηλλαγμένοι.

They entrusted themselves to the art, so that they are freed of reliance on chance but not of reliance on the art.

The parallel with the Periclean notion obviously extends beyond release from chance to the Hippocratic concept of techne as the force that opposes chance. Pericles stated his naval strategy partly in terms of the tyche-techne antithesis, and his statesmanship was based on a tyche-gnome antithesis.

The antithesis between tyche and deos in 2.42.4 is the most inclusive instance of, and thus climactic to, the five preceding antitheses of this sentence; furthermore, in the next chapter, where Pericles applies his description of the fallen soldiers' bravery to an exhortation to his audience, he maintains the same antithesis. One must first read the passage as a whole and then trace the single, main antithesis in its various statements.

τῶνδε δὲ οὔτε πλούτου τις τὴν ἔτι ἀπόλαυσιν προτιμήσας ἐμαλακίσθη
οὔτε πενίας ἐλπίδι, ὡς κἂν ἔτι διαφυγὼν αὐτὴν πλουτήσειεν,
ἀναβολὴν τοῦ δεινοῦ ἐποιήσατο· τὴν δὲ τῶν ἐναντίων τιμωρίαν
ποθεινοτέραν αὐτῶν λαβόντες καὶ κινδύνων ἅμα τόνδε κάλλιστον
νομίσαντες ἐβουλήθησαν μετ᾽ αὐτοῦ τοὺς μὲν τιμωρεῖσθαι, τῶν δὲ
ἐφίεσθαι, ἐλπίδι μὲν τὸ ἀφανὲς τοῦ κατορθώσειν ἐπιτρέψαντες, ἔργῳ
δὲ περὶ τοῦ ἤδη ὁρωμένου σφίσιν αὐτοῖς ἀξιοῦντες πεποιθέναι, καὶ ἐν
αὐτῷ τῷ ἀμύνεσθαι καὶ παθεῖν μᾶλλον ἡγησάμενοι ἢ [τὸ] ἐνδόντες
σῴζεσθαι, τὸ μὲν αἰσχρὸν τοῦ λόγου ἔφυγον, τὸ δ᾽ ἔργον τῷ σώματι
ὑπέμειναν καὶ δι᾽ ἐλαχίστου καιροῦ τύχης ἅμα ἀκμῇ τῆς δόξης
μᾶλλον ἢ τοῦ δέους ἀπηλλάγησαν.

᾽Καὶ οἵδε μὲν προσηκόντως τῇ πόλει τοιοίδε ἐγένοντο; τοὺς δὲ
λοιποὺς χρὴ ἀσφαλεστέραν μὲν εὔχεσθαι, ἀτολμοτέραν δὲ μηδὲν
ἀξιοῦν τὴν ἐς τοὺς πολεμίους διάνοιαν ἔχειν, σκοποῦντας μὴ λόγῳ
μόνῳ τὴν ὠφελίαν, ἣν ἄν τις πρὸς οὐδὲν χεῖρον αὐτοὺς ὑμᾶς εἰδότας
μηκύνοι, λέγων ὅσα ἐν τῷ τοὺς πολεμίους ἀμύνεσθαι ἀγαθὰ ἔνεστιν,
ἀλλὰ μᾶλλον τὴν τῆς πόλεως δύναμιν καθ᾽ ἡμέραν ἔργῳ θεωμένους
καὶ ἐραστὰς γιγνομένους αὐτῆς, καὶ ὅταν ὑμῖν μεγάλη δόξῃ εἶναι,
ἐνθυμουμένους ὅτι τολμῶντες καὶ γιγνώσκοντες τὰ δέοντα καὶ ἐν τοῖς
ἔργοις αἰσχυνόμενοι ἄνδρες αὐτὰ ἐκτήσαντο, καὶ ὁπότε καὶ πείρᾳ του
σφαλεῖεν, οὐκ οὖν καὶ τὴν πόλιν γε τῆς σφετέρας ἀρετῆς ἀξιοῦντες
στερίσκειν, κάλλιστον δὲ ἔρανον αὐτῇ προϊέμενοι.

Neither preferring the future enjoyment of wealth did any one of these men play the coward nor in the poor man's hope, that one might yet escape poverty and be rich, did any one of these delay terror. Taking vengeance on the enemy to be more desirable than future prospects (αὐτῶν), and at the same time believing this to be the fairest of risks, they wanted to run the risk (μετ᾽ αὐτοῦ), to punish the one (the enemy) and renounce the other (the future), having committed to hope the obscurity of success, and seeing fit in action to rely on themselves in regard to what presently lay before their eyes. And considering that in resistance itself and suffering they found safety rather than in submission, they escaped a disgraceful account of themselves and in their own person endured the deed. In the briefest moment they were, at the height of their glory, released from chance rather than from proper fear.

Such were these men, as befits the city. Those who survive them should pray to make safer choices but should not at all deem it right to have a less bold spirit in the face of the enemy, considering not only the advantages, on which one could expatiate to you who yourselves know as well as he—he could tell you how many benefits there are in defense against the enemy—but rather in fact looking upon the power of the city day by day and becoming lovers of her, and, when she seems great to you, reflecting that men acquired all this acting boldly, knowing their duty, and acting out of fear of disgrace, thinking it wrong to deprive the city of their bravery if they failed in some attempt and offering it to her as their fairest gift.

The following schematization represents in order the various expressions of the central antithesis (a through i) and the order in the sentence of the two halves of each expression (1 or 2):

42.4

(a.1) οὔτε πλούτου τις τὴν ἔτι ἀπόλαυσιν προτιμήσας ἐμαλακίσθη οὔτε πενίας ἐλπίδι, ὡς κἂν ἔτι διαφυγὼν αὐτὴν πλουτήσειεν

(a.2) τὴν δὲ τῶν ἐναντίων τιμωρίαν ποθεινοτέραν αὐτῶν λαβόντες, καὶ κινδύνων ἅμα τόνδε κάλλιστον νομίσαντες

(b.2) τῶν δὲ ἐφίεσθαι[76]

(b.1) ἐβουλήθησαν μετ᾽ αὐτοῦ τοὺς μὲν τιμωρεῖσθαι,

(c.1) ἐλπίδι μὲν τὸ ἀφανὲς τοῦ κατορθώσειν ἐπιτρέψαντες,

(c.2) ἔργῳ δὲ περὶ τοῦ ἤδη ὁρωμένου σφίσιν αὐτοῖς ἀξιοῦντες πεποιθέναι,

76. This schematization makes it all the clearer that there is corruption here. The reading of the MSS, retained by Jones-Powell in the Oxford Classical Texts edition and also by Luschnat in the new

(d.2) μᾶλλον ἡγησάμενοι ἢ [τὸ] ἐνδόντες σῴζεσθαι,[77]

(d.1) καὶ ἐν αὐτῷ τῷ ἀμύνεσθαι καὶ παθεῖν

(e.1) τὸ μὲν αἰσχρὸν τοῦ λόγου ἔφυγον

(e.2) τὸ δ᾽ ἔργον τῷ σώματι ὑπέμειναν

(f.1) καὶ δι᾽ ἐλαχίστου καιροῦ τύχης

(f.2) ἅμα ἀκμῇ τῆς δόξης μᾶλλον ἢ τοῦ δέους ἀπηλλάγησαν.

43.1

(g.1) τοὺς δὲ λοιποὺς χρὴ ἀσφαλ. εστέραν μὲν εὔχεσθαι

(g.2) ἀτολμοτέραν δὲ μηδὲν ἀξιοῦν τὴν ἐς τοὺς πολεμίους διάνοιαν ἔχειν

(h.1) σκοποῦντας μὴ λόγῳ μόνον τὴν ὠφελίαν

(h.2) ἀλλὰ μᾶλλον τὴν τῆς πόλεως δύναμιν καθ᾽ ἡμέραν ἔργῳ θεωμένους καὶ ἐραστὰς γιγνομένους αὐτῆς

(i.2) καὶ ὁπότε καὶ πείρα τοῦ σφαλεῖεν, οὐκ οῦν καὶ τὴν πόλιν γε τῆς σφετέρας ἀρετῆς ἀξιοῦντες στερίσκειν

(i.1) ἐνθυμουμένους ὅτι τολμῶντες καὶ γιγνώσκοντες τὰ δέοντα καὶ ἐν τοῖς ἔργοις αἰσχυνόμενοι.

Teubner edition of Books I and II (1960), is clearly illogical. As Gomme observes, "it would be contradictory as well as tasteless, after asserting that both rich and poor have abjured the charms of wealth, to add that in their last fight it was still their aim" (II, 132). We should emend either to ἀφίεσθαι with Poppo or to ὑφίεσθαι, either of which with the genitive can mean "to put something off." Since ὑφίεσθαι with the genitive is used of passions (LSJ s.v. ὑφίημι II) it seems the more likely. But for a Periclean use of ἀφίεσθαι with the genitive in the required sense, see 2.60.4.

77. For a plausible explanation of how the bracketed τό came into the MS, see J. H. Oliver, rev. of Kakridis, *Der thuk. Epitaphios*, *AJP* 85 (1964), 106.

On the negative side (the left-hand column) are the future, desire, hope, words (as opposed to deeds), and, finally, tyche. All these matters appear in conjunction again in Diodotus' analysis of revolutionary psychology (3.45.6): hope and passionate desire lead the revolutionary to rely on hope and, being obscure, prevail over present visible dangers. Eros or willfulness and hope (4.108.4, 6.24.3) and tyche and hope (3.97.2, 5.103–104; cf. Democr. B 176) appear together in contexts in which a disparaging view is taken of these traits.[78] In short, the complex of ideas in the left-hand column has several parallels in Thucydides which show that tyche finds an appropriate place on this side of the antitheses schematized. Furthermore, tyche, as the most general term, serves to sum up the others. The complex of ideas on the positive side is self-evidently consistent, and again deos, as the most general term in the series, is climactic, summing up the indications of bravery in a.2 to f.2.

In 43.1 Pericles continues the same antithesis. In i.1 *aischynomenoi* corroborates the semantics of deos proposed for 42.4.[79] Thus we have again, as in 2.37.2–3, a collocation of "proper fear" and the sense of shame. That this collocation should now appear in a military context is by no means surprising, since Pericles, having made the connection of δέος and αἰσχύνη in 2.37.2–3, turned immediately to the application of this thought to two areas, the pleasures of Athenian life, which he treats very

78. For hope as a negative concept in Thucydides, see Tudor Gardiner, "Terms for Power in Thucydides" (unpub. diss., Harvard University, 1968), p. 223.

79. See Appendix for the semantics of *deos*.

briefly (2.38), and then the Athenian military character, which he treats much more fully (2.39).[80]

Gignoskontes (i.1) is perfectly Periclean. Elsewhere Pericles contrasts gnome with both *elpis* (2.62.5) and tyche (1.144.4), and we hope to have shown that the gnome-tyche antithesis, implicit here again in 2.42.4–43.1, is central to Pericles' thought. On the negative side, there is an association of ideas in f.1, g.1 (ἀσφαλεστέραν), and i.1, namely, in tyche and *sphallesthai*. Pericles implicitly associates the two in 1.140.1, and one could say that *to sphallein* is the characteristic activity of tyche: ταῖς μὲν τύχαις ἐνδέχεσθαι σφάλλεσθαι τοὺς ἀνθρώπους (2.87.3; cf. 3.39.8, 43.5); cf. σφάλλει δ' ἐκείνους οὓς ἂν ὑψώσῃ τύχη (fr. adesp. 547.13N).

The positive side (the right-hand column) provides a strong confirmation of the interpretation of deos and aischyne in 2.37.3. The notion of law as consisting not in blind obedience but in inner conviction appears in 2.42.4–43.1 in the large number of subjective terms, that is, terms which describe the bravery of the fallen soldiers as originating in conscious choice or some inward sense of obligation: ποθεινοτέραν . . . λαβόντες; νομίσαντες (a.1); ἐβουλήθησαν (b.1); σφίσιν αὐτοῖς ἀξιοῦντες πεποιθέναι (c.2); τοῦ δέους (f.2); γιγνώσκοντες τὰ δέοντα καὶ . . . αἰσχυνόμενοι (i.1). In the same way Pericles puts the exhortation to the survivors in subjective terms: ἀξιοῦν . . . διάνοιαν ἔχειν (g.2); ἐραστὰς γιγνομένους (h.2); ἐνθυμουμένους (i.1). The Periclean understanding of Athenian citizenship in terms of the subjectivity of the citizen should be seen against the background, recently described so fully by Pierre Huart, of Thucydides' elaborate psychological

80. Cf. von Fritz, *Griech. Geschichtsschreibung*, Ia, 672.

vocabulary and analysis.[81] Once again the study of Pericles' words leads to a conclusion that has truth for Thucydides' own thought as well.

The subjectivity of Athenian citizenship is what makes it possible for the citizen to be "released from chance," that is, freed of the whims of fortune. In choosing to die for the city, the citizen places the continued existence of the city and the values it represents above the continued enjoyment of his own individual existence or whatever hopes for the future he may have. Patriotism of this sort is a release from fortune, because the city is considered itself to embody the values of the individual citizen so that he knows in advance—and all the more so if he risks his life in battle—that the individual mischance of his own death will not have destroyed what was most essential in him, his character as an Athenian citizen; and thus by his own briefest mischance (δι' ἐλαχίστου καιροῦ) he is freed of chance altogether, which is powerless over him. This subjective or self-conscious Athenian patriotism differs from the Spartan habit of unreflecting obedience to the state. With the Spartans, the individual is at the disposal of the state, and the individual's death can be considered only as a sacrifice to an objectively posited law which he has never freely taken upon himself; the Athenians do not have a law requiring bravery but act bravely when they must (2.39.4). The Spartans, with their lifelong cultivation of bravery (2.39.4), have never made a choice (cf. 2.40.3). The death of a Spartan in battle may ensure the safety of his city and may win individual fame for him, but since he has never made a free and conscious choice of the city's ends, which have rather been imposed

81. P. Huart, *Le Vocabulaire.*

upon him, the mischance of his death is chance *tout court.* From the city's point of view, he represents the loss of a fighting man; from his own point of view, he has always been the stakes with which the city will gamble for its existence if it must and which it has now lost.

The Periclean principle of subjectivity and release from chance, a principle which emerges from 2.42.4–43.1, is set in relief by the following chapter (2.44.1). As Pericles moves from the λόγος ἐπαινετικός (esp. 2.42.4) and the λόγος παραινετικός (2.43) to the παραμυθητικὸς εἰς τοὺς γονεῖς, his opportunities for innovation in thought shrink,[82] and indeed the very principle against which he has been at least implicitly polemical now appears:

Δι' ὅπερ καὶ τοὺς τῶνδε νῦν τοκέας, ὅσοι πάρεστε, οὐκ ὀλοφύρομαι μᾶλλον ἢ παραμυθήσομαι. ἐν πολυτρόποις γὰρ ξυμφοραῖς ἐπίστανται τραφέντες· τὸ δ' εὐτυχές, οἳ ἂν τῆς εὐπρεπεστάτης λάχωσιν, ὥσπερ οἵδε μὲν νῦν, τελευτῆς, ὑμεῖς δὲ λύπης, καὶ οἷς ἐνευδαιμονῆσαί τε ὁ βίος ὁμοίως καὶ ἐντελευτῆσαι ξυνεμετρήθη.

Therefore [i.e., because of the bravery of the fallen soldiers] I do not commiserate the parents of these men who are here; rather I shall comfort them. They know that they were raised in fortunes which often turn. But good fortune belongs to those who receive as their portion the most fitting death, as these here now—whereas you have the most fitting grief—and to whom a space of life has been measured out equally in which to be happy and in which to die (2.44.1).

As commentators have often pointed out, the Herodotean principle of the casualness of life (see especially Hdt. 1.32), the principle antithetical to what the present study shows to be Pericles' own, here makes an appearance,

82. Kakridis, *Der thuk. Epitaphios,* p. 95.

both in thought and in diction (ἐν πολυτρόποις . . . ξυμφοραῖς; cf. Eur. fr. 273N: τῆς τύχης οὐχ εἷς τρόπος; Thuc. 2.44.2 τὸ . . . εὐτυχές; λάχωσιν; εὐτυχίαις).[83] Pericles here adopts momentarily the Herodotean principle, since he is addressing the parents of the dead soldiers. One could even say that the Herodotean principle is reduced, by comparison with the preceding section of the Funeral Oration, to the status of a mere topos of consolation. The topical character of the passage is all the more apparent in the contrast between the traditionalism of the thought and the novelty of the expression. In diction, ἐνευδαιμονῆσαι and ἐντελευτῆσαι are neologisms, and "this use of epexegetic infinitives compounded with ἐν- is a late fifth-century mannerism."[84] In the syntax, abrupt changes of tense (present to future), of person (second person plural to third plural to second plural), of mood (indicative to subjunctive); inconcinnity (ἐνευδαιμονῆσαι—ἐντελευτῆσαι);[85] the strained, nearly anacoluthic quality of the relative clauses (οἷ ἂν τῆς . . . ; ὧν καὶ πολλάκις)—all this makes the passage perhaps the most difficult to read in the Funeral Oration and has attracted many emendations.[86] The present discussion will not take a position on the textual issues, since no

83. Gomme, II, 140–141.

84. E. R. Dodds, *Euripides: Bacchae* (Oxford, 1960), p. 141 on line 508. He gives references to further examples of this sort of infinitive.

85. Gomme, II, 140, emended to ⟨εὖ⟩ ἐντελευτῆσαι and this conjecture was accepted by O. Luschnat in the new Teubner edition of Thucydides I-II (1954).

86. For various conjectures, see Kakridis, *Der thuk. Epitaphios*, p. 98. Cf., on some of these, Jan Ros, *Die μεταβολή (Variatio) als Stilprinzip des Thukydides* (Vienna, 1938), pp. 271, 366. This work suggests what caution must be maintained in emending the inconcinnities in Thucydides (cf. n. 85 above).

matter how they are resolved, even if all changes were made in the direction of "normalization," which is the tendency in this passage, there would still remain a certain extravagance of rhetoric that would indicate how the thought is to be taken.

D. *The third speech of Pericles* (2.60–64)[87]

The third speech portrays Pericles as persevering both in his policy of forcing the issue with the Spartans and also in the principle of gnome by which he conducted this policy. What Pericles had said of men in war (πρὸς δὲ τὰς ξυμφορὰς καὶ τὰς γνώμας τρεπόμενοι [changing their policies in accordance with their fortunes] 1.140.1) has now in fact happened, not because of war but because of the plague: πρὸς γὰρ τὸ ἀνέλπιστον εὐθὺς τραπόμενοι τῇ γνώμῃ . . . οὐκ ἀντεῖχον (having immediately changed their minds in the face of the unexpected event, they did not stand firm) (2.51.4). But Pericles perseveres, in spite of the fact that the plague is an event which even he must admit was unexpected (2.61.3) and daemonic (2.64.2). Even in so describing the plague he appeals again to

87. For an excellent analysis of the structure and themes of this speech, see J. de Romilly, *Thucydides*, pp. 120ff. She comments on the importance of this speech thus: "by putting it in his work, alone, without any debate or discussion, and just before the praise of Pericles in II.65, presenting it almost as a political testament, he seems to have been particularly anxious to attract his reader's attention to certain aspects of Pericles' ideas considered for their own sake." The ideas that I discuss do not form part of de Romilly's subject, imperialism, and are not discussed by her. I have not been able to consult W. Plenio, "Die letzte Rede des Perikles (Th. II 60–64)," unpub. diss., University of Kiel, 1954.

intelligence and resolve as sufficient to pull the Athenians through.

Pericles' policy as it emerged in the first speech and in the speech in *oratio obliqua* rested on a calculation of the Athenian advantage over the Lacedaemonians, and also on the premise that chance was not a major factor in wars. If this premise and this policy were correct, there was no reason why even the plague should cause him to change his mind. Thus what must have appeared to the disgruntled Athenians as an external force, the back luck which brought the plague, appears to Pericles a subjective phenomenon, namely, their anger, from which he must try to dissuade them. Pericles regards the individual soul as the locus of chance; and he seems to deny implicitly that the city as a whole can be affected seriously by chance. Thucydides regarded the plague as a defeat for techne (2.47.4; cf. Lucr. 6.1179: *mussabat tacito medicina timore*) and also for human reason, since the causes of the plague were obscure (2.48.3); but Pericles, as regards techne, has nothing to say, apparently assuming that eventually the plague will pass and that this cure will suffice for want of any other. As regards causes, he is equally silent, since all that matters, given the assumption that the city as a whole is ultimately impervious to the plague and chance, is that he understand the causes of the people's anger (2.60.1).[88]

It is sufficient for Pericles to understand only causes of this sort, because this understanding will enable him to

88. Cf. Flashar, *Der Epitaphios*, p. 44: "... Steht ja das ganze Wirken des Perikles bei Thukydides von vornherein unter dem Zwiespalt zwischen der Rationalität des perikleischen Planes und der aus dem Augenblick urteilenden Reaktion der Menge."

win the people over again to his policies; his policies will maintain the freedom and strength of Athens; the freedom and strength of Athens, of the city as a whole, will be the redemption of individual misfortunes. In this Pericles corrects the Solonian view, which was mistaken in its simplicity: πᾶν ἐστι ἄνθρωπος συμφορή (man is altogether a thing of chance) (Hdt. 1.32.4). What Solon leaves out in his theory of human happiness is the city. The patriotism of Tellos who dies for Athens might be considered an aspect of his happiness, but the happiness of Cleobis and Biton is evidently independent of political considerations, and in fact Solon says nothing of the city in his general remarks about happiness (Hdt. 1.32.5–9). For Pericles the city was a defense against what had been regarded as the turbulent jealousy of the gods, and so it is fitting that, faced with what even he must refer to as the "daemonic," he begins by calling upon the Athenians to think not of their private misfortunes but of the good of the whole city, which is their only guarantee against these misfortunes.

Pericles twice refers to the plague in this speech, in two separate passages, and he has two different ways of allaying the anger and fear caused by the plague. Pericles begins the speech by stressing the primacy of the city. He then defends his own character: if the Athenians were right in following his policies previously, they are wrong in attacking him now. He goes on to say that it is necessary to fight. He has not changed his mind about this, but the people have. It is noteworthy that here Pericles puts the whole matter of the Athenians' misfortunes—he has in mind besides the plague the devastation of Attica by the Lacedaemonian invasion (2.62.3)—in terms of their effect upon the minds of the Athenians ($\gamma\nu\acute{\omega}\mu\eta\varsigma$, $\delta\iota\acute{\alpha}\nu\sigma\iota\alpha$, $\phi\rho\acute{\sigma}\nu\eta\mu\alpha$ 2.61.2–3). Only now does he mention the plague, somewhat obliquely (61.3). And here, implicitly resting his case on what he has already said about the primacy of the whole, he exhorts them to be worthy of the tradition of their city, to persevere, and to put the common good before their individual woes (61.4).

There intervenes between this mention of the plague and the second mention a rather complicated argument. After reiterating his naval policy, which is as valid as it ever was and the thought of which should compensate them for the loss of their lands, and after once more reminding them of their ancestors' virtue, he goes on to bid the Athenians go against the enemy not only with pride ($\phi\rho\sigma\nu\acute{\eta}\mu\alpha\tau\iota$) but also with disdain ($\kappa\alpha\tau\alpha\phi\rho\sigma\nu\acute{\eta}\mu\alpha\tau\iota$ 2.62.3; cf. the Corinthians' censure of this attitude: 1.122.4). This antithesis is based on the antithesis between gnome and tyche. Pride is associated with boasting and with ignorant good luck ($\dot{\alpha}\pi\grave{\sigma}$ $\dot{\alpha}\mu\alpha\theta\acute{\iota}\alpha\varsigma$ $\epsilon\dot{\upsilon}\tau\upsilon\chi\sigma\hat{\upsilon}\varsigma$); disdain belongs "to whoever trusts to his intelligence (gnome), too, that he is superior to his enemies, as you may do." The basis of this trust for the Athenians is their knowledge of their naval superiority, which Pericles has just reiterated. Pericles continues: "And since chance is equal, intelligence (*xynesis*) based on a sense of superiority provides a surer daring, and trusts less to hope, the strength of which lies in desperation, and more to intelligence (gnome) based on the facts, the foresight of which is more stable" (62.5).[89]

89. The phrase which I have translated "since chance is equal" is remarkable in that *homoias* is attributive, not predicative, as all commentators unaccountably take it to be. Pericles is not saying, "where

The rationalism of Pericles is in sharp contrast with the Spartan understanding of the gnome-tyche antithesis as it is expressed by Brasidas in his speech to the citizens of Acanthus. Brasidas assures the Acanthians that he is not seeking their friendship on false pretenses, in order to install a new oligarchical or tyrannical government. He states his reason for disclaiming such false pretenses in terms of the gnome-tyche antithesis (4.86.6):

ἀπάτῃ γὰρ εὐπρεπεῖ αἴσχιον τοῖς γε ἐν ἀξιώματι πλεονεκτῆται ἢ βίᾳ ἐμφανεῖ· τὸ μὲν γὰρ ἰσχύος δικαιώσει, ἣν ἡ τύχη ἔδωκεν, ἐπέρχεται, τὸ δὲ γνώμης ἀδίκου ἐπιβουλῇ.

If aggrandizement were at the bottom of the Spartan offer of friendship, it would be more honorable for the Spartans to use the strength which tyche has given them than scheming and treacherous gnome. The Spartan prefers the gifts of chance, which Pericles scorns, to the use of gnome, which Pericles considers the basis of secure policy.

It is characteristic of Pericles to speak of chance as he does in 2.62.5, but considering the situation and the state of mind of his audience, it is here that he gives his most impressive proof of a noble constancy of gnome. In returning here to gnome Pericles also reaffirms the principle of his military policy, that wars are won for the most part on the basis of gnome and capital (2.13). Since Pericles disparages chance and the superhuman in this last speech, not directly but more by refusing to consider them, the modern reader probably does not feel the full

the chances are equal" or "if chance is not against you," but "chance is the same for both sides," or, in Democritus' words, τὰ τῆς τύχης κοινὰ πᾶσιν (B293). Cf. Aesch. fr. 389N[3]: κοινὸν τύχη, γνώμη δὲ τῶν κεκτημένων; Petronius CXLI: Fortuna communis.

effect of his heroic rationalism. But Pericles in the *History* is unique in this; for it is not only the Spartan traditionalist Archidamus who thinks that "war is obscure" (2.11.4) and that the chances that befall men cannot be analyzed by reason (1.84.4), but even Athenians think that war is wont to become a matter of chance (1.78.1–2). ἐπιμὶξ δέ τε μαίνεται "Ἀρης (Ares is rage and confusion) (*Od.* 11.537).

When Pericles mentions the plague for the second time, he grants that it was beyond what was expected and aligns himself with traditional piety in his admonition to the Athenians φέρειν . . . χρὴ τὰ . . . δαιμόνια ἀναγκαίως (the divine must be borne of necessity) (2.64.2), a principle which he says is traditional with Athenians. This is Pericles' penultimate admonition to the Athenians, and whether this uncharacteristic passivity and piety is really Pericles' or whether he is adopting for rhetorical purposes the common point of view may be queried. For his ultimate admonition is of a piece with the outlook that has been traced in all the speeches: "those who in the face of misfortunes are least wounded in their minds (γνώμη) and most hold out in deed, these are the strongest, both men and cities" (2.64.6). Like the summons to a rational self-confidence, this ultimate statement is based on the gnome-tyche antithesis.[90] In his final statement Pericles exchanges the passivity implied in the traditional apothegm (φέρειν . . . χρὴ κτλ.)[91] with a call to action and reliance on intelligence.

---

90. Zahn, *Die erste Periklesrede*, pp. 58–59.

91. Commentators compare Soph. *Phil.* 1316–17; Eur. *Phoen.* 382, 1763; Dem. 18.97. To these could be added Eur. fr. 37N³: τὰς δὲ δαιμόνων τύχας/ὅστις φέρει κάλλιστ' ἀνὴρ οὗτος σοφός.

E. Comparison of the Periclean with certain traditional concepts of the city

The innovational character of the thought of the Thucydidean Pericles, which is all too easily lost to view, emerges more clearly from a comparison of the Periclean with certain traditional concepts of the city and of citizenship. The Periclean principle of gnome is innovational in three main respects: first, this principle carries with it a new humanism and secularism; second, this principle thus asserts the primacy of the city; third, in consequence of the primacy of the city, the old aristocratic ideal of ἡσυχία must be abandoned.

The secularism and humanism of Pericles emerge more clearly in comparison with Solon's concept of the polis. The main difference between Pericles and Solon is theological. The Thucydidean Pericles never mentions a god or the gods: he mentions only the gold-plated statue of Athena and he refers once, with doubtful piety, to *ta daimonia*.[92] Solon is above all a religious poet and statesman. Even his reforms of the Athenian constitution are an act of piety.

For this reason there is no real difference between the religious wise man who appears at the court of Croesus in the first book of Herodotus and the Athenian statesman described by Plutarch and by Aristotle in the *Athenian Constitution*. In Herodotus, Solon mentions the polis only once, in passing, and in his most general remarks about

92. Flashar, *Der Epitaphios*, p. 32, observes that it is only in 2.64.1 that the religious note is struck by Pericles. Flashar comments: "Im übrigen aber fehlt der ganze religiöse Bezug gerade auch da, wo man ihn erwarten würde. Offenbar glaubt Thukydides, so die eigentliche Haltung des Perikles richtig zum Ausdruck zu bringen."

human happiness he says nothing of the political dimension of human life (1.32.5–9). One sees even here, however, the grounds of political reform in Solon's critique of the harsh aristocratic code which made wealth and power necessary to happiness. The representative of this code is Croesus, whose claim to being *olbiotatos* of all men rests on his wealth (1.30.1–2) and who is astonished that Solon attributes to private men a greater happiness than to the king of Lydia (1.32.1). Solon's critique follows from his observation of the instability of human happiness, and he believes that this instability is caused by the god (1.33), who teaches that for mortals it is better to be dead than alive (1.31.4–5).

Pessimistic as this theology is, it yet points to the sort of reform which Solon in fact carried out. It softens the aristocratic code by implying a fundamental equality of all men before the god or gods. Since the human condition is essentially casual (1.32.4), all men are at least potentially equal. It is only a short step from the theological definition of man as mortal, according to which conventional distinctions between men are less important than their generic casualness of existence, to the political definition of man as citizen. The rich man, the aristocratic chief, the monarch or tyrant is only a mortal, and in the withering theological perspective of Solon his predominance shrinks to the proportions demanded by piety. But the Herodotean Solon is content with the negative implications of his theology for power and wealth and never expresses the political tendency of this theology. In the examples of human happiness chosen by Solon, the polis plays almost no part. The prosperity of Tellus' city is not apparently essential to Tellus' own happiness (1.30.4). Solon's point concerning Tellus' death is not its patriotism, a detail added by Plutarch (*Sol.* 27.4 ὑπὲρ τῆς πατρίδος), but the personal distinction achieved by one who died in battle.[93] In the tale of Cleobis and Biton, the polis is not mentioned. Their felicity is completely apolitical.

The comparison of mortal and god at the heart of Solon's theology implies a fundamental equality of all men in their abjectness. The political tendency of this comparison is political equality. Theological equality becomes political equality; and the fragments of Solon imply a development of this sort in Solon's thought. But at the same time the theological outlook is preserved in the political development. In the political thought of Solon, the citizen and the polis guide themselves by laws whose ultimate sanction is the divine. Mortals commit no crimes against one another which are not also crimes against the gods. The confiscation of land by creditors is a crime against Earth, the mother of Olympian gods. She will bear witness that Solon acted for the best in removing the boundary marks (which marked the confiscations), in order that the earth, which was enslaved, might be free (fr. 24D³).

Through hybris men commit injustice; but Zeus watches over the end (fr. 1.9–17D³). This is the familiar theological ethic of Solon. Solon's innovation is the political application of this ethic: the people (fr. 5.7–10D³) and the leaders of the people (fr. 3.7–8D³) are capable of hybris in their political roles. Thus Eunomia in checking

93. καί μιν Ἀθηναῖοι δημοσίῃ τε ἔθαψαν αὐτοῦ τῇ περ ἔπεσε καὶ ἐτίμησαν μεγάλως (1.30.5). With δημοσίῃ, cf. Thuc. 5.11.1 (the heroization of Brasidas) and Pl. *Rep.* 540c1 (the burial of the philosopher-king).

hybris (fr. 3.34D³) is to the polis what *sophrosyne* is to the individual. Solon's reforms are an act of piety in that he seeks to restore to, or to give to, Athens the moderation required by the gods.

The context of Solon's reflections on wealth makes clear the theological basis of his political reforms (fr. 1.63–76D³):

> Verily, Fate brings to mortals both evil and good; the gifts of the gods may not be declined. In every kind of activity there is risk, and no man can tell, when a thing is beginning, what way it is destined to take. One man trying to do his work well falls unexpectedly into great and bitter ruin; to another who blunders in his work the god grants good luck in everything, to save him from his folly. [71] In wealth no limit is set up within man's view; those of us who now have the largest fortune are doubling our efforts; what amount would satisfy the greed of all? Gain is granted to mankind by the immortals; but from it arises disastrous Folly, and when Zeus sends her to exact retribution, she comes now to this man, now to that.[94]

According to Solon's pessimistic theology, man's very mortality pushes him into error. Man is imperfect in comparison with the gods; man's imperfection compels him to strive for the sufficiency which will repair the imperfection of his mortal existence. But man lacks a definition of sufficiency; his condition therefore drives him to insatiety; man then overreaches himself and the gods punish him. It is easy to understand Solon's political reforms as a reflection of these beliefs. What Solon saw all around him in Athens was vast inequality of wealth, which is one of the most constant themes of the fragments. The *seisachtheia* and the redistribution of land are

94. The translation is by K. Freeman, *The Work and Life of Solon with a Translation of His Poems* (Cardiff, 1926).

a political remedy for the *ate* of mortal acquisitiveness. The Solonian constitution has divine sanction and is enforced by the promise of divine retribution against wrong-doers. Solon achieved his reforms "with the gods" (fr. 23.18D³).

Thus the reflections on wealth (71–76), which clearly imply the program of reform, appear side by side with a most bitter statement of archaic fatalism (63–70). The human competence and freedom of political reforms find their place within a scheme of human subjection to divine necessity. Nothing could be more alien to Pericles' concept of the polis than this sense of divine necessity. In the *History*, the archaic view emerges as the Peloponnesian principle. The Corinthians tell the congress of Peloponnesian allies (1.120.5):

πολλὰ γὰρ κακῶς γνωσθέντα ἀβουλοτέρων τῶν ἐναντίων τυχόντα κατωρθώθη. καὶ ἔτι πλείω καλῶς δοκοῦντα βουλευθῆναι ἐς τοὐναντίον αἰσχρῶς περιέστη.

Many ill-conceived plans succeed, meeting with still more ill-advised enemies. And still more plans that seem to have been well laid meet disgraceful reverses.

Their thought is remarkably close to lines 67–70 of the first fragment of Solon (quoted above), and it is nothing but an analysis of the apothegm of that spokesman of tyche, Archidamus: τὰς προσπιπτούσας τύχας οὐ λόγῳ διαιρετάς (the chances that befall us cannot be analyzed in words) (1.84.4). Appropriately, the Corinthians are disbelievers in the possibility of a consistent application of techne in warfare: they say of war (1.122.1): αὐτὸς ... ἀφ' αὑτοῦ τὰ πολλὰ τεχνᾶται πρὸς τὸ παρατυγχάνον (for the most part, it draws upon itself for its art, according to circum-

stances) (cf. Empedocles B 106). Here again the Peloponnesian principle is akin to the thought of Solon, for Solon
ranks the arts among the idle hopes and pursuits of
mankind (fr. 1.43ff.D³).[95] In short, the spiritual descendants of the Athenian Solon in the *History* are not the
Athenians, or at least not Pericles, but the Peloponnesians.[96]

It is worth returning to Solon, however, to get a fuller
account of the earlier, theological concept of the polis
from which Pericles departed, since there is no speech by
any of the Peloponnesians in the *History* which makes it so
clear as the fragments of Solon, taken in conjunction with
the Herodotean Solon.

For Pericles, chance is mere randomness. Chance is
defined subjectively, that is, from the human point of
view, and negatively, as that which is contrary to calculation. For Solon, the vicissitudes of life are an expression
of Moira and the gods' purposes, which mortals can
neither understand nor prevent. The polis, like the individual, can only tread cautiously and hope by moderation to avoid hybris. It is important to remember that the
popular belief in this ancient connection of tyche with the
gods persisted in Athens and was even in a sense official:
theoi and the phrase ἀγαθῆι τύχηι frequently appear together in Attic inscriptions and are coupled in the head-

95. Cf. Heinimann, *MH* 18 (1961), 110.

96. W. Wössner, *Die synonymische Unterscheidung bei Thukydides und
den politischen Rednern der Griechen* (Würzburg, 1937), p. 21, observes
of the argument made by the Spartan peace embassy in 4.18.5: "Diese
Worte gründen sich auf dieselbe Einsicht wie die Unterscheidung
Solons bei der Unterhaltung mit Kroisos Hdt. I 30. εὐτυχής bezeichnet
dort den Glückzustand des Augenblicks; ὄλβιος das wahre Glück, das
man erst nach dem Tode eines Menschen festellen kann."

ings of inscriptions.[97] There is also the fact that chance and the divine are associated again and again in Pindar and the tragedians.[98] Aristotle says, in reporting the various common opinions concerning tyche, "There are some who believe that tyche is a cause, but obscure to human reason as being something from the gods and rather daemonic" (*Phys.* 196b5–7). In his commentary on this passage, Simplicius preserves the curious fact that "At Delphi [the formula] 'Chance and Loxias, do you give answer to this person?' was the beginning of the consultation of the oracle" (Simpl. *Phys.* 333). Clearly Pericles manifests a consistent rationality to which most Athenians would not have attained, and which might even have been considered impious. One is reminded of the charge of impiety brought against Pericles' friend, Anaxagoras. In this light, it is easier to understand the obliquity of the treatment of tyche in the prooemium to the first speech—Thucydides does not wish to represent Pericles as foolishly iconoclastic.

In Pericles' concept, the polis has a new importance, since it stands between the individual citizen and the chances of life, provided that the individual citizen is willing to put the preservation of the whole city before his own self-interest. The polis is that standard of sufficiency missing in the theological ethic of Solon. On the one hand, the polis compensates the individual for his particular insufficiency and protects him against tyche; on the other hand, the polis serves as both the mode and the goal of that striving and acquisitiveness to which the

97. J. P. Traywick, "θεοί and ἀγαθὴ τύχη in Headings of Attic Inscriptions" (unpub. diss. Harvard University, 1968), pp. 71, 67–68.

98. For a survey, see K. Ziegler, *RE* 14, col. 1655.

theological mind of Solon saw no end but hybris and *ate*. In Herodotus, Solon observes that no mortal can possess every attribute of happiness just as no region can provide everything for itself (1.32.8). In the Funeral Oration, Pericles says that the Athenians have ἐκ πάσης γῆς τὰ πάντα (all things from the whole world) (2.38.2). Pericles says of his generation that it has made the city by every means self-sufficient (αὐταρκεστάτην) for war and peace (2.36.3). Solon also draws a comparison between the human condition as regards happiness and the human body: ὡς δὲ καὶ ἀνθρώπου σῶμα ἓν οὐδὲν αὔταρκές ἐστι (so no one person is self-sufficient) (1.32.8). But Pericles says of the Athenians (2.41.2):

τὸν αὐτὸν ἄνδρα παρ' ἡμῶν ἐπὶ πλεῖστ' ἂν εἴδη καὶ μετὰ χαρίτων μάλιστ' ἂν εὐτραπέλως τὸ σῶμα αὔταρκες παρέχεσθαι.

One and the same man from our city would present himself as self-sufficient for the most plans of action and with the most graceful versatility.

Pericles' words sound like a reply to the Herodotean Solon.[99] Athens is self-sufficient: what the rest of the world has is as much hers as what her own region produces. Through the self-sufficiency of his polis, the Athenian citizen also attains an individual self-sufficiency beyond what Solon had thought possible.[100]

It is the originality of Pericles, as Thucydides presents him, to have seen the essentially political character of man. The polis, not nature or the universe, is man's home. Man is in the world not as a bread-eating mortal beloved of or despised by the gods, but as the citizen of

99. Cf. Flashar, *Der Epitaphios*, p. 31.
100. Cf. Flashar, *Der Epitaphios*, p. 26.

this or that polis. In Athens, citizenship means, or should mean, the individual's choice of the city's ends. The individual fulfills himself through participation in the magnificence of Athenian political life. Even death, if it is a patriotic death, is an escape from tyche.

The humanism and secularism of Pericles are thus the basis of the second of the main innovational aspects of his concept of the city, the primacy of the polis. It is necessary to begin by anticipating a likely objection: the "Lycurgan" constitution established in Sparta a statism or totalitarianism in which individual freedom was unknown. Therefore, it might seem that the primacy of the city was a Spartan invention. But the Spartan constitution existed for the sake of war and for no other reason, as Aristotle observes (*Pol.* 1271a41–b10, 1324b5–10), and Thucydides traces the Spartan constitution to the continual fear of a helot revolt (4.80.3; cf. 5.23.3). The Spartan constitution does not, then, imply the primacy of the city but the total absorption of the citizen *in the defense of* the city. Paradoxically, the city in itself has nothing to offer the citizen in return. As Aristotle observes, no other virtue but valor was cultivated. Thus Sparta could not assert its primacy as Athens can, in the voice of Pericles, in the Funeral Oration. The Spartan constitution has no positive meaning for its citizens, but rather creates an armed camp. Tyrtaeus is thought to have reshaped the heroic ideal of arete into a Spartan civic ideal,[101] but Tyrtaeus addresses not citizens but warriors, who are exhorted to fight not for a certain constitution or way of

101. W. Jaeger, *Paideia: the Ideals of Greek Culture,* trans. Gilbert Highet (Oxford, 1946), I, 87ff.

life but for the *preservation* of the city, which is in their self-interest as individuals.[102] Thus the warriors addressed by Tyrtaeus do not differ essentially from Hector.[103]

Pericles is thus innovational in his concept of citizenship, according to which participation in civic life is the ultimate goal of the individual, and the citizen is willing to die for the city not simply to preserve the physical existence of his family but to ensure the continuance of the civic values represented by Athens. Pericles gives voice to an ideal of patriotism which has often been spoken of as if it were normal for all Greeks, but which was in fact abnormal.[104] When Thucydides says that, after Pericles, Athenian statesmen conducted affairs κατὰ τὰς ἰδίας φιλοτιμίας καὶ ἴδια κέρδη (following private ambition and private gain) (2.65.7), he speaks not of a new development in Greek politics but of a reversion to

---

102. Cf. L. Strauss, *The City and Man* (Chicago 1964), p. 170: "At the end of the address to the troops before a naval battle, the Peloponnesian commanders tell them that none of them will have an excuse for acting as a coward and if anyone tries to act cowardly he will be properly punished, while the brave ones will be honored properly. [2.87.9] The parallel to this conclusion in the address of the Athenian commander Phormio is his statement that the troops are about to engage in a great contest: they will either make an end to the Peloponnesians' hope for naval victory or else bring the fear regarding the sea nearer home to the Athenians. [2.89.10] The Peloponnesians appeal to the self-interest of the individual; the Athenian appeals only to what is at stake for the city."

103. For his "patriotism," see *Il.* 12.243. Cf. C. M. Bowra, *Early Greek Elegists* (Cambridge, Mass. 1938), pp. 66ff.

104. See N. M. Pusey, "Alcibiades and τὸ φιλόπολι," *HSCP* 51 (1940), 215–231; A.-H. Chroust, "Treason and Patriotism in Ancient Greece," *Journal of the History of Ideas* 15 (1954), 280–288.

the norm which is succinctly articulated by Alcibiades in Sparta in extenuation of his treason (6.92.4):

τό τε φιλόπολι οὐκ ἐν ᾧ ἀδικοῦμαι ἔχω, ἀλλ᾽ ἐν ᾧ ἀσφαλῶς ἐπολιτεύθην. οὐδ᾽ ἐπὶ πατρίδα οὖσαν ἔτι ἡγοῦμαι νῦν ἰέναι, πολὺ δὲ μᾶλλον τὴν οὐκ οὖσαν ἀνακτᾶσθαι.

I feel love of my city not when I am wronged but when I live securely as a citizen. I do not consider that I am now attacking a fatherland still my own, but rather that I am recovering one no longer mine.

That this statement is not a piece of a sophistry but is quite ingenuous is shown by the comparison of Alcibiades with the exiled Theognis, whose vernal longing for the ploughland of his native city (1197ff.Y²) is synonymous with a desire to crush the democracy and restore the rule of the aristocrats (847ff.Y²). His city is a "holy city" (604Y²), but his devotion to it includes a passion for vengeance on the opposing faction of his fellow-citizens (337–304Y²). The selfishness of citizenship as traditionally understood, to which the Periclean concept is obviously opposed, is epitomized in the tract by the Anonymous Iamblichus where the problems of individual arete and of *eunomia* are discussed separately and the word πολίτης does not occur. The discontinuity between the individual's aspirations and the requirements of civic life is implicit in Solon, too (fr. 3.26D³).

Even Nicias, whose patriotism is shown in various ways (5.16.1, 6.47), believes that a good citizen can be motivated by self-interest (6.8.2). The Nician patriotism is really a compromise between self-interest and the common good. This compromise, which is implicit in Nicias' reasons for seeking the Peace named after him (5.16.1), can be dissolved very abruptly in favor of self-interest, as

86

Pericles and Gnome

when Nicias' desire to preserve his own honor causes him to gamble with the whole army in his command (7.48.4).[105] In this respect, Nicias differs little from Alcibiades or from the Spartan Brasidas, who wished the war to continue for the reason that he was deriving honor from his successful campaign (5.16.1).

The old-fashioned patriot, in relinquishing self-interest in the name of the primacy of the city, must leave behind an earlier ideal of political life: ἡσυχία (quiet). The third of the main innovations in Pericles' concept of the city is the requirement of activity. Pericles says that Athenians consider the man who does not take part in political life οὐκ ἀπράγμονα ἀλλ' ἀχρεῖον (not unambitious but useless) (2.40.2). ἀπραγμοσύνη (not meddling in public affairs), a synonym for ἡσυχία,[106] was a conservative, gentlemanly ideal, as Pericles' harsh words on this subject make clear (2.63.2, 64.4). In demanding a renunciation of ἡσυχία, Pericles broke with the tradition according to which the goal of political life was tranquillity. This is the tradition reflected in Pindar's ἀσυχία φιλόπολις (city-loving quiet) (Ol. 4.16; cf. Pyth. 8.1–2) and in his prayer to Zeus that Hieron may lead the people σύμφωνον ἐς ἀσυχίαν (into harmonious quiet) (Pyth. 1.71; cf. fr. 109 Bgk.). In the History of Thucydides, the ideal of tranquillity lives on in such figures as Archidamus and Nicias, whose devotion to this ideal will be discussed in the next chapter. Pericles confirms what the Corinthians say in

105. Cf. K. J. Dover on this passage (7.48.4), quoted below, Chap. II, n. 61.
106. V. Ehrenberg, "Polypragmosyne: A Study in Greek Politics," JHS 67 (1947), 46; R. A. Neil, Aristophanes: Knights (Cambridge, 1901), pp. 208–209.

87

their attempt to stir the peace-loving Spartans into action: the Athenians were born neither to have ἡσυχία themselves nor to allow anyone else to have it (1.70.9).

The Corinthians regard this restlessness of the Athenians as native (n.b. πεφυκέναι 1.70.9; cf. 8.96.5). The Athenian ethos might thus be understood as the psychological basis of the polis as it was conceived by Pericles. Those who are restlessly active will run risks (cf. 1.70.3). Those who run risks acquire experience (1.18.3). Experience systematized becomes techne. Without risk and experience, techne declines (1.71.3, 6.18.6). A city that possesses techne can base its policies on gnome. In so doing, the city emerges from the Solonian state of things and asserts a proud humanism. At the same time, the individual citizen experiences the reflection of these historical developments in the growth of his own intelligence and in the possibility of his own cultivation. He can thus make a conscious choice of the city's ends, and the city acquires a primacy heretofore inconceivable. Thucydides has made Pericles the spokesman of this new concept of the city.

II

"The Lacedaemonians and Chance"[1]

A. The Corinthians' analysis of the difference between Sparta and Athens

After the Persian Wars the Greek world came to be polarized between the Athenian sailors and the Spartan landsmen (1.18.2). That the difference between the two cities was more than military was intimated in the difference in their hegemonies (1.19), and Thucydides has various means of elaborating the comparison. There are the parallel lives of Pausanias and Themistocles (1.128–138). Certain details seem to make tacit comparisons, for instance, the Spartan consultation of the oracle at Delphi before the war (1.118.3). But the speeches, above all, are Thucydides' way of comparing the rival cities.

The speech of the Corinthians in Sparta (1.68–71), with its detailed exposition of the differences between Athens and Sparta, cities nearly the opposite of one another (1.70.1), is programmatic. It provides the terms and the concepts by which both Thucydides in his own

1. In the Melian Dialogue, the Athenians scornfully couple the Lacedaemonians and chance (5.113).

voice (the Corinthians' main points are corroborated by Thucydides, 4.55.2, 8.96.4) and also the actors of the *History* understand events. The Corinthians establish the Spartan norm and the Athenian norm, by which one can measure the degree to which an individual manifests the character of a complete Athenian or a complete Spartan.

Archidamus is the complete Spartan: he possesses the virtues which he says are the characteristic Spartan virtues (1.79.2, 1.84.2).[2] Pericles is the complete Athenian: he possesses the virtues which he says are the characteristic Athenian virtues (2.34.6–8, 59.8, cf. in the Funeral Oration, e.g., 2.40.2–3). And what Archidamus and Pericles say substantiates the Corinthian analysis. There are, on the other hand, Athenian Spartans and Spartan Athenians. Brasidas, in employing techne (5.8.2) and tactics which another Spartan general rejected (5.9, cf. 3.30),[3] tactics more in keeping with Athenian daring than with Spartan slowness, and in his oratorical abilities, unusual for a Spartan (4.84.2), and in possessing ξύνεσις (4.81.2), has an Athenian dimension.[4] Nicias expresses views, especially of tyche, which are opposed to those of Pericles and also to those of Alcibiades, who is in some ways Pericles' spiritual descendant, and which are remarkably close to the views of Archidamus.[5]

2. Cf. Strauss, *The City and Man*, p. 149.

3. Brasidas speaks of κλέμματα *(furta belli)* in 5.9.5. Gomme, III, observes the inappropriateness of this to a Spartan. But where it suits his rhetorical purposes, Brasidas scorns ἀπάτη (4.86.6).

4. F. M. Wasserman, "The Voice of Sparta in Thucydides," *CJ* 59 (1964), 293: "As in his Pericles, Thucydides sees in Brasidas . . . the combination of 'modern' matter-of-fact efficiency with the aristocratic standards of a gentleman."

5. G. F. Bender, *Der Begriff des Staatsmannes bei Thukydides*

The difference between Athens and Sparta can be seen in the tyche-techne and tyche-gnome anthitheses. Pericles, who is the Athenian par excellence, is the exponent of techne and of gnome, especially of gnome in the sense of intelligent policy. The Spartans, too, think in terms of the tyche-gnome antithesis. They, however, grant tyche a wider scope than does Pericles, and they mean by gnome a tenacious adherence to their traditional ways. The Spartan view of tyche emerges, like every aspect of the comparison between Sparta and Athens, from the Corinthian speech, and therefore it is with this speech that one must begin. The first speech of Archidamus, in which the Spartan understanding of tyche first, and most clearly, appears, is in fact an answer to the Corinthians and a rebuttal of their criticisms of Sparta.[6]

The Corinthians begin by distinguishing between two results of the Spartans' confidence in their constitution and community. This confidence, the Corinthians say, makes the Spartans moderate but also ignorant of the outside world. Archidamus will defend the Spartan ignorance as not distinct from but rather an aspect of moderation and a virtue (1.68.1, 84.3).[7] The Corinthians complain that the Spartans defend themselves not by

---

(Würzburg 1938), p. 44: "Nikias sympathisiert mit Sparta, weil sein ganzes Wesen dort Verwandtes spürt." Cf. p. 48 for a comparison of details in the Corinthians' estimate of Sparta with corresponding details in what Thucydides says of Nicias.

6. Cf. L. Bodin, "Thucydide I.84," in *Mélanges Desrousseaux* (Paris, 1937), pp. 19–25.

7. The contrast between the ignorant *sophrosyne* of the Spartans and the *sophia* of the other Hellenes was a standard joke on the Spartans: Hdt. 4.77.

strength but by delay, a bad policy, since in this way they take the chance of facing a much stronger enemy. Archidamus will argue that, on the contrary, the Spartan delay provides more security against chance (1.69.4–5, 82).

After the Corinthians have made their own claims and have made specific complaints against present Spartan policy, they give a general statement of the differences between the Athenians and Spartans. Not all of these differences, of course, bear on the tyche-gnome antithesis. In general, the Corinthians view the difference as one between innovators and traditionalists. The Athenians are unhesitating, bold, hopeful. The Athenians run risks in the hope of gain. The pessimistic Spartans fear the loss of what they already have if they should try to increase it (1.70.1).

Since the Corinthians always have in mind their objective of persuading Sparta to undertake war immediately, they attempt to present the comparison between Sparta and Athens in especially provocative terms. Therefore they conclude their survey of the differences by saying that the Athenians were born to allow neither themselves nor anyone else to live in peace (ἡσυχία 1.70.9). They go on to explain to the Spartans what the conditions of peace are (1.71.1). For a city at peace, unchanged customs are best; but for a city in Sparta's position, threatened by Athens, technical innovation is necessary. The Corinthians draw a contrast between peace and techne (1.71.3; cf. 1.70.2: the Spartan refusal to ἐπιγνῶναι). The Athenian restlessness and technical innovation menace the Spartan peacefulness. That the Corinthians have directed their remarks to something prized by Spartans, their tranquillity, is shown by the recurrence of this note in the speech of Archidamus, who urges the Spartans to deliberate καθ' ἡσυχίαν (1.83.3, 85.1).

It is with a view to the Spartan love of peace and tranquillity that the Corinthians introduce the only concrete example in the whole of their analysis of the general differences between Athens and Sparta: the Athenians consider a festival nothing but the discharge of duty (1.70.8). And this detail is penultimate in the long series of comparisons, just preceding the conclusion, according to which the Athenians are a threat to the tranquillity that the Spartans love so much. One can imagine how incredible it would have seemed, and how menacing, to the Spartans that there was a city which did not love festivals. For the old-fashioned (1.71.2; cf. 1.10.2) Spartans, since they were celebrating a festival, even overlooked the Athenian fortification of Pylos (4.5); and after their great victory at Mantinea, they immediately dismissed their allies and went home, since it was time to celebrate the Carnea (5.75). In not following up their victory, they were the opposite of the Athenians (1.70.5; cf. 4.14.3, of the Athenians after Pylos). Even the Syracusans do not immediately follow up their great victory in the harbor, because there happens to be a festival of Heracles (7.73). Athenians, on the other hand, hope to turn the traditional love of festivals to military advantage: they hope to surprise the Mytilenaeans outside their walls celebrating the festival of Apollo Maloeis (3.3). In short, the Corinthians wish to impress upon the Spartans that the Athenians have changed fundamentally the conditions of life in Hellas.

B. Archidamus' analysis and defense of the Spartan constitution[8]

The speech of Archidamus (1.80–85) in reply to the Corinthians begins with the observation that the older men in his audience, like him, will not desire war, since they know that it is neither a good thing nor a predictable thing (ἀσφαλές 1.80.1). No doubt the young have a different idea (cf. 2.8.1). The old Spartans do not desire war, because they are peace-loving: there is nothing to be gained, but something to be lost (cf. the Corinthians 1.70). It is better to stay at home and follow one's ancestral customs. As for the other side of Archidamus' opening observation, the unpredictability of war, this is a point to which he returns again and again (1.82.6, 84.3; 2.11.4). Even with his use of the word ἀσφαλές he has signaled the characteristic Spartan respect for tyche, since the opposite of *asphaleia* (security) is τὸ σφάλλεσθαι, and this is the function of tyche (see the discussion of 2.42.4–43.1 in Chap. I. sec. C).

Archidamus' second point concerns this war in particular, as opposed to war in general. "This war about which you are now deliberating would not be the smallest war, if one should reflect on it moderately" (1.80.2). Thus does the theme of moderation make its entrance; and what follows in the next two sections of the speech (1.80.3–83) are Archidamus' moderate recommendations of strategy. He outlines the Spartans' disadvan-

8. For an appreciation of Archidamus, see F. M. Wasserman, "The Speeches of King Archidamus in Thucydides," *CJ* 48 (1953), 193–200. Wasserman suggests similarities between the Thucydidean Archidamus and the contemporary characterization of Theseus in Sophocles and Euripides, for which see H. Herter, "Theseus der Athener," *RM* 88 (1939), 311–322.

tages. The Spartans are landsmen against sailors, and the Athenians are superior in finances, which even Archidamus considers the sinews of war, and which especially should be taken into consideration in the face of a war of long duration. His general view of the strategy of the war is the same as Pericles'. The Spartans, Archidamus thinks, should wait, make fuller preparations, and then πεφραγμένοι ἴμεν (we shall go fortified). He seems to use the image of a moving fort.

Archidamus then turns to a defense of the Spartan sluggishness deprecated by the Corinthians. This sluggishness, he says, is the same as "conscious moderation" (1.84.2). "Moderation" (σωφροσύνη) is paraphrased by "orderliness" (τὸ εὔκοσμον): "we become skilled in war and of good counsel through *orderliness,* the former because a sense of shame has the greatest share in moderation" (1.84.3). In other words, the two virtues, skill in war and goodness of counsel, which Archidamus seems to regard as especially Spartan, both derive from moderation, which was the same as sluggishness, or what seemed to be sluggishness to the Corinthians. Archidamus has an explanation of each virtue. He derives skill in war from moderation as follows: moderation (σωφροσύνη/τὸ εὔκοσμον) leads to a sense of shame (αἰδώς/αἰσχύνη), which leads to bravery (εὐψυχία).[9] The virtue of sound-

---

9. The connection of αἰδώς and τὸ εὔκοσμον is asserted in a gnomic fragment of Lycophronides (ca. 300 B.C.):

οὔτε παιδὸς ἄρρενος οὔτε παρθένων
τῶν χρυσοφόρων οὐδὲ γυναικῶν βαθυκόλπων
καλὸν τὸ πρόσωπον, ἀλλ᾽ ὃ κόσμιον πεφύκει
ἡ γὰρ αἰδὼς ἄνθος ἐπισπείρει

ness of judgment comes from the Spartan education, which teaches strict obedience to the laws, a contempt for useless cleverness, a healthy respect for the enemy, sound preparation for war, and the belief "that our neighbors' intelligence is the equal of our own and that the chances which befall men cannot be analyzed by reason." "We always prepare in deed against our enemies as if they were of good counsel, and one ought not to base one's hopes on the assumption that they will make mistakes, but on the assumption that we ourselves have made reliable preparations. One ought not to believe that one mortal differs much from another. He is the strongest who is reared on the barest minimum" (1.84.3–4).[10]

In the same way that the Athenian restlessness is related to technical innovation, so, according to Archidamus' analysis, Spartan sluggishness is related to a sense of a general limitation imposed on human intelligence by the power of chance. Of the two main Spartan

---

(D. L. Page, *Poetae Melici Graeci* [Oxford, 1962], no. 843). For αἰδώς as the source of bravery, see C. E. F. von Erfa, "αἰδώς und verwandte Begriffe in ihrer Entwicklung von Homer bis Demokrit," *Philologus* Supp. 30 (1937), passim. The notion of αἰδώς as a source of bravery appeared in a work contemporary with Thucydides in Timotheus' allusion, in his *Persai*, to Homer (*Il.* 13.121): σέβεσθ' αἰδῶ συνεργὸν ἀρετᾶς δοριμάχου (Page, no. 789).

10. ἐν τοῖς ἀναγκαιοτάτοις παιδεύεται. See LSJ s.v. ἀναγκαῖος II.3 and 4 for the application of this word to the necessities of life. With Archidamus' sentiment, compare the well-known: ὁ δὲ πόλεμος ὑφελὼν τὴν εὐπορίαν τοῦ καθ' ἡμέραν βίαιος διδάσκαλος (3.82.2). Thucydides' apparently portentous figure of speech has reference to a drab fact: *volgus alimenta in diem mercari solitum* (Tac. *Hist.* 4.38.6). When Thucydides says that war is a "harsh teacher," he means, in Archidamus' words, that war rears the people on the barest minimum of such necessities as food.

virtues, one, sound judgment, is traced ultimately to tyche. For Athenians, sound judgment means defiance of tyche in the name of gnome or techne. This antithesis emerges clearly in Thucydides' account of the naval engagement near Naupactus.

C. *Spartan analysis of success and failure*

1. *The naval engagements near Naupactus* (2.83–92)[11]

In the first action of this episode, just outside the entrance to the Gulf of Corinth, Phormio hems in the defensive circle of the Peloponnesian fleet and waits for the morning breeze, which always blows down from the gulf. The breeze, when it comes, drives the Peloponnesian ships against one another. The Athenians attack them in their confusion and win an easy victory (2.84).

The Spartans at home suspect cowardice, because, as Thucydides explains, they underestimated the importance of Athenian naval experience in which, according to Pericles, the Athenian technical ability had its origin. The Spartans send out advisers, Timocrates, Brasidas, and Lycophron, to Cnemus, who was the admiral in the first battle, and demand another encounter. Cnemus, Brasidas, and the other Peloponnesian commanders encourage the sailors, explaining the previous defeat in terms of chance and minimizing the importance of inexperience (2.87.2–3). Bravery counts for more than experience and understanding: "without bravery no technical skill can stand up against danger" (2.87.4).

11. For an analysis of Thucydides' manner of narrating these naval engagements, see J. de Romilly, *Histoire et raison chez Thucydide* (Paris, 1956), pp. 138–150.

In terms of the tyche-techne antithesis, the previous defeat is attributed to tyche. But Phormio with his experience knew that the breeze would come, and Thucydides observes that the Spartans underrated the value of experience. The Spartans have mistaken techne for tyche. The Peloponnesian commanders speak in terms of a gnome-tyche antithesis (2.87.3). It soon becomes clear that they mean by gnome resolution or courage. The antithesis does not have the same meaning for them which it has in Pericles' thought. The Peloponnesians maintain, in effect, that the gnome-tyche antithesis, where gnome is understood in an ethical rather than a rational sense,[12] is more fundamental than the techne-tyche antithesis. The second encounter provides a test of their theory.

In the first stage of this second battle the Peloponnesians' ruse is successful in luring the Athenian fleet into the gulf, where the Athenians are driven ashore and disabled. The ships would have been taken but for support from a Messenian land force. Eleven Athenian ships escape, however, and flee to Naupactus, pursued by twenty Peloponnesian ships. One of the Athenian ships falls far behind the rest, and one Leukadian ship far outstrips the pursuing force. Outside the harbor of Naupactus there happens to be anchored a transport ship. Maneuvering around it, the Athenian rams the Leukadian amidships and sinks her.

The unexpectedness of this event—one notes the language of chance (γενομένου τούτου ἀπροσδοκήτου τε καὶ

---

12. Gnome is coupled with the Archidamian αἰδώς (cf. sec. B of Chap. II) by Theognis (635Y²) ἀνδράσι τοῖσ' ἀγαθοῖσ' ἔπεται γνώμη τε καὶ αἰδώς.

παρὰ λόγον 2.91.4)—threw such a fright into the pursuing squadron that it fell into disorder. The Athenians then attacked and carried the day. One of the Spartan generals, Timocrates, who was aboard the Leukadian ship, killed himself, and his body washed ashore at Naupactus.

Once again the Spartan gnome proves inferior to tyche, and not only is the Spartan principle, based on the gnome-tyche antithesis, where gnome has an ethical sense, proved wrong, but the techne-tyche antithesis, which the Spartans repudiated, is here vindicated. For the Athenian techne, as exemplified in the maneuver around the transport, showed that it could utilize tyche, as exemplified in the coincidence of the transport's location (ἔτυχε κτλ. 2.91.3).[13] Timocrates kills himself out of a sense of shame, but he was defeated not because of moral weakness on his part but because of Athenian skill.[14]

2. *Pylos*

The Spartan interpretation of their defeat at Pylos emerges both in the speech of the Spartan ambassadors in Athens, when they come to make peace, and also in the anecdote of the Spartan prisoner who was taunted by some one of the Athenian allies. In the speech, the Athenian victory is attributed to tyche; in the anecdote, to

13. For the cooperation of techne and tyche cf. Hdt. 1.168.1: συν-τυχίη χρησάμενος καὶ σοφίη; Democritus on the breeding of mules, in Aelian, D. K. II.125.13ff.; Agathon fr. 6 N: τέχνη τύχην ἔστερξε καὶ τύχη τέχνην.

14. For similar Spartan suicides, cf. Hdt. 1.82.8, 7.232. Timocrates does not realize that he is fighting in what has become the παλαιὸς τρόπος (cf. 1.49.1–3).

techne in the pejorative sense of "base stratagem," "guile," or the like.

a. The speech of the Spartan ambassadors in Athens (4.17–20). After the defeat of the Spartan fleet in the harbor of Pylos, the Spartan hoplites on Sphacteria are cut off. The Spartans, seeing that they can do nothing, make a truce and send ambassadors to Athens to sue for peace. Although this is their purpose, they deliver what is more a sermon on tyche than a suit for peace. After a brief prooemium, they admonish the Athenians not to be carried away by good luck and not to hope foolishly for more than they have already gained (4.17.4). We were undone neither by lack of power nor by arrogance through superior power. We had the same resources as ever, but we made a mistake in judgment, as anyone may do.

The contrast between the Athenian and the Spartan outlook comes out in the Spartan echo (4.18.2) of a phrase of Pericles: ἀπὸ δὲ τῶν αἰεὶ ὑπαρχόντων γνώμῃ σφαλέντες, ἐν ᾧ πᾶσι τὸ αὐτὸ ὁμοίως ὑπάρχει (deceived in our judgment, though our resources were as usual, as may happen to anyone); cf. Pericles (2.62.5) ἡ ξύνεσις ... ἐλπίδι ... ἧσσον πιστεύει ... γνώμῃ δὲ ἀπὸ τῶν ὑπαρχόντων, ἧς βεβαιοτέρα ἡ πρόνοια (sagacity trusts not to hope but to intelligent policy based on available resources, since the foresight of such policy is more certain). In Pericles' understanding, gnome is the basis of a rational self-confidence; in the Spartan understanding, gnome is generally fallible. Here the Spartans are thinking of the rational side of gnome, to which they obviously attribute very little strength; when they oppose gnome to tyche in their exhortation to the sailors in the episode in the

Corinthian Gulf, they conceive of gnome as resolution or courage. This is obviously the more Spartan sense of gnome. Gnome as rational judgment will have little meaning for them, since they are so impressed by the power of chance. For the Spartans, it is a foregone conclusion that chance will overcome gnome in the sense of rational judgment; therefore they oppose to chance their traditional understanding of gnome, namely, a stubborn resistance, an unwillingness to give up the position assigned one (cf. 2.87.9: "do not leave the post at which you are stationed" with Tyrt. 7.15–16, 9.15–17D³).

The Spartan ambassadors caution the Athenians: do not think that chance will always be on your side (4.18.3). Prudent or moderate men—and this is the virtue on which Spartans pride themselves—know that the length of wars is not in their hands but in the hands of chance (18.4).[15] You now have the opportunity, by agreeing to terms, of leaving for the future an unthreatened reputation for might and intelligence, whereas if you continue the war and meet a reversal, your present success will be considered a matter of chance (18.5). This Spartan argument is later vindicated by the Spartan victory at Mantinea, after which, Thucydides says, the Greek world considered that Pylos was a matter of tyche and the Spartans were still the same in gnome, that is, they were still brave men (5.75.3). Thucydides' remark implies that it was common to view events in terms of the gnome-tyche antithesis, and that the common view resembled the Spartan. Gnome was the mettle which resisted tyche. Here is a corroboration of the observation that Pericles'

15. R. C. Seaton, *CR* 14 (1900), 223–224, conjectures ἐς τοῦτο for τούτῳ in 18.4.

emphasis on the rational dimension of gnome is innovational.

b. The anecdote. After the capture of the Spartan hoplites on Sphacteria, there was surprise in the Greek world that Spartans would give themselves up uncompelled by starvation or any other necessity,[16] and there was the suspicion that those who had given themselves up were inferior to those who had died fighting. Some one of the Athenian allies taunted one of the Spartan prisoners in Athens by asking him if the dead were brave, implying that those who had been taken prisoner were cowards. The Spartan replied that it would be a valuable arrow—ἄτρακτος, the word the Spartan uses, also means "spindle" and thus implies effeminacy[17]—that could separate the brave from the cowards, meaning that it was the one who fell afoul of rocks and arrows who perished (4.40). Since "it is not often that Thucydides relates such anecdotes,"[18] it would be useful to know what lay behind his decision to include this particular anecdote out of the many he must have known. The value of the anecdote is that it so neatly capsulates the antithesis between the

16. Cf. *Gnomologium Vaticanum e Codice Vaticano Graeco* 743, ed. Leo Sternbach (Berlin, 1963), no. 575.

17. On this word, see Gomme, "The Interpretation of καλοὶ κἀγαθοί in Thuc. 4.40.2," *CQ* NS 3 (1953), 65–68.

18. Gomme, III, 480. Cf. J. de Romilly, "L'Utilité de l'histoire selon Thucydide," in *Histoire et historiens dans l'antiquité* (Entretiens sur l'antiquité classique IV) (Vandoeuvres - Genève 1956), p. 60: "De même que la sûreté des previsions établies par les chefs dépend du caractère lucide et exhaustif de l'enquête qu'ils mènent, de même la valeur de l'analyse élaborée par Thucydide dépend de caractère lucide et exhaustif de la sienne. *Il peut laisser de côté ce qui est purement anecdotique,* c'est-à-dire ce qui ne se rattache pas à la chaine des causes et des conséquences indispensables" (my italics).

"The Lacedaemonians and Chance"

Athenians and the Spartans, as this antithesis appears to the Spartans.[19] What lies behind the Spartan's reply can be understood in general as the aristocrat's scorn for the underhanded stratagem by which he has been undone, and in particular as the hoplite's scorn for the archer. This scorn will be found to involve the characteristic Spartan concept of the gnome- or techne-tyche antithesis.

The Athenian ally, an Ionian, knows that the Spartans believe in the natural superiority of Dorians to Ionians, and thus the Ionian taunts the Spartan with the phrase καλοὶ κἀγαθοί. As Gomme observes of this expression: "when social it is a title adopted by aristocrats or the rich . . . who claimed these virtues as exclusively theirs, or by Dorians in opposition to Ionians and islanders, as here." But "unlike τὸ εὐγενές, it does not imply social status only, but the possession of a certain ἀρετή—the ἀρετή of Achilles: conspicuous and individual courage in battle, a good carriage, athletic prowess, generosity, and courtesy."[20] As Gomme well observes, the Spartan's reply, which answers καλοὶ κἀγαθοί with ἀγαθοί, limits the former concept to a single kind of *arete*, namely, bravery.[21] The bravery of the Spartan prisoners is not in question since, under the conditions of battle on Sphacteria, it was never put to the test. The Spartan's reply is

19. Herodotus (e.g. 7.56) used the pointed anecdote: see H. R. Immerwahr, "Historical Action in Herodotus," *TAPA* 85 (1954), 20–21.

20. Gomme, III, 480.

21. Gomme, *CQ* NS 3 (1953), 65. That the Spartan had another reason for his reply is suggested by Strepsiades' comparison of the "beasts" (θηρία) he sees in the *phrontisterion* to the prisoners from Sphacteria (Ar. *Clouds* 184–186): the physical appearance of the Spartan prisoners was no longer handsome.

in the aristocratic and also the heroic tradition, and its sources can be found in Pindar and in Homer.

In *Isthm.* 4 Pindar compares the Cleonymids in the days before Melissus' recent victory on the Isthmus to Ajax, the type of unrewarded merit. "There is obscurity of fortune (τύχας) even for those who strive, before they reach their utmost goal. For fortune gives both success and failure. And fortune lays hands on and trips up the better man with the guile (τέχνᾳ) of the lesser men" (32–37 Bury). The example is Ajax.

One MS (D) reads τέχνα. Most editors prefer the dative (B and apparently the scholiast) on the principle of *lectio difficilior*. Techna then becomes the agent of tycha, which might be surprising considering that these concepts are sharply antithetical elsewhere (especially in the Hippocratic *De Arte*), but in the light of the Spartan reasoning about their first naval defeat, Pindar's usage is explicable. For the Spartans, gnome, in the sense of resoluteness or courage, was superior both to the techne of the Athenians and also to tyche. These two concepts, then, techne and tyche, could be taken together as one side of a more fundamental antithesis, the other side of which was the unchangeable gnome of the Spartans, and which here, in Pindar, appears as the innate arete of the Cleonymids (cf. *Isthm.* 3.13–14), exemplified by the *alka* of Ajax—arete which has finally, as was inevitable, been brought to light by Melissus, after chance and the guile of inferior men (so Pindar implies) had kept it in darkness for so long.

But when Pindar describes the virtues of Melissus which enabled him to win the pancration, it turns out that since Melissus was of small stature (53ff.) he had to combine the shrewdness (μῆτιν 51) of the fox with leontine spirit. As the scholiast says, Melissus defeats a larger man τέχνη.[22] Melissus, then, is guilty of just the sort of guile, which, in connection with tyche, was said to overcome the better man. Pindar seems to excuse Melissus with the sentence χρὴ δὲ πᾶν ἔρδοντ' ἀμαυρῶσαι τὸν ἔχθρον (one must do everything to obliterate his adversary) (52). Furthermore, it might have seemed that since the natural superiority of the aristocratic Cleonymids would finally have its day in any case, the means to Melissus' victory were less important than the end. We find the same sort of moral ambiguity (from a non-Spartan point of view) in certain Spartan statements in the *History*. In the anecdote of the Spartan prisoner in Athens the departure from conventional hoplite warfare is scorned (4.40.2); but Brasidas has no misgivings about tricky tactics, which he recommends in the same context in which he reminds his men of the customary superiority of Dorians to Ionians (5.9).[23] One recalls the epic code of honor, according to which a successful ambush was as glorious as the vanquishing of an enemy in regular combat. But that the Spartan position is inconsistent appears from the fact that the same kind of tactics which Brasidas recommends were earlier proposed by an Elean named Teutiaplus;

22. For the connection of τέχνη and μῆτις see the discussion of *Iliad* 23 below and n. 26. The heroic version of Melissus' achievement is the enchaining of Ares and Aphrodite by Hephaestus (*Od.* 8.266–366). The swiftest of the gods is caught by Hephaestus χωλὸς ἐὼν τέχνῃσι (332).

23. Cf. n. 3 above.

and Thucydides says simply that "he could not persuade Alcidas" (3.30).[24]

The aristocratic view of the Spartan in the anecdote is reflected in Homer's account of the chariot race in *Iliad* 23, which constitutes a sort of apology for Menelaus.[25] Antilochus, who has been advised by Nestor to use μῆτις (313ff.) in turning the post (323ff.), goes beyond his father's advice and craftily (n.b. τεχνήσομαι 415) forces Menelaus off the track in an opportune place.[26] Antilochus not only uses guile, but chance, that is, the lot, gives him the most advantageous starting place (352–357). Antilochus combines the advantages of techne and tyche. He has the best of both but he does not venture to pass Diomedes, because Diomedes is favored by Athena. The combination of techne and tyche is opposed not only by the divine but also, as in the passage of Pindar discussed above, by natural excellence, for the poet says that the contest for second place between Antilochus and Menelaus was very close, even in spite of Antilochus' guile, and if they had run farther, Menelaus, the best (357), would have won (526–527), as would have

24. On the text, see C. P. Bill, "τὰ κοινὰ τοῦ πολέμου," *CP* 32 (1937), 160, for an excellent defense of the καινόν of C² in 3.30.4, with reference to Cic. *Ep. ad Att.* 5.20.3 and Arist. *EN* 1116b7, where the same corruption (κοινόν) has occurred. H.-J. Schulz, "Zu Thukydides 3,30,4," *Hermes* (1957), 255–256, argued well against Steup's κοινόν, but, ignorant of Bill's note, proposed καιρόν. On the contrast between Alcidas and Brasidas, see H. D. Westlake, *Individuals in Thucydides* (Cambridge, 1968), pp. 136, 142–147.

25. For an analysis of the chariot race, see S. Benardete, "The *Aristeia* of Diomedes and the Plot of the Iliad," ΑΓΩΝ No. 2 (1968), 10–11.

26. For μῆτις as the source of techne, see Empedocles B 23.2; Clemens regarded μῆτις as Homer's paraphrase of Mousaios' τέχνη: Mousaios B 4 = D.-K. I.22.22.

been fitting. Excellence would have defeated guile and the luck of the draw. Antilochus beat Menelaus κέρδεσιν, οὔ τι τάχεϊ γε (by guile, not by speed); compare 322 and 709, where μῆτις and κέρδεα are implicitly associated.

Turning from the aristocratic point of view reflected in the anecdote to the specific issue of hoplite versus archer, one finds that, although the contrast of archer and hoplite goes back to Homer, it was still alive in the second half of the fifth century. The Homeric example is Alexander, against whom τοξότα could be leveled as a term of reproach (11.385). The epic view of the archer is not, however, unambiguous: there were respectable bowmen, and Alexander is not always described as an inferior warrior.[27] But when Homer represents his heroes as scorning the archer he perhaps reflects a prejudice of his own time. At the beginning of the seventh century, when the cities of the Lelantine plain fought against one another, they made an agreement banning missile weapons. Strabo saw an inscription to this effect (Strabo 448).[28]

In the discussion of Pericles, it was observed that his constant stress on the navy must have been a response to some part of the Athenian citizenry which still retained a traditional, perhaps Hesiodic view of sailing, even in spite of Salamis and the Athenian empire, or which clung to an aristocratic view, according to which only the traditional army, with the hoplites as the core, supported by cavalry or slingers, as the case might be, could be consid-

27. W. B. Stanford, *Sophocles' Ajax* (London, 1963), pp. 199–200.
28. Cited by Albin Lesky, *A History of Greek Literature*, trans. James Willis and Cornelis de Heer (New York, 1966), p. 55. Cf. Archil. fr. 3.4–5 D³.

ered the basis of military policy. Now another archaic tradition, which sets the hoplite above the archer, who is regarded as a lower-class sort, also persists into the second half of the fifth century, and it is for this reason that Thucydides' anecdote concerning the Spartan prisoner is so telling. Euripides, in his *Heracles,* shows Lycus' scorn of Heracles as bowman. The bow is the coward's weapon. It is no test of εὐψυχία (162; cf. Archidamus' use of this term, discussed above). Lycus is on the side of a kind of fighting at which the Spartans excelled.[29] Again in the fourth episode of Sophocles' *Ajax,* Menelaus scorns Teucer as bowman (1120). To this Teucer replies οὐ γὰρ βάναυσον τὴν τέχνην ἐκτησάμην (the art that I possess is not vulgar). It may not have been a lower-class techne but still it was a techne, and, as we have seen, the descendants of Menelaus who appear in Thucydides' *History* do not rate techne very high. That Menelaus had contemporary relevance appears likely: Bowra has brought out certain similarities between Menelaus in the *Ajax* and the Thucydidean Archidamus.[30]

To conclude, the anecdote expresses, from the Spartan point of view, the theme of Spartan gnome, namely, aristocratic bravery, versus both Athenian techne, which the Spartans would consider banausic and guileful,[31] and also tyche, under the conditions of which there is no test of bravery. To be killed by a missile is to be killed by tyche

29. Cf. Wilamowitz, *Euripides Herakles* (Bad Homburg vor der Höhe, 1959), III, 45.

30. *Sophoclean Tragedy* (Oxford, 1944), p. 50.

31. On this conservative concept of techne, see also L. Camerer, *Praktische Klugheit bei Herodot: Untersuchungen zu den Begriffen* μηχανή, τέχνη, σοφία (Cologne, 1965).

(cf. Arist. *Rhet.* 1362a6–10). By implication the reply of the Spartan prisoner couples techne and tyche and contrasts them with the Spartan gnome. In this way, the anecdote admirably capsulates the theme adumbrated in the episode of the naval battles near Naupactus.

D. The Spartan character of Nicias[32]

Nicias, the pacificist forsaken by his people, the pietist forsaken by the gods, the cunctator forsaken by his own strategy, was an Athenian with a Spartan heart. At times Nicias echoes Archidamus, while his rival, Alcibiades, echoes Pericles, in such a way that the antithesis in terms of which the war was originally conceived seems to be reestablished. Again the contrast between Nicias and Demosthenes is the contrast between Nicias' procrastination, uncharacteristic of an Athenian, and the much more characteristically Athenian strategy of Demosthenes, who mounts an attack immediately upon his arrival at Syracuse.[33]

But at the same time the course of events has outrun

32. For studies of the Thucydidean Nicias, see Ivo Bruns, *Das Literarische Porträt der Griechen* (Berlin, 1898), pp. 16–22; cf. pp. 64–70; G. F. Bender, *Der Begriff*, pp. 38–57; H. D. Westlake, "Nicias in Thucydides," *CQ* 35 (1941), 58–65; H. D. Westlake, *Individuals in Thucydides* (Cambridge, 1968), pp. 86–96, 169–211; O. Luschnat, *Die Feldherrnreden im Geschichtswerk des Thukydides, Philol.* Supp. XXXIV (1942), passim; H. A. Murray, "Two Notes on the Evaluation of Nicias in Thucydides," *BICS* 8 (1961), 33–46; Leo Strauss, *The City and Man*, pp. 200–209.

33. 7.42.3. The adverse opinion on Nicias expressed here is Thucydides': see G. Donini, "Thuc. 7,42,3; Does Thucydides Agree with Demosthenes' View?," *Hermes* 92 (1964), 116–119; Dover's note on this passage (7.42.3).

the Athenian-Spartan antithesis in terms of which Pericles, and also Archidamus, planned strategy. Athens faces in Syracuse a city like herself (as Nicias himself observes: 6.20.3; cf. 7.55.2, 8.96.4). In rejecting Pericles' wise counsel not to expand their empire, the Athenians also give up the advantages of Pericles' strategy, which pitted Athenian wealth and naval prowess against Spartan land army and want of capital, and "reaching out for more" they attack a naval democracy like their own. The story of Nicias is part of the story of the Sicilian expedition. Thematically, un-Athenian Nicias is the foil to an Athens bent on its own ruination, while factually he is in large part the cause of this ruination.

It is curious that history gave Thucydides the person of Nicias whose spirit was so unlike the dominant Athenian spirit of his time and whose story would thus develop in opposition to the story of his city, even though the same defeat awaited both. The story of Nicias unfolds in three main episodes. First, in securing the Peace he acts on motives which would have gladdened the heart of Archidamus but which could never become the motives of the Athenians described by the Corinthians (and Thucydides considered their description correct: cf. 1.70 with 8.96.4). It is as if Thucydides had extended Heraclitus' proverb to cities and imagined that on the principle ἦθος πόλει δαίμων (cf. Heraclitus B 119), the Athenians would inevitably abandon the Peace. Alcibiades is simply the recrudescence of the true Athens, with his scorn of chance and his willingness to run all risks (6.16.4). In the second episode, Nicias struggles to defend the Peace against Alcibiades. Nicias believes that he is opposing the youthful rashness of Alcibiades, but in reality it is the spirit of Athens which speaks through Alcibiades, the new generation that has grown up in a city of renewed fortune and hope. Finally the circle is drawn, and Nicias is again at the head of an Athenian army. Wrong-headed in his strategy, after previous military success, prostrate with nephritis, he epitomizes in his own person the hopelessness of the Athenian campaign. His words signal the peripety (7.11.4; cf. 4.29; later Thucydides makes this peripety explicit: 7.71.7). At the same time, Nicias, who had wished to make the least commitment to chance (5.16), finds himself at the mercy of chance (7.77.1–4).

1. *Peace*

The Nicias who seeks peace has already emerged as an eccentric in the Pylos episode, when he dared (τολμῆσαι 4.28.2), with a characteristically negative daring, and in a completely unexpected fashion, to call Cleon's bluff and step down from the office of strategos. Nicias' motives in seeking peace are equally eccentric and unexpected of a man in his position. Unlike the motives of the Spartan peacemaker, Pleistoanax, Nicias' have nothing to do with his city's internal politics, nor is there any external compulsion working upon him. Nicias is described as

βουλόμενος ἐν ᾧ ἀπαθὴς ἦν καὶ ἠξιοῦτο, διασώσασθαι τὴν εὐτυχίαν, καὶ ἔς τε τὸ αὐτίκα πόνων πεπαῦσθαι καὶ αὐτὸς καὶ τοὺς πολίτας παῦσαι καὶ τῷ μέλλοντι χρόνῳ καταλιπεῖν ὄνομα ὡς οὐδὲν σφήλας τὴν πόλιν διεγένετο

wishing to preserve his good luck, and to be quit of toils himself and to end the citizens' toil and to leave for the future the reputation that he had gone through life without causing any harm to the city (5.16.1).

Such are Nicias' motives, and he defends the Peace in similar terms (5.46.1): εὖ ἑστώτων τῶν πραγμάτων ὡς ἐπὶ πλεῖστον ἄριστον εἶναι διασώσασθαι τὴν εὐπραγίαν (since their affairs were in a good state, it was best to preserve their prosperity as long as possible).

"To preserve to the end his prosperity" (5.16.1) is explained (καί may be taken as exegetical) by two closely connected motives (n.b. ἔς τε τὸ αὐτίκα . . . καὶ τῷ μέλλοντι χρόνῳ): (1) surcease of his own and of the citizens' toil, and (2) leaving behind him the reputation of never having harmed the city. As for (1), if what the Corinthians say is true, that it is the Athenians' nature to spend their whole lives in toil and danger and that the Athenians consider unbothered tranquillity more a calamity than toilsome activity (1.70.8), then Nicias goes against the Athenian grain and (2) may be doomed from the start. Nicias' personal motives are incompatible with the city's character: this incompatibility will appear less strange in the light of the discussion below of the connections between Archidamus and Nicias.

In both (1) and (2) Nicias' motives combine a personal and a patriotic element, as does the main proposition that they explain (βουλόμενος through εὐτυχίαν), where εὐτυχίαν is both Nicias' and Athens' (cf. 5.46.1). In (2) the patriotic element is clearly subordinate: he wished to leave for posterity the reputation of having reached the end of his life (διεγένετο) without having caused his city any harm. It is only thus that he can preserve to the end (διασώσασθαι) his and his city's prosperity. The δια-compounds intimate the characteristic Nician outlook underlying these motives. Such compounds are common in contexts in which the instability of human affairs is expressed (Alc. fr. 138; Sem. fr. 7.99; Pind. *Nem.* 7.99; Bacch. 11.3, fr. 5.53; Hdt. 5.92.3). In some of these places it is of course said that tyche causes this instability.

The concern with preserving prosperity *to the end,* which entails a fitting death (cf. 7.48.4 and sect. D.4 below), is precisely what is required by the Herodotean Solon (1.32.5–7). It was his dictum that no man can be called blessed until the end of his life, and this dictum was based on the belief that human life is subject to chance (Hdt. 1.32.2–5). Aristotle observes that it would follow that no one is ever happy while he is alive but only after death (*EN* 1100a10–18), and Nicias appears to have felt that his happiness was subject to this condition. What will survive him is a good name, the reverberation in the future of the good repute in which he is now held (ἠξιοῦντο 5.16.1). This present good repute is integral to his prosperity. *Nec sunt enim beati quorum divitias nemo novit* (Apul. *Met.* 5.10).[34] It must be maintained to the end, so as to extend in an unbroken line into posthumous fame. Yet Nicias will prove the truth of what Amasis told Polycrates: "I cannot remember that I ever heard of any man, who, having been constantly successful, did not at last utterly perish" (Hdt. 3.40). So Nicias will suffer a disastrous reversal of his hopes, as catastrophic bad luck follows upon cherished good luck, just as in the Herodotean cycle of fortune (1.209).

Here, in addition to his motives for peace, other details of Nicias' character in which he appears rather eccentric by Periclean standards should be recalled. The offer of

34. Cf. Petronius C: Immo vero nolo habere bona, nisi quibus populus inviderit.

resignation from command made during the Pylos episode is repeated (παρίημι . . . τὴν ἀρχήν are the emphatic closing words of Nicias' reply to Alcibiades: 6.23.3). But the Athenian who abstains from public life is considered useless, according to Pericles (2.40.2). In fact, Nicias' quietism flatly contradicts Pericles' exhortation to toil and defense of the empire: the Athenians must not flee toil (2.63.1; cf. 5.16.1, 6.18.6); to give up the empire, which they possess as a tyranny, would not be to avoid (cf. 5.16.1) but to take risks (2.63.2).[35] Nicias acknowledges the right of individual self-interest (6.9.2), a principle unknown to the Corinthians' paradigmatic Athenians (1.70.6). Nicias is a lover of peace (consider the comparison below of Nicias with Archidamus); the paradigmatic Athenian is by nature unpeaceful (1.70.9).

Nicias, with his piety, his self-concern, and his quietism, is clearly not at home in the Periclean Athens described in the last section of Chapter I. His piety, which has just been discussed, could take the form of disastrous superstition (7.50.4). The humanistic self-reliance of Pericles is unknown to Nicias, who says, concerning the Sicilian expedition, that he knows πολλὰ μὲν ἡμᾶς δέον εὖ βουλεύσασθαι, ἔτι δὲ πλείω εὐτυχῆσαι, χαλεπὸν δὲ ἀνθρώπους ὄντας (we must have much good counsel and still more good fortune, and that is difficult for mortals) (6.23.3). The pious distrust in human planning is the opposite of the scorn of tyche shown by Pericles in the prooemium to his first speech.

Nicias' piety is also egotistical.[36] In his final exhortation

---

35. Cf. Bender, *Der Begriff*, pp. 43–45.
36. Cf. Bruns, *Das Literarische Porträt*, p. 17.

to the army (7.77), he attempts to inspire his men with hope by presenting himself as an example of one who is as badly off as they but expects a favorable turn of events because of his justice and piety. The self-concern of Nicias, which is not, of course, unmixed with patriotism, is shown in his un-Periclean desire to avoid risk[37] in order to release himself and his fellow-citizens from toil. But the selfish side of Nicias revealed in his motives for seeking peace comes into the open in his "personally chosen" (ἰδίᾳ 7.48.4) death, by which he hopes to avoid disgrace and to preserve the fair name that was one of his concerns in seeking peace. Nicias' choice of death is reminiscent of Leonidas' decision at Thermopylae to send away the allies in order that he and the Spartans might have more glory (Hdt. 7.220.2).

Nicias' quietism is likewise opposed to the Periclean concept of Athenian citizenship. Nicias' position is labeled ἀπραγμοσύνη (not meddling in public affairs) by Alcibiades (6.18.5), who, as will be seen, revives certain Periclean notions. A city like Athens, which is not ἀπράγμων, as Nicias would have it, is destroyed by ἀπραγμοσύνη, according to Alcibiades (6.18.7). ἡσυχία (quiet) is not permitted Athens (6.18.3). To defend the Athenian presence in Sicily will be to defend Athenian πολυπραγμοσύνη (meddlesomeness) (6.87.3). Thucydides has made it clear that the character of Nicias is conservative and un-Athenian in terms of the Periclean concept of Athens.

But the quietism of Nicias has further implications. Once the Periclean concept has established itself and

37. Cf. Gomme, III, 663 on 5.16.1.

can be appealed to as a norm, as by Alcibiades and Euphemus, the character of Nicias may appear simply eccentric or individualistic. Nicias' attitudes find parallels in the individualistic ethics of Democritus and in the eccentric Amphion of Euripides' *Antiope*.

The desire for quietude, the retreat from the public realm, the resistance to the allure of good fortune—all this is Democritean: "The man who wishes to have serenity of spirit should not engage in many activities, either private or public, nor choose activities beyond his power and natural capacity. He must guard against this, so that when good fortune strikes him and leads him on to excess by means of (*false*) seeming, he must rate it low, and not attempt things beyond his powers. A reasonable fulness is better than overfulness" (Democr. B3).[38]

Democritus' admonition is generally in keeping with the Solonian dictum, but the notion of a retreat from activity and public life is new. Greek literature of the fifth century and before does not abound in examples of such shrinking souls. The Persian Otanes' οὔτε γὰρ ἄρχειν οὔτε ἄρχεσθαι ἐθέλω (I wish neither to rule nor to be ruled) (Herod. 3.83.2) must have sounded strange and oriental to Greek ears, for τὸ ἄρχειν ἥδιστον (to rule is sweetest) (Arist. *Rhet.* 1371b26; cf. Hdt. 4.147.3).[39]

---

38. The translation is by K. Freeman, *Ancilla to the Pre-Socratic Philosophers* (Cambridge, Mass., 1948).

39. Perhaps Xenophon (*Anab.* 1.9.4) makes a critical allusion to Herodotus' report of Otanes when he says of the sons of the Persian nobles: εὐθὺς παῖδες ὄντες μανθάνουσιν ἄρχειν τε καὶ ἄρχεσθαι. For what may be another, similar echo of Hdt. by Xen., cf. Hdt. 7.237 συμβουλευομένου ἂν συμβουλεύσειε τὰ ἄριστα with Xen. *Anab.* 2.1.17: συμβουλευομένοις συνεβούλευσε τάδε. But the juxtaposition of active and passive forms is, it must be admitted, commonplace: see H. Herter,

Nicias' life was dedicated to arete (7.86.5), and a traditional definition of arete given by Meno in the Platonic dialogue named after him is: ruling men (73c); but it is Nicias who twice offers to resign his command. In passing, it should be pointed out that the aristocratic ideal of *arche* is not to be identified with the Periclean concept of the primacy of the city, according to which the life of each citizen is absorbed in the city in war and peace. In his Democritean desire for serenity of spirit, Nicias opposes an aristocratic ideal that he might have been expected to maintain, even if he was not a citizen in the Periclean sense.

In fifth-century Greek literature the best parallel to Nicias is Euripides' Amphion. In the *Antiope,* one of his last plays, Euripides presented an antilogy between Amphion and his brother, Zethus, representatives of opposite ways of life, the musical and the practical, the apolitical and the political, the private and the public. It must be admitted at the outset that the comparison of Nicias with Amphion is only partial. The poet Amphion, with his dedication to τὰ καλά (fr. 198 N), goes beyond Nicias in spirituality. We do not know from Thucydides what positive description Nicias might have given to a retreat from public life. In the *History* such a retreat inevitably has a negative sense. There is also the fact that at a certain point in the play Amphion abandons inactivity,[40] and when he does, he follows a Periclean

---

"Das Königsritual der Atlantis," *RM* NS 109 (1966), 257, n. 107. For the unreasonableness of wishing neither to rule nor to be ruled, cf. Xen. *Mem.* 2.1.12; cf. Eur. *IA* 19–20.

40. Bruno Snell, *Scenes from Greek Drama* (Berkeley and Los Angeles, 1964), pp. 73–74.

principle, in acting on gnome (if fr. 220 N may be attributed to Amphion).[41]

It is rather in his ethics, as he defends his way of life against Zethus, that Amphion resembles Nicias. Accepting the Solonian view that mortal life is at the mercy of chance, Amphion concludes that one should seek as much pleasure as possible (fr. 196 N). Nicias, too, believes that it is difficult for mortals to be happy (6.23.3). He wants to avoid pain (5.16.1), no doubt to enjoy the pleasures of peace. Nicias was presumably more restrained in his expectations of peace than Aristophanes' Trygaeus, and yet Trygaeus shows what a hedonistic aspect peace might wear. In fragment 194 Amphion praises the ἥσυχος (the peaceful man) as the best friend and the best citizen and forbids risks. "For I like neither the overbold sailor nor the chief of state." Whoever makes himself busy in many undertakings when he can live pleasantly as an ἀπράγμων is a fool (fr. 193 N). According to Alcibiades, Nicias wants to be this ἀπράγμων (6.18.5). One might suspect a common origin of the views of Amphion and Nicias in Democritus.

Nicias' ends in seeking peace may, then, be understood as conservative against the background of the Periclean concept of the city, or they may point to a new sort of individualism. Thucydides may have thought of the character of Nicias as a combination of an old and a new ethics. In any case, the means by which Nicias hopes to attain the ends of peace, namely, "the least commitment to chance," will appear as peculiar as these ends. At first sight, however, it appears that there is nothing nonsensical about Nicias' means. Thucydides explains how Nicias expected to achieve the ends already discussed (5.16.1):

41. Snell, *Scenes from Greek Drama*, p. 89, so attributes it.

νομίζων ἐκ τοῦ ἀκινδύνου τοῦτο ξυμβαίνειν καὶ ὅστις ἐλάχιστα τύχῃ
αὐτὸν παραδίδωσι, τὸ δὲ ἀκίνδυνον τὴν εἰρήνην παρέχειν.

believing that this would result from avoidance of risk and if
one committed himself to chance as slightly as possible, and
that peace provided avoidance of risk.

Since war is the realm of fortune (1.78.2; cf. Archidamus'
views, sec. B above; cf. 4.18.4), peace is security; and then
there is also the matter of quitting when one is ahead. But
Nicias understands peace in a special sense: freedom
from danger and the least commitment to chance. It is as
if Nicias underestimated the scope of chance, within
which, as it turned out, there were no secure precincts. In
fact, Nicias' belief that he could preserve his *eutychia*
(prosperity) by exempting himself from tyche is quite
contrary to Greek common sense, as Aristotle shows in
Physics 2.5, where, on the basis of his own analysis of
tyche, he shows what is reasonable in various common
opinions about tyche and related matters. If we set
Aristotle's remarks about eutychia next to Nicias' line of
reasoning about eutychia, we see at once how implausible
Nicias' reasoning is:

Νικίας . . . βουλόμενος . . . διασώσασθαι τὴν εὐτυχίαν . . . νομίζων ἐκ
τοῦ ἀκινδύνου τοῦτο ξυμβαίνειν καί ὅστις ἐλάχιστα τύχῃ αὐτὸν
παραδίδωσι (5.16.1).

With which compare Aristotle, *Physics* 197a30–32:

ἔτι ἀβέβαιον ἡ εὐτυχία εὐλόγως. ἡ γὰρ τύχη ἀβέβαιος, οὔτε γὰρ ἀεὶ
οὔθ' ὡς ἐπὶ τὸ πολὺ οἷον τ' εἶναι τῶν ἀπὸ τύχης οὐθέν.

Again prosperity (eutychia) is reasonably considered unstable.
For chance (tyche) is unstable. For nothing that comes from
chance can be forever or for a long time.

From Aristotle's point of view eutychia shares in the
instability of tyche. This is also Nicias' view, but Nicias

believes that he can exempt himself from tyche and preserve his eutychia on grounds different from those on
which it was won. Nicias' desire is, in effect, to reify that
eutychia which was gained in action and which could only
be gained in action. Nicias' desire is to make a thing out of
a deed, contrary to the necessary connection of eutychia
and action, which Aristotle explains as follows (1 97b1–5):

ἡ μὲν γὰρ τύχη καὶ τὸ ἀπὸ τύχης, ἐστὶν ὅσοις καὶ τὸ εὐτυχῆσαι ἂν
ὑπάρξειεν καὶ ὅλως πρᾶξις. διὸ καὶ ἀνάγκη περὶ τὰ πρακτὰ εἶναι τὴν
τύχην (σημεῖον δ᾽ ὅτι δοκεῖ ἤτοι ταὐτὸν εἶναι τῇ εὐδαιμονίᾳ ἡ εὐτυχία
ἢ ἔγγυς, ἡ δ᾽ εὐδαιμονία πρᾶξίς τις. εὐπραξία γάρ).

Chance and the results of chance belong to those capable of
prosperity and of action in general. Therefore chance must
concern actions, as is indicated by the fact that prosperity
(eutychia) is believed to be the same, or nearly the same,
as happiness (*eudaimonia*), and happiness is a certain
action—doing well (*eupraxia*).

Nicias' desire to preserve his eutychia is from the ordi-
nary point of view (n.b. δοκεῖ) logically impossible.
Eutychia cannot be transferred from activity to quietude
and kept as a possession. Nicias learns by suffering the
illogic of his thought.

2.   *The end of the Peace: The debate of Nicias and Alcibiades*
(6.8.3–26)[42]

The second episode in the story of Nicias is his futile
effort to persuade the Athenians to rescind their decision
to send aid to Egesta and to reestablish Leontinoi. Nicias
believed that, on these pretexts, Athens reached out for
control of all Sicily. Nicias' debate with Alcibiades follows

42. On this debate, see K. von Fritz, *Griech. Geschichtsschreibung*, Ia,
727–731; Ib, 316–317; Daniel P. Tompkins, "Stylistic Characterization in Thucydides: Nicias and Alcibiades," *YCS* 22 (1972), 181–214.

in the *History* close upon the Melian dialogue, and Thucydides makes Nicias echo a rather striking metaphor used by the Athenians. The Athenians tell the Melians not to rely on Hope, who, for those who stake everything they own on one throw of the dice (ἀναρριπτοῦσι), becomes known when they are undone and leaves them no second opportunity of guarding against her now that she is known (5.103.1). Nicias asks the Athenians to reverse their decision on behalf of their fatherland, which now stands the hazard (ἀναρριπτούσης) of the greatest danger ever (6.13.1). It happens that the hopeful and more than hopeful mood of the Athenians (6.24.3) is of the same sort as that condemned by the Athenians in the Melians. By poetic justice the Athenians fall prey to the same passions which they believe are ruinous (cf. 6.24.3 also with Diodotus' analysis of revolutionary psychology, where ἔρως and hope are linked: 3.45.5). Nicias' repetition of the metaphor from dicing seems to underline the fact that he is addressing a city that is subject to the same psychological forces which led to the defeat, destruction, and enslavement of the Melians.

Appropriately, therefore, Nicias is the one who at Syracuse restates the futile moral position of the Melians, when it is too late for the Athenians to save themselves (7.77; cf. 5.104). The debate between Nicias and Alcibiades stands between the Melian dialogue and the Syracusan disaster. The reader, with his hindsight, knows that Nicias' arguments will not prevail. In any case, Nicias is arguing against a decision that has already been made, and this seems characteristic of him. What then is the function in the *History* of this debate? Its function is like that of the speech of Archidamus

(1.80–85) already discussed. Archidamus stated policies whose rejection by the Spartans he could have anticipated (1.79.2).[43] But these principles and policies are not less Spartan for this reason; in fact, they are more Spartan than the zealousness of Sthenelaidas. Archidamus' speech has little to do with the hard facts of the commencement of the war. Its value is, rather, thematic. It answers the critical one-sided views of the Corinthians by showing that what the Corinthians take for vices are really virtues. The first speech of Nicias in the debate with Alcibiades has equally little to do with the hard facts of the causes for the Sicilian expedition. This speech, too, is thematic. It evokes the principles which the expedition violates and thereby provides an antithetical framework on the basis of which the events can be analyzed. In fact there is a remarkable consistency in the story of Nicias within the story of the Sicilian expedition, since he maintains to the end the outlook expressed in his Peace and in the defense of that Peace.

Because Nicias' principles are to some extent Spartan, we have an evocation, just before the disaster at Syracuse, of the antithesis between Sparta and Athens developed in the speeches of the Corinthians, Archidamus, and Pericles. The fact that Alcibiades' speech recalls Pericles, in general and in some details, strengthens this evocation of the antithetical terms and concepts in which the participants originally conceived of the war. We can think then of the Athenian defeat at Syracuse as the defeat at once of the Spartan and of the Athenian principles:

43. Gomme overlooks this passage when he says, "Spartan opinion was divided and both sides are important and must be represented," I, 255.

events have outrun the antitheses which once appeared fundamental and which were the basis of Archidamus' and of Pericles' policies. These antitheses have collapsed in Athens, since the expedition is Periclean in concept, to the extent that its promoter, Alcibiades, is Periclean, while its strategy is Spartan, to the extent that Nicias is Spartan and guides its strategy. At the same time Syracuse presents itself as a new Athens (consider 7.21.3) in Dorian dress (6.80.3, 82.2; 7.5.4). Each of the combatants is to some degree a combination of Athenian and Spartan. Alcibiades tips the balance (6.15.3–4). His defection, with the death of Lamachus, leaves the Athenian force in the hands of the Spartan Nicias, while Syracuse, with Alcibiades now guiding the policy of its ally Sparta, has a greater proportion of the Athenian character. This paradox is adumbrated in the debate of Nicias and Alcibiades.

In the prooemium of the first speech in the debate with Alcibiades Nicias shows himself solidly in agreement with the Corinthian analysis of the difference between Athens and Sparta: Nicias will not oppose the Athenian character by attempting to persuade the Athenians $\tau\grave{\alpha}$ . . . $\dot{\upsilon}\pi\acute{\alpha}\rho\chi o\nu\tau\alpha$ $\sigma\acute{\omega}\zeta\epsilon\iota\nu$ (to preserve what they have) (6.9.3). To preserve what one has would after all be characteristic not of Athens but of Sparta, as is clear from the Corinthians' use of the very same phrase of the Spartans (1.70.2). Other points made by Nicias square with the Corinthians' analysis. Since the Athenians are runners of risks ($\kappa\iota\nu\delta\upsilon\nu\epsilon\upsilon\tau\alpha\acute{\iota}$ 1.70.3, 1.70.8), Nicias will not try to dissuade the Athenians from that practice (6.9.3). But Nicias cautions the Athenians not to be too much in love with what is out of sight ($\dot{\alpha}\pi\acute{o}\nu\tau\omega\nu$ 6.13.1), though the

Athenians always expect to gain something ἀπουσίᾳ (1.70.4).[44] Nicias' position is somewhat like that of Archidamus at the allies' conference in Sparta before the outbreak of the war. Nicias calls for lengthier deliberations: let us not be persuaded οὕτω βραχείᾳ βουλῇ περὶ μεγάλων πραγμάτων (by such brief deliberation concerning weighty matters) (6.9.1); Archidamus pleads (1.85.1): μηδὲ ἐπειχθέντες ἐν βραχεῖ μορίῳ ἡμέρας περὶ πολλῶν σωμάτων καὶ χρημάτων καὶ πόλεων καὶ δόξης βουλεύσωμεν ἀλλὰ καθ' ἡσυχίαν (let us not hastily decide in the brief space of a day about many lives, possessions, cities, and honor, but at leisure). This last phrase, already used once previously by Archidamus (1.83.3), will be used by Nicias, that other admirer of tranquillity (6.25.2). Both Nicias and Archidamus recommend to their city that it preserve what it already has (1.70.4, 6.10.5). Both call for moderation: εἰ σωφρονοῦμεν 6.11.7; εἰ σωφρόνως τις ... ἐκλογίζοιτο 1.80.2. Both counsel against trusting to bad luck on the enemy's part (1.84.4, 6.11.6). Both distinguish between the older and younger members of their audience (1.80.1, 6.13.1). The disdain of the enemy which is a virtue for Pericles is a vice for both Nicias and Archidamus (1.84.3–4, 6.11.6).

Alcibiades on the other hand recalls Pericles. Whereas Nicias wished to make the least commitment to chance, Alcibiades defends his hauteur on the grounds of the exceptional magnitude of his risks. Pericles had taught that the greatest honor comes from the greatest risks (1.144, 2.64); Alcibiades has adopted this principle and

---

44. Dover, in Gomme, IV, on 6.13.1, points out that τῶν ἀπόντων had "more emotional associations for the Greeks than for us."

applied it to his own career. "It is not unjust that a man who is proud of himself[45] be not equal to the rest, since when he fares ill his share of the disaster is far from equal. As we are shunned when our luck is bad[46]—in the same way endure to be looked down upon by us when our luck is good; or else treat us equally [when our luck is bad] and thus demand equal treatment from us [when our luck is good]" (6.16.4). Perhaps there is some mockery of ἰσονομία in τὰ ἴσα νέμων.[47] Alcibiades argues: in general you do not treat the unfortunate equally with the fortunate; therefore the fortunate have a right to treat you as unequally as you treat the unfortunate; since I am exceptionally fortunate, and thus risk exceptionally bad treatment from you if my luck should change, I have a right to treat you with exceptional arrogance. Alcibiades maintains his right to those exceptional honors which Pericles had said come from exceptional risks. Alcibiades seems to apply to his own individual case what Pericles had said of Athens; but Pericles had also spoken, in the Funeral Oration, of Athens as the city in which individual arete had scope. According to Pericles, Athens allowed the display of the older aristocratic virtue (see Chap. I, sec. C), and thus Alcibiades has not gone beyond the Periclean concept of Athens in arrogating to himself such grandeur.

As Nicias faces the Sicilian expedition in an Archida-

45. ἐφ' ἑαυτῷ; cf. LSJ s.v. ἐπί B.III.1.

46. There was a proverb that bad luck was contagious: see G. M. Browne and L. Koenen, "Zu der griechisch-koptischen Rezension der Menandersentenzen," *ZPE* 8 (1971), 105–108.

47. For ἰσονομία as a democratic slogan, see E. R. Dodds, *Plato: Gorgias* (Oxford, 1959), p. 266, on 483c5.

mian state of mind, so Alcibiades faces the expedition in a
Periclean state of mind, even if it is an expedition that
Pericles would not have countenanced. Alcibiades finds
the same weaknesses in the Sicilians which Pericles had
found in the Peloponnesians—they are of mixed race;
selfish and thus without the necessary capital for war;
without common counsel (1.141.6–7, 6.17.2–4).[48] Like
Pericles, Alcibiades would rely on naval preeminence
(περιουσίᾳ 6.17.7; cf. 1.141.5, 2.13.2). Alcibiades' insis-
tence on the necessity of empire, of ruling or being ruled,
and the consequent impossibility of tranquillity, is a re-
statement of a theme which first emerges in the speech of
the anonymous Athenians at Sparta, who speak of the
Athenian empire as the result of necessity (1.75.3), and
of the maintenance of this empire as the necessary alter-
native to risk of rule by others (1.76.1). Pericles, from
whom Alcibiades has here taken his text, elaborates this
theme in his final speech in the *History* (2.63). The comparison of Alcibiades and Pericles also comes out in Alcibiades' verbal echoes of Pericles: ὥσπερ καὶ οἱ πατέρες
ἡμῶν ... ἐς τάδε ἦραν αὐτά 6.18.6; οἱ γοῦν πατέρες ἡμῶν ... ἐς
τάδε προήγαγον αὐτά 1.144.4; ὥσπερ καὶ ἄλλο τι 6.18.6;
Pericles has used this same phrase at 1.142.9.[49]

But the conclusion of Alcibiades' speech above all else
marks him as an Athenian according to the Corinthian

48. W. Peremans, "Thucydide, Alcibiade et l'expédition de Sicile en
415 av. J. C.," *AC* 25 (1956), 340–344 defends πολιτειῶν (6.17.2) of the
MSS against πολιτῶν of editions now generally in use.
49. For other, less close, verbal similarities between the speech of
Alcibiades and the speeches of Pericles, see A. W. Gomme, "Four Passages in Thucydides," *JHS* 71 (1951), 78. Gomme considers Alcibiades the political heir of Pericles. Cf. Plut. *Alc.* 1–7.

definition and as the intellectual descendent of Pericles (6.18.6):

νομίσατε . . . τὴν πόλιν, ἐὰν μὲν ἡσυχάζῃ, τρίψεσθαί τε αὐτὴν περὶ αὑτὴν ὥσπερ καὶ ἄλλο τι, καὶ πάντων τὴν ἐπιστήμην ἐγγηράσεσθαι, ἀγωνιζομένην δὲ αἰεὶ προσλήψεσθαί τε τὴν ἐμπειρίαν καὶ τὸ ἀμύνεσθαι οὐ λόγῳ ἀλλ' ἔργῳ μᾶλλον ξύνηθες ἕξειν.

The Athenians should believe that "the city if it remains at peace will more than anything else wear itself out in internal struggle, and everyone's knowledge [or the knowledge of all things] will grow old; but if the city engages in struggle, it will continually acquire experience, and will be accustomed to defend itself not in word but in deed" (6.18.6). The sequence of subjects, which is A-B-A,[50] helps to define the difficult τρίψεσθαί τε αὐτὴν περὶ αὑτὴν ὥσπερ ἄλλο τι. This expression would refer to factions and debates,[51] as distinguished from external conflicts. Now, since such a development, namely, self-attrition, cannot be said to be true of simply anything (ἄλλο τι), perhaps Gomme is correct in taking ἄλλο τι as a superlative of sorts.[52] Alcibiades' observation recalls the Corinthian comparison of the city with the canons of a techne—what is new is best—and also Pericles' stress on the value of Athenian *empeiria* and naval technology, even if Alcibiades lacks Pericles' moderation.

Furthermore, in opposing peace as unsuited to Athenian customs and character, he corroborates the Corinthians' concluding point, that the Athenians are by

50. As Dover points out, in Gomme, IV, 255.
51. As LSJ say, s.v. τρίβω III.1, "internal struggle." Cf. Classen-Steup, *Thukydides*, VI (Berlin, 1905), 49, who translated, "ohne Einwirkung von aussen."
52. Gomme, I, 459. This was also the view of Classen and Steup, *Thukydides*, I, 370.

nature unpeaceful (1.70.9). Alcibiades' concluding sentence, following upon the sentence quoted above, is (6.18.7):

παράπαν τε γιγνώσκω πόλιν μὴ ἀπράγμονα τάχιστ' ἄν μοι δοκεῖν
ἀπραγμοσύνης μεταβολῇ διαφθαρῆναι, καὶ τῶν ἀνθρώπων
ἀσφαλέστατα τούτους οἰκεῖν οἳ ἂν τοῖς παροῦσι ἤθεσι καὶ νόμοις, ἢν
καὶ χείρω ᾖ, ἥκιστα διαφόρως πολιτεύωσιν.

It is my opinion that a city not fond of quiet would be very quickly destroyed by a change to quietude, and that those men live most securely who administer their state with the least divergence from the existing character and laws, even if these be inferior.

This sentence applies to international politics the principle which Pericles had maintained of Athenian politics: that the man who abstained from political life was considered useless (2.40.2). According to Alcibiades, Athens has conducted itself in the world as Pericles had said the Athenian citizen must conduct himself in Athens. Consequently Athens cannot with impunity withdraw from activity in the world as Nicias wishes, any more than Nicias can withdraw from the public life of Athens.

In his reply to Alcibiades, Nicias again uses the device which he used against Cleon, and again the device fails. In attempting by the recommendation of such vast preparations to bluff the Athenians into a change of mind, Nicias succeeds only in inflaming their desire for the venture. His bluff is a latter-day version of the speech of Agamemnon to the Greek army in *Iliad* 2, and equally unfortunate. Although this first reversal of Nicias' expectations is only preliminary to the larger peripety of the defeat in Sicily, one can speculate with Dover that Nicias' failure in the assembly prepared for the peripety, for "if a smaller force had been sent, it might not have secured in the first year success enough to justify prolonging its efforts, and the whole adventure might have ended more in accordance with Nicias' wishes."[53] Nicias not only fails in his objective: he causes an outcome exactly the opposite of what he had intended. In fact Thucydides thinks of Nicias' career in terms of peripety. Thucydides observes of the effect on the Athenians of Nicias' reply to Alcibiades: τοὐναντίον περιέστη αὐτῷ (the opposite befell him). This verb is used elsewhere of reversals of expectation and of tyche (1.32.4, 76.4, 78.2; 4.12.3) and more often metaphorically, of war, fear, danger, or suspicion (3.54.5; 4.10.1, 34.3, 55.1; 5.73.1; 6.61.4; 8.2.4, 15.1) than literally (1.106; 4.4; 5.7; 5.10; 7.83; 8.108). The Spartans plan their resumption of the war in 414 on a putative reversal of guilt: τὸ παρανόμημα . . . ἐς . . . τοὺς Ἀθηναίους . . . περιεστάναι (7.18.3). When Thucydides uses this verb of Nicias he clearly implies peripety—reversal and defeat of hopes. So perhaps in the beginning of the first speech, where Thucydides makes Nicias say, "I fear less than others for my own person" (6.9.2), Thucydides intends the reader to think of another reversal, the nephritis which afflicted Nicias at Syracuse. Similarly, in the reply to Alcibiades, Nicias uses the analogy of founding a city in hostile territory (6.23.2), an analogy which Thucydides will echo, as if to stress the peripety (7.77).[54]

53. *Thucydides: Book VI* (Oxford, 1965), p. 32.
54. C. Mossé, "Armée et cité grecque," *REA* 65 (1963), 290–297, wishes to make literal sense of Nicias' hortatory statement to the army in 6.77.4–5 that it will be a city and a fatherland wherever it halts. Mossé fails to consider 6.23.1–4, 37.1, 63.3; 7.77. For an interpretation of 7.77.4–5 see Tompkins, *YCS* 22 (1972), 203.

In this final speech, Nicias again shows his spiritual kinship with Archidamus. Like Archidamus, he details the enemy's advantages (1.80.3, 6.20.4). The burden of the speech is παρασκευή, which was Archidamus' theme (1.82.3, 84.4). Nicias concludes, however, that the Athenians will need not only vast preparation but luck, which is difficult for mortals (6.23.2). Nicias repeats nearly verbatim the words that Thucydides had used in analyzing Nicias' motives in seeking peace (6.23.3, 5.16.1)—"I wish to sail having entrusted myself as little as possible to chance."

The desire to avoid commitment to chance, the offer to step down from office (6.23.3), which recalls the Pylos episode—these traits again sum up the paradoxical character of Nicias. By making Nicias describe himself thus at the end of this speech, which marks a juncture in the story of the Sicilian expedition, Thucydides again establishes the foil to the Athenian principles represented by Alcibiades. It is tempting to think of Nicias as a choral figure, who expresses a moderation and piety against which the heroic impulses of Athens loom all the larger; and yet Nicias does not stand outside and comment upon the action but is himself an actor.

3. *Nicias at war*[55]

The Nicias who wished to exempt himself from chance and to preserve in peace his good fortune outlives peace and gives up his eutychia to tyche. We understand the Sicilian expedition as the final collapse of the proud

55. For a review of Nicias' military career in Thucydides, see Bender, *Der Begriff*, pp. 38–43; Westlake, *CQ* 35 (1941), 58–65; Westlake, *Individuals*, pp. 86–96, 169–211.

rationality of Pericles largely through the character and the words of Nicias. Having sought peace out of a desire to avoid a confrontation with tyche, Nicias is the ideal spokesman of an interpretation of the disaster in terms of tyche. His own peripety is also Athens' peripety. Nicias, who had wished to commit himself as little as possible to chance, ends his days at the mercy of chance (7.77.1). Though he had wished to preserve his good name by never harming the city, he is mainly responsible for bringing Athens to its worst defeat. Nicias dies in the possession of his arete and nothing else: he is like Glaucon's "statue" of the just man who is stripped of everything but his justice (Pl. *Rep.* 361d4–6).

Nicias, reluctant to command (6.8.4), opposed to the expedition, continues his opposition even when the Athenians have reached Rhegium. He attempts to persuade his fellow-generals, Lamachus and Alcibiades, to limit the objectives of the mission to Selinus. He does not want to waste the city's money on further risks (6.47; cf. 6.10.5, 12.1): in the same way that he wanted to preserve his own prosperity and fair name, he wants Athens to preserve what it has.

Before the first battle at Syracuse, Nicias displays his characteristic cautiousness, even though it seems unwarranted by the situation,[56] and yet he strikes a Periclean note. Nicias maintains that the Sicilian *episteme* is inferior to the Sicilian courage, and this fact is advantageous to the Athenians (6.68.2).[57] Thucydides corroborates Nicias' point (6.69.1), and Hermocrates admits it (6.72.3). Yet the Athenians here face an enemy of a

56. Dover, *Thucydides: Book VI* (1965), p. 76.
57. On this speech, see Luschnat, *Die Feldherrnreden,* pp. 72–80.

character like their own. The Syracusans quickly man a fleet (7.7.4). Hermocrates advises them that they will acquire naval experience just as the Athenians, not born with their ability, were forced to do by the Mede (7.21.3). And the Syracusans show an Athenian capacity for technical innovation in their ships (7.36). Therefore Nicias' repetition of the theme of the Athenian technical superiority on the occasion of the last battle in the harbor—"show that 'even in misfortune and weakness your *episteme* is stronger than the other's lucky strength," with its Periclean ring (εὐτυχούσης ῥώμης 6.63.4; cf. Pericles' ἀπὸ ἀμαθίας εὐτυχοῦς 2.63.5; note also the theme of καταφρόνησις in both contexts)—this repetition sounds hollow, since we no longer believe that it is a matter of Athenian skill and knowledge versus Syracusan strength or bravery. This antithesis is obsolete.

And even if Nicias uses this characteristically Athenian antithesis, it is perhaps only a rhetorical topos for him, since he shows himself as Spartan as ever and as un-Athenian in failing to follow up his initial success.[58] Nicias was formidable when he first arrived at Syracuse, but he was scorned when he did not press on but sailed away (in late 415) to winter in Catana (7.42.3).[59] Nicias is not one of those paradigmatic Athenians who follow up victories (1.70.5).

In the spring of 414, the Athenians return to Syracuse and begin to throw a blockading wall around the city. Just before they complete this operation, Gylippus arrives. Nicias refuses battle. Thucydides makes no comment on

58. Dover, *Thucydides: Book VI*, p. 77, on 6.71.2.
59. Cf. n. 33 above.

his decision, as he made no comment on the generals' decision to withdraw from Syracuse the preceding autumn (6.71), but we cannot help feeling that Nicias' inactivity is characteristic. Gylippus saves Syracuse from circumvallation (7.2.4).

Nicias resolves to fortify Plemmyrium, now paying more attention to the war at sea (7.4.4). Previously, then, Nicias had been paying more attention to the war on land. Historical circumstances—the necessity of investing Syracuse—as well as his own proclivities had made a Spartan landsman of Nicias. Alas, in reverting to a naval strategy, Nicias chooses the wrong base of operations (7.4.6). Gylippus completes his countervallation of Epipolae. The Athenians, unable now to invest the city, are thrown on the defensive. Nicias sends a letter to Athens.[60] "We the besiegers are besieged" (7.11.4). His words recall a remark of Thucydides about the Athenians at Pylos (4.29.2) and intimate a comparison of Athenian good luck there with bad luck here, a comparison which Thucydides will make explicit (7.71.7). Nicias' previous rhetorical offer to give up his command, an offer made on two separate occasions, is now seriously meant: afflicted with nephritis, he asks to be replaced (7.15.1).

After the arrival of Demosthenes (7.42) and the unsuccessful attack on Epipolae (7.42.6–45), the generals confer. Demosthenes would return to Athens immediately

---

60. On this letter, see Westlake, *Individuals,* p. 192, who points out that it has the dramatic function of foreshadowing and thus makes the situation seem more desperate than the preceding narrative had implied; cf. Dover, in Gomme, IV, 386–387.

(7.47). Nicias hesitates (7.48). Nicias has some reason to believe that the Athenians may yet prevail. But his motives in delaying are also selfish (7.48.4):

οὔκουν βούλεσθαι αὐτός γε ἐπιστάμενος τὰς Ἀθηναίων φύσεις ἐπ' αἰσχρᾷ τε αἰτίᾳ καὶ ἀδίκως ὑπ' Ἀθηναίων ἀπολέσθαι μᾶλλον ἢ ὑπὸ τῶν πολεμίων, εἰ δεῖ, κινδυνεύσας τοῦτο παθεῖν ἰδίᾳ.

He for his part, knowing the characters of Athenians, did not want to die unjustly at the hands of the Athenians on a dishonorable charge but preferred to run the risk of suffering a private death, if he must, at the hands of the enemy.

The desire to avoid a disgraceful accusation is the desire, already noticed by Thucydides, to preserve a fair name (5.16.1). Nicias' choice, despite the fact that he is the general of a whole army, of a "personally chosen" (ἰδίᾳ) death at the hands of the enemy (which would preserve at least some measure of honor) recalls that Nicias who wished to preserve his own good luck (5.16.1) (which Alcibiades said the city should put to use) and who maintained that a man was no worse a citizen for looking out for his own person and his own interests (6.9.2; contrary to the paradigmatic Athenians: 1.70.6).[61]

When Nicias has come around to the opinion of the other generals and is prepared to sail away, there is an eclipse of the moon. With what Thucydides calls excessive superstition, Nicias refuses to stir for the period of thrice nine days stipulated by the seers, and so seals the

61. Dover, in Gomme, IV, 426 on 7.48.4: "Nikias' pride and consequent cowardice in the face of personal disgrace lead him to put forward as disgraceful a proposition as any general in history: rather than risk execution, he will throw away the fleet and many thousands of other people's lives, and put his country in mortal peril. Even Grote's condemnation (vi.145f.) of his 'guilty fatuity' on this occasion may be thought unduly temperate."

doom of the expedition (7.50.4). There now appears clearly this religious side of Nicias' character, intimated previously in his remark that it is difficult for mortals to be lucky. In Nicias' final speech in the *History* (7.77), he will argue a theodicy on the basis of which he hopes for better luck.

But in the exhortation to the army before the final naval engagement (7.61–64),[62] Nicias oddly combines an exhortation to hopefulness on the ground that tyche may contribute to success (7.61.3)—an exhortation contrary to both Athenian and Spartan principles—with the familiar Athenian principle of the superiority of Athenian episteme (7.63.4). The appeal to this Athenian principle is here meaningless, since the Athenians have been forced to fight a land battle on ships in the old-fashioned style, in which episteme and techne have no scope (7.62.2; cf. 1.49.1–2). As Mme. de Romilly has shown, this battle is a *contre-épreuve* of the battle of Naupactus.[63]

In his final words in the *History,* Nicias attempts to strengthen the spirit of the army for the overland retreat from Syracuse. He exhorts the troops to have hope and not to blame themselves for their misfortunes and sufferings. His grounds for this exhortation are most difficult to follow.[64] The argument falls into two parts, both theodical but different in emphasis.

In the first part, having begun with the statement that the troops should have hope, Nicias uses himself as an example (7.77.1–3):

62. On this speech, see Luschnat, *Die Feldherrnreden,* pp. 84–94.
63. *Histoire et raison,* p. 158.
64. Luschnat, *Die Feldherrnreden,* pp. 101–105; Dover, in Gomme, IV, 453–454; Tompkins, *YCS* 22 (1972), 197–199.

' Καὶ ἐκ τῶν παρόντων, ὦ Ἀθηναῖοι καὶ ξύμμαχοι, ἐλπίδα χρὴ ἔχειν
(ἤδη τινὲς καὶ ἐκ δεινοτέρων ἢ τοιῶνδε ἐσώθησαν), μηδὲ
καταμέμφεσθαι ὑμᾶς ἄγαν αὐτοὺς μήτε ταῖς ξυμφοραῖς μήτε ταῖς
παρὰ τὴν ἀξίαν νῦν κακοπαθίαις. [2a] κἀγώ τοι οὐδενὸς ὑμῶν οὔτε
ῥώμῃ προφέρων (ἀλλ᾽ ὁρᾶτε δὴ ὡς διάκειμαι ὑπὸ τῆς νόσου) οὔτ᾽
εὐτυχίᾳ δοκῶν που ὕστερός του εἶναι κατά τε τὸν ἴδιον βίον καὶ ἐς τὰ
ἄλλα, νῦν ἐν τῷ αὐτῷ κινδύνῳ τοῖς φαυλοτάτοις αἰωροῦμαι· [2b]
καίτοι πολλὰ μὲν ἐς θεοὺς νόμιμα δεδιήτημαι, πολλὰ δὲ ἐς ἀνθρώπους
δίκαια καὶ ἀνεπίφθονα. [3] ἀνθ᾽ ὧν ἡ μὲν ἐλπὶς ὅμως θρασεῖα τοῦ
μέλλοντος, αἱ δὲ ξυμφοραὶ οὐ κατ᾽ ἀξίαν δὴ φοβοῦσιν.

The obscurity of the thought in this passage lies in the
contradiction between the logic and style on the one
hand and the main assertion on the other. The three
sentences beginning with sentence 2 contain these three
propositions in sequence: (2a) In my present ill-health
and misfortune, I am reduced to the level of the lowliest
of you; (2b) and yet I have lived in the continuous obser-
vance of religious customs and of justice toward men
without arousing envy; (3) therefore I have hope, and, as
far as desert is concerned,[65] our misfortunes do not
terrify me. Thus, in this last sentence, Nicias comes
around to the first sentence of his speech (77.1). The
verbal responsions of 77.3 to 77.1 are obvious, and one
can now see that 2a and 2b follow from the thought
suggested by παρὰ ἀξίαν: *I certainly do not deserve my
suffering.* The logical sequence of the three sentences
(paraphrased above) in support of this point is thus precisely the reverse of what it ought to be. The logic of
Nicias' argument for the assertion of 77.1 runs as follows:
(1) You should have hope: (3) I have hope as far as desert

65. On this interpretation of the Greek, see Dover, in Gomme, IV,
453, against Schwartz' conjecture.

is concerned, (2b) because I have led a blameless life, (2a) though at present I am reduced to the level of the lowliest of you. Nicias is using an *a fortiori* argument: if *I* still have hope, there is all the more reason for you to have hope. This argument has a remarkably anfractuous form in its main outline, which is complicated by the rather strained antithesis between strength and prosperity and by the parenthesis (ἀλλ' ὁρᾶτε . . .). Even apart from other considerations, the form of the argument by itself seems to belie the possibility of hope. The first sentence of 77.3, while insisting on hope, yet admits that the misfortunes *are* alarming.[66]

Three of the particles in 77.2 combine to give the impression of a speaker whose statement is of such personal urgency that its import is less weighty than the emotion inspiring it—in this case fear or despair. The particles are τοι, δή, and που. The first and the last occur only three times each in Thucydides.[67] In Gildersleeve's memorable words, "τοι is an appeal for human sympathy, as που is a resigned submission to the merciless *rerum natura*."[68] δή should be interpreted as emotional and pathetic, and the parenthesis in which it occurs is well translated: "But see! See how ravaged I am by disease."[69]

In the second part of the argument designed to inspire

---

66. Again, see Dover, in Gomme, IV, 453.

67. On τοι, see J. D. Denniston, *The Greek Particles*² (Oxford, 1959), p. 539; on που, Tompkins, *YCS* 22 (1972), 198.

68. B. L. Gildersleeve, "Brief mention," *AJP* 33 (1912), 239–240 = *Selections from the Brief Mention of Basil Lanneau Gildersleeve*, ed. C. W. E. Miller (Baltimore, 1930), p. 256.

69. The translation is Tompkins', *YCS* 22 (1972), 199.

the troops with hope, Nicias envisages a rather different theodicy (77.3–4):

τάχα δὲ ἂν καὶ λωφήσειαν· ἱκανὰ γὰρ τοῖς τε πολεμίοις ηὐτύχηται, καὶ εἴ τῳ θεῶν ἐπίφθονοι ἐστρατεύσαμεν, ἀποχρώντως ἤδη τετιμωρήμεθα. ἦλθον γάρ που καὶ ἄλλοι τινὲς ἤδη ἐφ᾽ ἑτέρους, καὶ ἀνθρώπεια δράσαντες ἀνεκτὰ ἔπαθον. καὶ ἡμᾶς εἰκὸς νῦν τά τε ἀπὸ τοῦ θεοῦ ἐλπίζειν ἠπιώτερα ἕξειν (οἴκτου γὰρ ἀπ᾽ αὐτῶν ἀξιώτεροι ἤδη ἐσμὲν ἢ φθόνου), . . .

(Our calamities) might perhaps be lightened. Our enemies have had enough success, and if some god was jealous of our expedition, we have now been sufficiently punished. Others in the past have attacked their enemies and having done what mortals will do, have suffered what can be borne. So it is fair that we now hope for gentler treatment from the god. For we are worthier of pity than of jealousy.

Here it is not a matter of the gods' rewarding an individual man's piety, but of the gods' retributive justice, according to which the one who commits a crime must himself suffer what he has done (Aesch. *Ag.* 1564; *Cho.* 311; Hes. fr. 286 Merkelbach and West). It may be that the Athenians had incurred divine enmity. In that case, the enemy has had enough success and the Athenians have suffered enough. The enemy's good luck was, Nicias implies, the Athenians' punishment. In keeping with his hortatory purpose, Nicias works a slight variation on the traditional concept of *lex talionis:* others have committed mortal crimes (i.e., such as mortals are likely to fall into willy-nilly) and have suffered *what can be borne* (ἀνεκτά). Thus the traditional theodicy wears, contrary to what might have been expected, a potentially benign aspect. Again Nicias inverts the Herodotean concept of the envy of the gods, which Herodotus always finds over-

turning and abasing the prosperous, and expects a contrary movement, from bad luck to good again, since what
has happened to the Athenians may now happen to the
Syracusans. The paradoxical character of Nicias'
thought also appears in his statement that "we are now
more worthy of pity than of envy" (7.77.4). There was a
proverb that it is better to be envied than pitied (Pind.
Pyth. 1.85; Hdt. 3.52) but this proverb applied of course
to relations among men. Nicias, in speaking of the relations of men and gods, in effect reverses the proverb: it
would be better to be pitied than envied.

4. *Nicias and Pericles: The thematic structure of the* History

As Pericles was characterized by gnome, so Nicias is
characterized by his pious concern with tyche. To the
unparalleled summary and analysis of Pericles' career
(2.65) there corresponds the unparalleled psychological
analysis of Nicias (5.16.1) and the remarkable final
judgment on him (7.86.5). As both the speeches of Pericles in many respects and many details of the narrative
were guided by Thucydides' understanding of Pericles in
terms of gnome, so the career of Nicias from the time of
the Peace—in Thucydides' reports of his speeches and of
his deeds—is presented in terms of tyche. The main
terms of the psychological analysis—eutychia and tyche
(5.16.1)—are carried through Books 6 and 7, especially
in Nicias' speeches.

In his concern with tyche, Nicias has an old-fashioned
Spartan character. He might well have spoken of tyche as
the Spartans do in Athens when they come to plead for
the prisoners taken on Sphacteria. The debate of Nicias
and Alcibiades, with its echoes of Archidamus by the one

and of Pericles by the other, reestablished the antitheses expressed by the Corinthians and the leaders of the rival cities at the time of the outbreak of the war. But now the course of events gives these antitheses a bizarre twist. With the defection of Alcibiades to Sparta and Spartan adherence to his advice, the spirit of the Athens that entered the Peloponnesian War now belongs to the enemy. There is also the fact that Syracuse is, despite its being a Dorian city, a latter-day Athens in crucial respects. The death of Lamachus leaves the Spartan Nicias in sole command of the force in Sicily, and by the time the more characteristically Athenian Demosthenes arrives, the Athenians have lost their advantage. Thematically, then, the Athenian debacle is the defeat of Sparta by Athens. This conclusion squares well with the view that the Funeral Oration is an apology for Periclean Athens written after the end of the war. With supreme irony, Thucydides, through his characterization of Nicias, gives the Sicilian disaster a meaning exactly the opposite of its factual meaning.

Thucydides' opinion of Nicias was negative.[70] The Periclean type, Alcibiades, could have made a success of the expedition.[71] Nicias was excessively superstitious, and Thucydides does not have to pass judgment on the theodicy of Nicias' last speech to the troops. Nicias' death

70. See Westlake, *CQ* 35 (1941), 58–65, and *Individuals*, pp. 185, 187, 281 (contrast of Nicias and Gylippus), 193–194 (Nicias' letter: 7.11–15), 198 (on 7.48); K. von Fritz, *Griech. Geschichtsschreibung*, Ia, 739ff.; cf. Dover's acidulous outline of Nicias' career, in Gomme, IV, 461–462.

71. On the relation of 6.15.4 to 2.65.11, see K. von Fritz, *Griech. Geschichtsschreibung*, Ib, 318 (n. 110).

comes eight days later.[72] His piety meets the same end as the Melians'. But if Thucydides' opinion of Nicias was negative, how explain the famous judgment (7.86.5)? This judgment is nearly always quoted and discussed out of context. In the context, Thucydides tells how Nicias surrendered himself to the Spartan general, Gylippus, because the Spartans were well disposed toward him on account of his good offices on behalf of the prisoners from Sphacteria (7.86.4). But some of the Syracusans who had been in communication with him and feared he might reveal this fact and also the Corinthians, who feared further troubles from him, had him executed. Thucydides then says (86.5):

καὶ ὁ μὲν τοιαύτῃ ἢ ὅτι ἔγγυτατα τούτων αἰτίᾳ ἐτεθνήκει ἥκιστα δὴ ἄξιος ὢν τῶν γε ἐπ᾽ ἐμοῦ Ἑλλήνων ἐς τοῦτο δυστυχίας ἀφικέσθαι διὰ τὴν πᾶσαν ἐς ἀρετὴν νενομισμένην ἐπιτήδευσιν.

He died for this reason or one very close to this, least worthy of Hellenes in my time to come to this misfortune, since his whole life had been led in accordance with arete.

This judgment bears on the sort of death that Nicias met and is not a reflection on the goodness or badness of his career.[73] To be executed by enemies to whom one has surrendered is a death without glory, exactly the sort of death that Nicias had intended to avoid by staying at Syracuse and dying in battle (7.48.5: n.b. κινδυνεύσας). Nicias has utterly failed to preserve to the end his eutychia and to fulfill the requirement of the Solonian

72. On the chronology of the retreat, see Dover, in Gomme, IV, 455. Of course one does not know if Nicias was executed on the same day he surrendered.
73. Dover, in Gomme, IV, 462.

141

dictum (cf. 5.16.1). His good fortune has suffered a complete reversal. Thucydides' judgment on Nicias is thus limited to the kind of death he died and is made from the point of view of Nicias' own expectations.[74] This judgment is thus like others in the *History* which are not absolute but are made from the point of view of the subject or of those affected by the subject. Thucydides' evaluation of Brasidas is a case in point.[75] It is fitting that Thucydides uses δυστυχία to describe Nicias' death. No doubt Nicias himself, who saw his life in terms of τύχη, would have used the same word.

Although the thematic structure of the *History* reverses the apparent meaning of the Sicilian disaster in such a way that a bitter apology for Athens is implicit, Thucydides surely did not think that Sparta and Syracuse had become Athenian in any but a strategical sense. The broader Periclean understanding of gnome and techne had already been lost in Athens itself, for that matter. Alcibiades was not the son but the ward of Pericles. What ultimately survived the Periclean enlightenment was the memory of it and its preservation by Thucydides.

74. Strauss, *The City and Man,* p. 208; cf. p. 150. It is not necessary to invoke some dramatic change in the figure of Nicias as Westlake does, *Individuals,* p. 201. Cf. Bruns, *Das Literarische Porträt,* p. 8: "Thukydides vermeidet es, in eigener Person die handelnden Personen zu beurtheilen." Bruns' Thucydidean *Stilgesetze* have never received the consideration they deserve.

75. 4.81.1: n.b. δοκοῦντα; 81.3: n.b. δόξας; cf. 5.16.1. There is no contradiction, because the judgments of 4.81 are not absolute.

III

Thucydides and the Antitheses of Techne-Tyche and Gnome-Tyche

A. The technical character of Thucydides' methodology[1]

1. *The problem*

Thucydides characterizes persons and cities in terms of gnome, techne, and tyche, and these concepts give the *History* a certain thematic structure according to which the Sicilian disaster has a meaning opposite to its factual meaning. The question remains whether Thucydides' stated methods of historiography can be understood in terms of these antitheses, and, if so, whether these methods, too, are then a vindication of the Athenian principle, as the success of Syracuse seemed ironically to be. Perhaps Athens is victorious at the level of historiography, having been defeated in history. Thucydides would, on this supposition, have seen rationality as the

1. It is necessary to be clear about what "technical" might mean in the case of a fifth-century author. In general, Greek technology, both in theory and in its products, at least down to the time of the marvel ous machines of the Alexandrian engineers, is radically different from modern technology (cf. J.-P. Vernant, "Remarques sur les formes et les limites de la pensée technique chez les Grecs," *Revue d'Histoire des Sciences* 10 (1957), 205–225 = *Mythe et pensée chez les Grecs*, II, Paris, 1971, 44–64). Greek technical thought belongs to the realms not of *poiesis* but of *praxis*. The most prominent examples are

province of the thinker and writer and impossible or rarely possible for the actor in history.

As regards the rationality of historical action, Thucydides faces a dilemma. If he believes that the rationality expressed by Pericles and generally by the Athenian temperament can be maintained by the actors in history, how does he reconcile this belief with the tale he must tell of the eventual defeat of Athens? For if Pericles' disdain of tyche, as in the prooemium of the first speech, was justified, ought not Athens to have fared better? Does Thucydides then side more with the Spartans' and Nicias' deference to tyche? If so, how does Thucydides reconcile this position with the Athenian achievement, acknowledged by him in various ways, and not least in his presentation of Pericles? For if the Archidamian view, apparently borne out by events, was valid, was not the Spartan moderation, with all its diffidence before tyche, preferable, and ought not one to have seen through the outward show of Athens (cf. 1.10.2–3)?

The prevailing explanation of these difficulties rests partly on the apparently technical character of Thucydides' *History*. Since Thucydides presents his work

medicine and rhetoric, but the art of warfare was well covered (cf. Heinimann, *MH* 18 (1961), 109, n. 19). The goal of techne is success. Thucydides' ὠφέλιμον (1.22.4) seems to bring him into the sphere of this technical thought, but many reservations are necessary (see sec. 2 below). His goal was *to saphes* (see sec. 3 below), i.e., not an immediate practical goal. On the other hand, his methodology (see sec. 3 below), as distinguished from his goal in writing the *History*, has undeniable affinities with contemporary technical thought, and thus one may speak of the "technical character" of his methodology. This character appears immediately in his statements about his methods, which are such that we are also indeed entitled to speak of a Thucydidean "methodology."

as "useful" and "a possession forever" (1.22.4), he must have regarded human nature, political and military affairs, and perhaps even the natural environment as liable to rational prediction and control, at least to some degree. Despite the defeat of Athens in the Peloponnesian War, the characteristic Athenian rationality can and should be the guide of historical action. The well-known remarks of the plague and on *stasis* would support this conclusion. Thucydides' undeniable affinities with Ionian science,[2] with the rationalism of the sophists, with the technical aspirations of the Hippocratics, and with the skepticism and psychologizing of Euripides have contributed to the picture of Thucydides as political scientist or perhaps even political engineer. Thus Thucydides emerges as a partisan of Athens, the home of the intellect, innovation, and the arts. Indeed the magnificence of the speeches given to Pericles entices one to connect Thucydides' views with the views expressed by the Thucydidean Pericles. The positivistic, scientific interpretation of Thucydides is thus corroborated by a political-biographical interpretation.[3] The scion of an aristocratic family breaks away from the values presumably instilled in him by his upbringing and becomes the panegyrist of Pericles and the defender of Athenian democracy in its Periclean moment.[4]

2. Cf. C. Mugler, "Sur la méthode de Thucydide," *Lettres d'humanité* 10 (1951), 20–51.

3. For a polemical survey of these two trends in Thucydidean scholarship, see H.-P. Stahl, *Thukydides: Die Stellung des Menschen im geschichtlichen Prozess*, Zetemata 40 (Munich, 1966), pp. 12–35.

4. For Thucydides as a partisan of democracy, see Guido Donini, "The Attitude of Thucydides to the Government of the Five Thousand" (unpub. diss., Harvard University, 1966) = *La Posizione di Tucidide verso il governo dei cinquemila* (Turin, 1969).

And yet, to return to the scientism of Thucydides, how much do the style and tone of Thucydides have in common with fragment B 1 of Anaxagoras, or fragment B 1 of Thrasymachus, or with the Hippocratic *De Arte?* How much do they have in common, with regard to clarity, even with a Euripidean *rhesis?* The style and tone of Thucydides, to take first things first, do not at all express the optimism that might be expected of a thoroughgoing rationalist. And, as for the supposed partisanship of Thucydides, how does one reconcile this with the aristocratic tone of the work (see sec. A.2 below), the favorable judgment on the Peisistratids (6.54.5) and the Constitution of the 5000 (8.97.2), and the statement that "the Chians were the only ones besides the Lacedaemonians I saw who combined prosperity and moderation" (8.24.4), and the favorable judgments on non-Periclean types (e.g., 8.68.1 on the oligarch Antiphon)?

One can question the supposed partisanship of Thucydides as much as the supposed scientism. But if one questions the scientism of Thucydides' outlook, what is one to make of his claim of utility and indeed of the various methodological utterances, with their scientific ring? What did Thucydides mean when he said his work might be judged "useful"? Did he believe that the historian's hindsight could become the statesman's foresight, and that thus his work would influence the future course of history? Or was its usefulness of some other, unpractical, sort?

It will be necessary to review in detail the statement of the work's usefulness, as well as the other programmatic and methodological passages. Here the attempt will be made to survey all of the passages from a single point of view, and thus to search for a conceptual unity underly-

ing them. That single viewpoint is the gnome-tyche antithesis. To anticipate the conclusion, the conceptual
unity which emerges is the practical or historical identity
of the terms of these logical antithesis. The programmatic and methodological statements show that
Thucydides thought of himself as distinguishing that
which came about by chance from that which was orderly
and reasonable. To the actor in history, however, history
never manifests a pure principle or law; on the other
hand, history never manifests the purely random. The
actor in history always experiences history as a mixture of
that which is amenable to reason and that which is impervious to it.

It is characteristic of Thucydides' narrative, which is
based on the logical antithesis of gnome or techne and
tyche, to present the double nature of history as a unity,
that is, from the actor's point of view, while at the same
time rendering history more intelligible than it could
have been to any actor at any time. The speeches in the
History are of the greatest importance in securing this
intelligibility. It is because of Thucydides' ability to maintain the strictest standards of historiography and at the
same time to represent history from the point of view of
the actors that the work has its marvelous combination
of the intellectually intelligible and the dramatically
immediate.[5]

With regard to the gnome or techne-tyche antithesis,
then, both Athenians and Lacedaemonians are right, or
both are wrong—wrong in their one-sidedness. Clearly
Thucydides' method has closer affinities with the Athe-

---

5. It is this combination that de Romilly has so well analyzed in *Histoire et raison*.

nian principle of gnome than with the Spartan diffidence before tyche. But to some degree what the method discovers is the validity of the Lacedaemonian principle at least from the point of view of the actors in history. Further discussion of this point will have to await a more detailed examination of Thucydides' method.

If this description of Thucydides' concept of history is accepted provisionally, a question concerning the ultimate grounds of his methodology can also be raised here. Did he proceed from facts to laws arrived at somehow inductively? Or aprioristically from laws to facts? From which side did Thucydides unmask what we might call the duplicity of history? On the other hand, considering the *unity* of particulars and general principles in Thucydides, we see that the question of the ultimate grounds of his methodology may have been put in the wrong terms. If this was an original unity of perception, and not a synthetic unity based on induction or deduction, then we are forced to imagine other grounds. Here it may be necessary to invoke the nearly forgotten Romantic concept of historiography. In this concept, the matrix of the combination of fact and law in historiography is art. A. W. Schlegel said in one of his lectures: "True history rests on a synthesis of the given and real with the ideal, but not through philosophy, since this rather neutralizes (*aufhebt*) reality and is completely ideal. But history should be completely in reality and yet at the same time ideal. This is nowhere possible except in art."[6] In fact, this concept has never completely lost cur-

6. "Auch die wahre Historie beruht auf einer Synthesis des Gegebenen und Wirklichen mit dem Idealen, aber nicht durch Philosophie, da diese die Wirklichkeit vielmehr aufhebt und ganz

rency. Sir Ronald Syme in the British Academy "Lecture on a Master Mind" for 1960 observed: "Diagnosis and narration are conducted with supreme literary power. The ancients (and who shall hold them superseded?) assumed that history is close kin to poetry and drama. Thucydides' theme is in itself a tragedy, by the facts—the ruin of an empire."[7] In considering the fundamental impulse of Thucydides' method, it may be necessary to go back to some such interpretation.

Fortunately Thucydides has made it possible, through various methodological and programmatic statements, to conduct an investigation of his method at a less profound but better illuminated level. Such investigation begins, of course, with what Thucydides himself says about his method.

2. *The usefulness of the* History (1.22.4)[8]

If the provisional account of Thucydides' concept of history is accepted, namely, the concept of an ineluctable

---

ideal ist: Historie aber ganz in jener und doch zugleich ideal sein soll. Dieses ist nirgends als in der Kunst möglich." Quoted by A. D. Momigliano, *Studies in Historiography* (New York and Evanston, 1966) p. 89, n. 29. In the essay "Friedrich Creuzer and Greek Historiography" Momigliano gives a good portrait of the Romantic school and shows how important Greek historiography was to this school's theorizing on historiography in general. And the most important Greek historian was Thucydides: "The revolution that places Thucydides at the head of all the ancient historians is the Romantic revolution," Momigliano, p. 218.

7. *Thucydides,* p. 55.

8. See Stahl, *Thukydides,* p. 15; Luschnat, *RE* Supp. XII, col. 1234; de Romilly, "Utilité"; Patzer, *Das Problem,* pp. 74–77, 89–97; Gomme, I; A. Grossinsky, *Das Programm des Thukydides* (Berlin, 1936), pp. 60–73; von Fritz, *Griech. Geschichtsschreibung,* Ia, 530–533, and Ib, 247–250, esp. the lengthy n. 15.

unity of the particular or adventitious and the general or universal, then one sees it is necessary to understand some qualification of the "usefulness" which Thucydides attributes to his work. For how perfect could rational calculation be, how useful could the *History* as a handbook of such calculation be, if the laws of human nature and of politics never manifested themselves but in adventitious forms?

The usefulness of his work Thucydides states as follows (1.22.4):

καὶ ἐς μὲν ἀκρόασιν ἴσως τὸ μὴ μυθῶδες αὐτῶν ἀτερπέστερον φανεῖται· ὅσοι δὲ βουλήσονται τῶν τε γενομένων τὸ σαφὲς σκοπεῖν καὶ τῶν μελλόντων ποτὲ αὖθις κατὰ τὸ ἀνθρώπινον τοιούτων καὶ παραπλησίων ἔσεσθαι, ὠφέλιμα κρίνειν αὐτὰ ἀρκούντως ἕξει. κτῆμά τε ἐς αἰεὶ μᾶλλον ἢ ἀγώνισμα ἐς τὸ παραχρῆμα ἀκούειν ξύγκειται.

The absence of the fabulous will, I fear, detract from the charm of my work. But if it be found useful by those who wish to know the exact nature of events that once took place and, by reason of human nature, will take place again in similar or analogous form, that is enough. My work has been composed, not for the applause of today's hearing, but as a possession forever (Finley, *Thucydides*, p. 108).

αὐτῶν and αὐτά refer to the ἔργα, as distinct from the speeches (1.22.1–2).[9] Thus Thucydides has already limited the usefulness of his work to the narration of the deeds alone. The speeches, with their potential character (see sec. 5 below), depend upon a prior understanding of the deeds. Therefore the narration of the deeds has the sole claim to usefulness.

9. Patzer, *Das Problem*, p. 74 and n. 169. A. Grosskinsky, *Das Programm des Thukydides* (Berlin, 1936), p. 77, asserts, without arguing the matter, that αὐτά and αὐτῶν refer to both the speeches and the deeds, i.e., to the work as a whole.

Furthermore, the usefulness is in some way a recompense for τὸ μὴ μυθῶδες, for the strictest possible factual accuracy (cf. ὅσον δυνατὸν ἀκριβείᾳ 1.22.2), which is assumed to be unpleasurable. The usefulness of the work is then connected with the deeds as distinct from the speeches and with factuality as distinct from the mythic.

Again the usefulness of the work is for a limited group, for ὅσοι βουλήσονται. It is not, for example, for *hoi anthropoi* in general, who accept hearsay uncritically (1.20.1; cf. 6.60.1). In the restriction of the intended usefulness of the work to a limited group, one hears the Thucydides who, as Hobbes said, "had in his veins the blood of Kings." This restriction is in keeping with the aristocratic outlook betrayed in such remarks as ὅπερ φιλεῖ ὅμιλος ποιεῖν (2.65.4); ὅπερ φιλεῖ δῆμος ποιεῖν (8.1.4); οἷον δὴ ὄχλος . . . ποιεῖν (6.63.2), and in the view expressed by Thucydides and by speakers in the *History* that men's minds are generally the slaves of present events (especially in wartime: 3.82.2; 1.140.1, 21.2).

Further, the usefulness is limited to τῶν τε γενομένων τὸ σαφὲς σκοπεῖν καὶ τῶν μελλόντων ποτὲ αὖθις κατὰ τὸ ἀνθρώπινον τοιούτων κτλ. Those who desire this will find the work useful. τὸ σαφὲς σκοπεῖν says nothing of practical utility.[10]

---

10. A. M. Parry, "λόγος and ἔργον in Thucydides" (unpub. diss., Harvard University, 1957), p. 105: "he says nothing of putting this clear image to any practical use." The view that Thucydides meant some sort of practical application when he spoke of the possible "usefulness" of his work was criticized as early as 1842, by Roscher: see Stahl, *Thukydides*, p. 15, n. 19. The interpretation of Thucydides' ὠφέλιμον as meaning χρήσιμον goes back at least as far as Lucian, *How to Write History*, 42. Cf. Polybius 3.31, where "work of instruction" appears to replace κτῆμα ἐς αἰεί.

Finally, the usefulness is limited to τῶν τε γενομένων ...
καὶ τῶν μελλόντων . . . κατὰ τὸ ἀνθρώπινον. The
category of "the human" in Thucydides is defined not
solely in terms of the laws of human nature, but also
with reference to the external conditions or physical
universe within which human nature finds its place.
This interpretation of κατὰ τὸ ἀνθρώπινον is confirmed
by the distinction made in the next chapter (1.23) between sufferings of human and political origin, on the
one hand, and sufferings of external and nonhuman
origin, on the other.[11] The latter, no matter how over-
whelming, are regarded as contingent (see sec. 6 below).

In summary, then, Thucydides' statement of the usefulness of his work is qualified by its reference to deeds
as distinct from speeches and the possibly unpleasurable
factuality of the narration of the deeds; by the expectation of a limited audience; by the nonpractical character
of the usefulness; and by the implicit distinction, soon
made explicit, between events of human and of
nonhuman origin, and the restriction of the usefulness
to events of the former class.

There remain for discussion apropos of the usefulness of the *History* two other passages, the remarks pref-
atory to the description of the plague (2.48.3) and to
the description of *stasis* (3.82.2). The first of these, with
its promise of such an account of the symptoms as
would enable recognition of the plague if it should ever
occur again, has often been brought into relation with
Thucydides' statement of the usefulness of his work as a
whole—as if the *History* as a whole had this medical

11. Cf. Stahl, *Thukydides*, p. 33; E. Topitsch, "Ἀνθρωπεία φύσις und
Ethik bei Thukydides," *Wiener Studien* 61–62 (1943–1947), 50–67.

character, and as if the description of the plague were a confirmation of this character. But, first of all, in renouncing etiology in his description of the plague (2.48.3), Thucydides broke with one of the departments of Hippocratic medicine, whereas he is quite confident that he knows that cause of the war. Furthermore, as in 1.22, Thucydides speaks not of practical utility but of knowledge: . . . ἀφ' ὧν ἄν τις σκοπῶν . . . μάλιστ' ἂν ἔχοι τι προειδὼς μὴ ἀγνοεῖν, ταῦτα δηλώσω (2.48.3). With σκοπῶν here compare σκοπεῖν (1.22.4). Gomme well observed: "It may be noted that even here, where the future practical benefits of an accurate description are obvious, Thucydides confines himself to the hope, or the expectation, that it will result in knowledge (μὴ ἀγνοεῖν); he does not necessarily expect a cure, he is not giving practical advice."[12]

Thucydides was struck by the superhuman character of the plague. He mentions the plague first in the class of disasters of nonhuman origin. The plague χαλεπωτέρως ἢ κατὰ τὴν ἀνθρωπείαν φύσιν προσέπιπτεν ἑκάστῳ (2.50.1) and ἀνθρωπεία τέχνη (2.47.4) was of no avail. If there was no single cure for the plague (2.51.2) and what helped one hurt another, then clearly the plague was a superhuman phenomenon in that it was essentially unamenable to scientific medical procedure. We must conclude that Thucydides had slight hope for the immediate practical usefulness of his account of the plague; and this conclusion is in keeping with the specific, severe limitations set upon the usefulness of the work as a whole.

In the famous introductory chapter on *stasis* (3.82)

12. Gomme, II, 150. Cf. A. Parry, "The Language of Thucydides' Description of the Plague," *BICS* No. 16 (1969), 106–118.

Thucydides speaks of recurrence in such a way as to recall 1.22. But in 3.82 he states baldly the inevitability of *stasis*, with the single qualification: "as long as human nature remains the same" (3.82.2). It cannot be assumed that ἀνθρωπεία φύσις (3.82.2) means the same as τὸ ἀνθρώπινον (1.22.4).[13] The latter refers to the objective limitations set upon human plans and aspirations, the former to psychology.[14] Therefore it is improper to draw inferences from the one concerning the other.

In each place, then, in which Thucydides speaks of the future and of the usefulness of his work, he does not expect immediate practical utility. In this sense Thucydides' *History* is not a technical effort, since it does not have the same goals as the Hippocratic writings or such fifth-century technical works as the rhetorical treatises of Thrasymachus (schol. Ar. *Aves* 880; cf. D. H. *Is.* 20) and Gorgias (Diog. 8.58) or Democritus' manuals on farming, tactics, and hoplite fighting (D.-K. II.149–150).[15] When Thucydides speaks of foreknowledge apropos of the plague (προειδώς: 2.48.3), he does not mean foreknowledge but prognostication once the plague has begun.[16] Since Thucydides knows of no cure, he cannot intend immediate practical utility by his description. On the other hand, there might yet be some practical value. For example, it might be useful to know

13. As by Grosskinsky, *Das Programm,* p. 69; Topitsch, *Wiener Studien* 61–62 (1943–1947), 53.

14. de Romilly, "Utilité," p. 55.

15. Felix Heinimann, *MH* 18 (1961), 108, n. 19, points out that we have no complete collection of all the evidence concerning the sophistic technai. Heinimann in the lengthy footnote cited brings together evidence for fields other than medicine and rhetoric.

16. Cf. von Fritz, *Griech. Geschichtsschreibung,* Ia, 530–531.

that those who had the plague and recovered were im-
mune. As for the *History,* as a whole, the qualifications set
upon its usefulness are now clear. What positive usefulness it has beyond these qualifications is not clear. There
is the temptation to think of the events described as
conferring their own sort of immunity, so that what
began as exile became a more profound detachment
from active life. But the question must be deferred
whether the *History* can be conceived of as a theoretical
work.

3. *To saphes* (1.22.4)

It is obvious from Thucydides' statements that he
wished to secure factual accuracy. But this factual accuracy is not the sufficient condition for history in the
Thucydidean sense but only the necessary condition for
τὸ σαφές, with which Thucydides associates the immortality of his work. τὸ σαφές emerges from the facts, the
contingent particulars, and thus comes to be the opposite
of the particulars as being freed of the contingent. Thus,
at the level of historiography, but not of events, there is
an escape from that which happens merely by chance
and contrary to reason. In this sense the *History* belongs
to the technical spirit of the fifth century, for an opposition to tyche was so much a part of this spirit, as is clearly
revealed in the Hippocratic *De Arte.* Thucydides differs,
of course, from the Hippocratic writer in that
Thucydides does not seem to believe that his work will be
useful in defeating chance in practice but only intellectually, that is, the *History* will free the mind from chance, by
allowing the mind to distinguish sharply between τὸ
σαφές, the general principle, and the particulars, which

are from the practical point of view to some extent always unpredictable and to that extent always a matter of chance.

Thucydides' use of the word σαφές supports the concept of Thucydidean historiography just proposed. As for the relation of this word to factuality, Patzer well observed that in 1.22.4 it applies both to the past and to the future, and therefore factuality cannot be part of its meaning, since the facts of the future are not yet known.[17] τὸ σαφές is that which emerges out of the facts, which are themselves ascertained by ἀκρίβεια.[18]

In 1.22.4, the sentence in which σαφές appears, with its declaration that the work is a possession forever, comes as the conclusion to the Archaeology and to the statement of method (1.22.1–3). Thus we can think of τὸ σαφές as the product of the method demonstrated in the Archaeology and promised in chapter 22.1–3. This methodology is based on ἀκρίβεια as regards both words and deeds (1.22.1 and 2). Thucydides describes himself as going over others' reports ὅσον δυνατὸν ἀκριβείᾳ περὶ ἑκάστου (1.22.2). Because of the connection of *akribeia* with factual exactness, it is not surprising that Thucydides uses it of reckoning time (1.97.2, 5.20.2).

τὸ σαφές, on the other hand, being the clarity which transcends factual exactness, is used mostly in juridical and political contexts (1.32.1, 34.1, 140.5; 3.40.7; 4.22.2, 4.50.2). The most illustrative use of the word occurs at

17. Patzer, *Das Problem,* p. 76.
18. "Das eigentliche Wort, mit dem Thukydides die durch Kritik erreichbare Genauigkeit des Tatsachwissens gebraucht, ist ἀκριβής . . . . Die in ἀκριβής festgehaltene Grundvorstellung ist die des *glatten Sich-Deckens* . . . Diesen festen Bezug auf die Tatsächlichkeit in ihrer Vereinzelung hat das Wort σαφής nicht . . . ," Patzer, *Das Problem,* p. 77, n. 174.

the end of the excursus on Harmodius and Aristogeiton in Book 6, where it is used thrice in a short space (6.60.2 and 4, 61.1). Since the Athenians lacked a factually exact account of the matter (n.b. ἀκριβὲς οὐδὲν λέγοντας 6.54.1) and trusted to hearsay (ἀκοῇ 6.60.1), which mankind generally accepts too uncritically (1.20.1), they suspected a plot against the democracy (6.60.1). Historical ignorance leads to ignorant suspicion. Ignorant suspicion leads in turn to ignorant action, unilluminated by τὸ σαφές (6.60.2–61.1). Yet, ironically, this want of illumination had a beneficial effect. Whether or not those executed were guilty of mutilating the herms, the city was clearly benefited by the trials and executions (6.60.5). One notes the difference between the perspective of the historian and of the Athenians. What from the historian's perspective was only a coincidence or bad luck (ξυντυχίαν 6.54.1; δυστυχίᾳ 6.55.4)—matters which the historian's method discriminates from general historical laws—became a historical force in ending the regime of the Peisistratids: and then later the ignorant recollection of the event caused ignorant trials and executions. Here is a striking indication of the difference between history raised to the level of τὸ σαφές and history as it appears to or is made by certain individuals at certain times.

That Thucydides thought in these terms is clear from his remarks on the great night battle at Syracuse, when Demosthenes mounted an attack on the Syracusans' counterwall. Thucydides is speaking of the difficulty of finding out just what happened in this battle (7.44.1):

Καὶ ἐνταῦθα ἤδη ἐν πολλῇ ταραχῇ καὶ ἀπορίᾳ ἐγίγνοντο οἱ Ἀθηναῖοι, ἣν οὐδὲ πυθέσθαι ῥᾴδιον ἦν οὐδ' ἀφ' ἑτέρων ὅτῳ τρόπῳ ἕκαστα ξυνηνέχθη. ἐν μὲν γὰρ ἡμέρᾳ σαφέστερα μέν, ὅμως δὲ οὐδὲ ταῦτα οἱ παραγενόμενοι πάντα πλὴν τὸ καθ' ἑαυτὸν ἕκαστος μόλις οἶδεν· ἐν δὲ νυκτομαχίᾳ, ἣ μόνη δὴ στρατοπέδων μεγάλων ἔν γε τῷδε τῷ πολέμῳ ἐγένετο, πῶς ἄν τις σαφῶς τι ᾔδει;

At this point the Athenians fell into great confusion and distress. From neither side was it easy to discover how each particular event took place. For in daytime the combatants see more clearly but still they do not see everything—only their particular location, and this with difficulty. In a night battle, the only one in this war fought by large armies, how could anyone perceive anything clearly?

In the second of these two sentences it is apparent that Thucydides contrasts τὸ σαφές with individual perception of individual facts.[19] In the first sentence, Thucydides complains of the difficulty he experienced in finding out the facts. Clearly Thucydides wanted not the facts alone, for their own sake, but the facts as a basis for τὸ σαφές, which is the legacy of his work to posterity (1.22.4).

This contrast between *akribeia* and *to saphes,* and the transcendence of the former by the latter, is at the heart of Thucydides' method. This contrast appears in all of Thucydides' methodological statements in language so similar in each place, in some respects, that it could almost be called formulaic. These similarities make it clear that Thucydides' purpose was to liberate himself from the individual perspective and from the particular facts.[20] Quotation and schematization bring out the points in question.

19. Thucydides preserves here the sense of the Homeric σάφα εἰδέναι, namely, visual clarity: see W. Luther, *"Wahrheit" und "Lüge" im Ältesten Griechentum* (Leipzig, 1935), pp. 61–63. But Thucydides seems to mean a clear *over*view.

20. This conclusion is corroborated by the meaning of σκοπεῖν, which refers not to the perception of individual facts but to a purview: Patzer, *Das Problem,* pp. 74–76 and n. 173.

		ὡς/ ὅπως	τις/ τι	ἕκαστος/ ἑκασταχοῦ/ ἑκάτερος	τυγχάνω/ παρατυγχάνω/ ξυντυχία
The deeds 1.22.2	τὰ δ᾽ ἔργα . . . οὐκ ἐκ τοῦ παρατυχόντος πυνθανόμενος ἠξίωσα γράφειν, οὐδ᾽ ὡς ἐμοὶ ἐδόκει.				X
The speeches 1.22.3	ἐπιπόνως δὲ ηὑρίσκετο, διότι . . . οὐ ταὐτὰ περὶ τῶν αὐτῶν ἔλεγον, ἀλλ᾽ ὡς ἑκατέρων τις εὐνοίας ἢ μνήμης ἔχοι.	X	X	X	
Plague 2.48.3	λεγέτω μὲν οὖν περὶ αὐτοῦ ὡς ἕκαστος γιγνώσκει καὶ ἰατρὸς καὶ ἰδιώτης	X		X	
Plague 2.51.1	τὸ μὲν οὖν νόσημα, πολλὰ καὶ ἄλλα παραλιπόντι ἀτοπίας, ὡς ἑκάστῳ ἐτύγχανέ τι διαφερόντως ἑτέρῳ πρὸς ἕτερον γιγνόμενον, τοιοῦτον ἦν ἐπὶ πᾶν τὴν ἰδέαν.	X	X	X	X
Stasis 3.82.2	καὶ ἐπέπεσε πολλὰ καὶ χαλεπὰ κατὰ στάσιν ταῖς πόλεσι. . . . μᾶλλον δὲ καὶ ἡσυχαίτερα καὶ τοῖς εἴδεσι διηλλαγμένα, ὡς ἂν ἕκασται αἱ μεταβολαὶ τῶν ξυντυχιῶν ἐφιστῶνται.	X		X	X
Chronology 5.20.2	σκοπείτω δέ τις κατὰ τοὺς χρόνους καὶ μὴ τῶν ἑκασταχοῦ ἢ ἀρχόντων ἢ ἀπὸ τιμῆς τινος ἐς τὰ προγεγενημένα σημαινόντων τὴν ἀπαρίθμησιν τῶν ὀνομάτων . . . οὐ γὰρ ἀκριβὲς ἐστιν, οἷς καὶ ἀρχομένοις καὶ μεσοῦσι καὶ ὅπως ἔτυχέ τῳ ἐπεγένετό τι.	X	X	X	X
Introduction to Sicilian Expedition 6.2.1	ἀρκείτω δὲ ὡς ποιηταῖς τε εἴρηται καὶ ὡς ἕκαστός πη γιγνώσκει περὶ αὐτῶν.	X		X	

The passages cited comprise all the most important methodological statements in Thucydides, with one exception, 5.26. In 5.26 Thucydides is defending the consistency and detachment of his own perspective. In all the places just cited Thucydides rejects perspectival limitation (ὡς), the individual (ἕκαστος), the discrete (τις, τι), the contingent (τυγχάνω, etc.). We shall see later that τυγχάνω in these (and other) places does indeed have the connotation of chance, of the adventitious or the contingent. Thucydides wishes to pass from "the changes of the contingent" (αἱ μεταβολαὶ τῶν ξυντυχιῶν 3.82.2) to the ἰδέα (2.51.1). A comparison with Plato suggests itself,[21] a comparison which must, however, presently be qualified in an important sense.

The idiom ὡς ἕκαστος (2.48.3, 51.1; 3.82.2; 6.2.1) calls for comment. Thucydides often uses this idiom to express the "changes of the contingent" as opposed to what was generally the case. Thus it can form part of a μὲν-δὲ construction, in which one half of the antithesis expresses the general, and the other half expresses the various particulars that escape the general observation of the first half (3.107.4; 4.32.2, 96.7; 5.4.3, 56.4, 57.2; 6.69.1, 76.3, 77.2; 7.13.2). The idiom can also have this function independently of the μὲν-δὲ construction (3.81.3; 4.58; 6.44.2). Thus it is not surprising that the idiom is used in connection with τυγχάνω (with 2.51.1 [Plague] cf. 4.25.2, 93.4) and ξυντυχία (with 3.82.2 [stasis] cf. 3.45.4; 7.57.1). Thucydides' use of the idiom provides strong corroboration of the interpretation of the methodological statements under discussion.

The distinction made by Thucydides in these places

21. E.g. *Phaedo* 108d.

resembles Heraclitus' distinction between the *logos,* which is common, and ἰδία φρόνησις (B4). We have seen that for the sake of his *logos* (cf. ἀξιολογώτατον 1.1.1) Thucydides wished to go beyond particular, private points of view to the general idea. Herein lies the technical character of Thucydides' method. For it is the aim of techne to defeat chance, and in going beyond the particular and private, Thucydides was going beyond "the changes of the contingent" and thus securing for his work a technical competence. This intention was already implicit in 1.22.4 in the qualification of past and future events by κατὰ τὸ ἀνθρώπινον. The neuter substantive adjective expresses a concrete generality ("in accordance with the way of mankind") or an abstraction ("in accordance with the human") and surely not concrete particularity. Thucydides' method has therefore an aim quite different from that of modern historiography.[22]

Two further examples will illustrate the technical character of Thucydides' method. First, this character appears in the dating by winters and summers (5.20). This device may, in fact, have been taken over from technical works on agriculture, though Herodotus had already shown the way.[23] That Thucydides succeeded in attaining the accuracy of reckoning he wanted is doubtful, unless the text is emended. But what is important for present purposes is his aim, which was obviously technical in the present sense. In abandoning dating by local magistracies and priesthoods, he sought to transcend

22. Patzer, *Das Problem,* pp. 91–93.
23. Gomme, III, 702; for Herodotus' dating of Xerxes' campaign against Greece by summers and winters, see M. Pohlenz, *Herodot: Der Erste Geschichtschreiber des Abendlandes* (Berlin and Leipzig, 1937), pp. 198–199.

the discrete and particular, "the changes of the contingent."[24]

A second example shows the application of Thucydides' method, namely, the replacement of particular, contingent, and thus fallible points of view by a general point of view, by actors in the *History* who use this method to solve a certain practical problem. Those of the besieged Plataeans and Athenians who undertake to escape from Plataea construct ladders to throw against the Lacedaemonian containing wall. They calculate the height of the wall in a place where the bricks happen to be exposed (an example of tyche and techne cooperating) (3.20.3):

κλίμακας ἐποιήσαντο ἴσας τῷ τείχει τῶν πολεμίων· ξυνεμετρήσαντο δὲ ταῖς ἐπιβολαῖς τῶν πλίνθων, ᾗ ἔτυχε πρὸς σφᾶς οὐκ ἐξαληλιμμένον τὸ τεῖχος αὐτῶν. ἠριθμοῦντο δὲ πολλοὶ ἅμα τὰς ἐπιβολάς, καὶ ἔμελλον οἱ μέν τινες ἁμαρτήσεσθαι οἱ δὲ πλείους τεύξεσθαι τοῦ ἀληθοῦς λογισμοῦ, ἄλλως τε καὶ πολλάκις ἀριθμοῦντες καὶ ἅμα οὐ πολὺ ἀπέχοντες.

They measured [the wall] by the layers of bricks, where their [i.e., the Lacedaemonians'] wall facing them [the Plataeans] happened not to be plastered. Many counted the layers at the same time, and it was likely that some persons would err but the majority would hit upon the true calculation, especially since they counted often and they were not far away [from the wall].

24. 5.20.2 appears in the Jones-Powell text with certain transpositions of words and emendations. But it is possible to make sense of the MSS' reading, which is as follows: σκοπείτω δέ τις κατὰ τοὺς χρόνους καὶ μὴ τῶν ἑκασταχοῦ ἢ ἀρχόντων ἢ ἀπὸ τιμῆς τινὸς τὴν ἀπαρίθμησιν τῶν ὀνομάτων ἐς τὰ προγεγενημένα σημαινόντων πιστεύσας μᾶλλον. "Let one make his observations according to [natural] divisions of time and not (make his observations of) the reckoning up of the names of persons in each locality who, either as magistrates or on the basis of some office, [thus] signify [something] in regard to past events, since

Thucydides recognizes in the technique of counting the same principle which he had himself applied in judging evidence. οἱ μέν τινες were likely to err. In the same way, in certain methodological statements, Thucydides rejected that which was a matter of τις or τι, the particular, which is the contingent.

4. *The "second preface"* (5.26)

The only important methodological or programmatic statement not included in the schematization presented

---

he rather trusts [to them]." Even Classen's deletion of ἐς is unnecessary. ἐς can be translated "in regard to." ἀπαρ. is the object of σκοπ., not of κατά understood, as Classen thought. Thus πιστεύσας is connected, contrary to Gomme, with the rest of the sentence, even though it governs no dative (as by Schültz' and Wilamowitz' emendation): it is a well-known principle of Greek prose style that when a finite verb and a participle in agreement with the subject of that verb have the same object, the object is stated only once, even if the finite verb and the participle govern different cases, as here (Smyth 1634–35). Thucydides writes σκ. . . . τὴν ἀπαρ. since he is thinking of the names as a list on a stele, i.e., the names are already "reckoned up." σημαίνω of a stele is to be expected (cf. 2.43; 6.55).

I do not have an opinion on the extremely vexed questions of how Thucydides computed his "ten years and a few days more or less." But I do not think that accuracy of computation or even factual accuracy was Thucydides' primary aim in writing the *History*. As for 5.20, one can at least observe that Thucydides twice states his computation, first in 5.20.1 in the more specific form of "*just ten years and a few days more or less.*" Then, having defined and justified his technique of computation, he again states his conclusion but this time in a less rigorous form, "on the basis that half of each year is a unit, ten summers and an equal number of winters" (5.20.3). Here he says nothing of the slight discrepancy mentioned in the first computation. Thucydides wished to emphasize not so much the *precise* length of time as the generality and clarity which his system of dating and of computing time had achieved in abandoning the dating and computing by particular, local systems.

above is 5.26. But this chapter is perfectly consistent with the present interpretation of the places assembled in the schematization, for here Thucydides gives an account of and a defense of the adequacy of his own perspective. First of all he wishes to show that he is writing about a single war. Scholarship on the "Thucydidean question" began with the hypothesis that 5.26 was a "second preface" written sometime after the recommencement of hostilities, or at the end of war, when Thucydides perceived that the Archidamian War was not a separate war. According to this interpretation, ὁ αὐτός Thucydides means "the same Thucydides who wrote Books 1–5.25," stressing single authorship.

But in fact *ho autos* stresses the unity of the war by stating that unity, the object which Thucydides has in view, from the side of the observing subject, the historian himself, who is "the same" in his opinion that he is still observing and describing the same war. *Ho autos* is an idiom which has several parallels in the *History*. Not unexpectedly, the most striking of these occurs in a speech of Pericles (2.61.2): καὶ μὲν ὁ αὐτός εἰμι καὶ οὐκ ἐξίσταμαι. Elsewhere, *ho autos* is specified by the dative of gnome (cf. Soph. *OT* 557):

3.38.1 ἐγὼ μὲν οὖν ὁ αὐτός εἰμι τῇ γνώμῃ
5.75.3 γνώμῃ δὲ οἱ αὐτοὶ ἔτι ὄντες
2.87.3 δίκαιον . . . νομίσαι . . . ταῖς μὲν τύχαις ἐνδέχεσθαι
σφάλλεσθαι τοὺς ἀνθρώπους, ταῖς δὲ γνώμαις τοὺς αὐτοὺς
αἰεὶ ὀρθῶς ἀνδρείους.

These three places suggest what is meant by *ho autos* in 5.26 and 2.61.2, that is, a mental or intellectual constancy and perhaps also a moral constancy, an unwillingness to be shaken from one's resolve.[25] The same notion can be expressed as in 1.140.1: τῆς μὲν γνώμης αἰεὶ τῆς αὐτῆς ἔχομαι (cf. Antiphon 6.7).

When Thucydides describes himself as *ho autos* in 5.26.1 he has in mind chiefly the period of truce which he is about to describe. From Thucydides' point of view, to believe that the truce was not a part of the whole war is to commit the fallacy which his method is designed to avoid—the fallacy of mistaking a particular "change of the contingent" for a general clarity. In the case of the truce, the fallacy would be to regard a specious peace not as a particular phase of the whole war, as it really was, but as distinct from the war.

In 5.26.5 Thucydides defends the adequacy of his perspective on other grounds. From the beginning of the war he was old enough to perceive what was going on. He paid attention. Through exile he came to see the war from both sides. He had the leisure for his undertaking.

In sum, 5.26 serves the purpose of the *History* by showing why the individual perspective of Thucydides is reliable. Thucydides must defend himself in this way since his method discriminates between individual perspective and general truth. To put the matter another way, the methodology of the *History* implies that the only valid individual perspective will be the historian's own. The use of *autos* does not point to a division in the work but to Thucydides' understanding of the unity of the war. Thus

25. For moral connotation, cf. the discussion of 1.140.1 in Chap. I, sec. A. This idiom can be varied with ὁμοῖος: ἡμεῖς δὲ ὁμοῖοι καὶ τότε καὶ νῦν ἐσμέν (Thuc. 1.86.2); cf. Hes. *OD* 114: αἰεὶ δὲ πόδας καὶ χεῖρας ὁμοῖοι; Pl. *Symp.* 173d4: ἀεὶ ὁμοῖος εἶ [sc. σεαυτῷ].

it is better to think of 5.26 not as a "second preface" but as a methodological disgression.[26]

5. *The speeches* (1.22.1)[27]

It is in terms of this distinction between the idea, arrived at through the technical character of method, and the contingent or adventitious that one must understand what Thucydides says of the speeches in his work. Thucydides distinguishes implicitly between his treatment of the speeches and of the deeds by contrasting, in the case of the speeches—while there is nothing similar in what he says of the deeds—between ὅσα . . . εἶπον with ὡς . . . ἂν ἐδόκουν ἐμοὶ . . . εἰπεῖν (1.22.1), between what and how, between facts and potentiality.[28] Thucydides will not report ὅσα . . . εἶπον, but the potential speeches, which

26. John H. Finley, Jr., *Three Essays on Thucydides* (Cambridge, 1967), p. 168. For the form of the opening sentence of 5.26 (Γέγραφε δὲ <u>καὶ</u> ταῦτα ὁ αὐτὸς Θουκυδίδης . . .), cf. the opening words of Phocylides, frs. 1–4: <u>καὶ</u> τόδε Φωκυλίδου.

27. Luschnat, *RE* Supp. XII, cols. 1167–79 gives a résumé of scholarship on 1.22.1. As he suggests several times, the conditions for a satisfactory interpretation of 1.22.1 are that equal weight be given to each part of Thucydides' statement and that this statement so interpreted square with Thucydides' practice as discernible in the speeches. But Luschnat's understanding of the central antithesis in Thucydides' statement is in terms of art and truth: "Die Schwierigkeiten, vor denen die modernen Interpreten stehen, liegen fast ausschliesslich in dem Nebeneinander (besser: Ineinander) von Künstlerischem und Wahrheitsanspruch, das sich in I 22 nicht zu der Einheit verbindet. die sie im Werke selbst zu sehen meinen" (col. 1169). As will be seen, my own understanding of the central antithesis 1.22.1 differs from Luschnat's; and I hope it will shed light on Thucydides' practice in composing the speeches.

28. Cf. Gomme, I, 140, n. 1. But no matter how one construes the μέν-δέ construction, one cannot escape the contrast noted. Gomme's paraphrase, by the way, amounts to a tautology.

are defined as περὶ τῶν αἰεὶ παρόντων τὰ δέοντα. τὰ δέοντα are implicitly contrasted with ἡ ξύμπασα γνώμη τῶν ἀληθῶς λεχθέντων, that is (as most scholars agree), the main point of what was actually said, the particular recommendation of policy.[29] τὰ δέοντα then, by contrast with what was actually said, are ἃ ἔδει ἑκάστους εἰπεῖν or γνῶναι, what ought to have been said or understood.

Thucydides implicitly distinguishes between the form in which the speech was actually delivered and what ought to have been the subject matter. *Ta deonta* is used by Socrates in *Phaedrus* 234e6 in the sense of the requisite subject matter as distinguished from the style, and this same distinction between form and content underlies Pericles' γνῶναι τὰ δέοντα καὶ ἑρμηνεῦσαι ταῦτα (2.60.5). It has been observed that "the fact that τὰ δέοντα could mean what we call moral duties shows that duties were not thought of primarily as either impositions on the person or as originating in a person's 'moral sense' (as with us) but as *requirements of the case which were there to be fulfilled.*"[30] When Thucydides says that in the speeches he has given what he considers ta deonta he refers to the objective political or military requirements of the particular case, whether or not the speaker actually had a grasp of the requirements. For example, there is general agreement between the speeches of Archidamus and

29. On "the general line of the speaker's argument," A. Andrewes, "The Mytilene Debate," *Phoenix* 16 (1962), 64ff. Andrewes argues, however, that in practice Thucydides diverged from this principle and introduced matter "foreign to the real speech and occasion" (p. 69). The Mytilene debate represents the "later" treatment of speeches.

30. S. Benardete, "χρή and δεῖ in Plato and Others," *Glotta* 43 (1965), 293. My italics.

Pericles in their analysis of the conditions under which and the means by which a long war between Athens and Sparta would be fought. Both show a grasp of ta deonta, though on another level there is a great difference between the Athenian and the Spartan leader. But it is the fact that they state ta deonta in more or less the same terms (cf. the discussion of chremata in Chap. I) that shows Thucydides' practice in presenting ta deonta in the speeches. Everyone would agree that it is most unlikely that historically such verbal correspondences between speeches occurred. In such places we are concerned with what Thucydides considered ta deonta, what the speakers should have perceived whether they did or not in fact. Thus the speeches in Book 1 contain many statements of the ἀληθεστάτη πρόφασις of the war, which Thucydides says was ἀφανεστάτη λόγῳ (1.23.6).

Ta deonta thus stands for the apodosis of a condition of which the unexpressed protasis is: "if they had had a total grasp of their situation."[31] But still ta deonta are always limited to a particular situation, as each speech is limited to such a situation. Therefore, no speech can be identified with Thucydides' own view. The whole war is not a situation about which there can be a speech in the way that actors in the *History* can make speeches about particular situations. At best there can be provisional speeches before the war begins, but of necessity these are made in the face of the unknown future. The war is a series of situations. The meaning of the war is in the process. In order to present the process as a process but

31. Cf. O. Regenbogen, *Thukydides politische Reden* (Leipzig, 1949), p. 19.

at the same time to render it intelligible, Thucydides composes the speeches on the grounds of a contrast between the ideal and the real speech in each situation, and presents each speech as an amalgamation of the two.

The distinction between the two components of the speeches in the *History* corresponds to the distinction, discussed above, between τὸ σαφές and the contingent particularity. But here that all-too-glib comparison of Thucydides with Plato comes in for a crucial qualification. Thucydides either could not or would not distinguish between his own grasp of τὸ σαφές and the enunciation of it by various persons in the *History*. Thus, the actors in the *History,* thanks to the dual nature of the speeches, appear to be living the truth which is in one sense only the historian's own, but in another sense only their own, since this truth is nothing apart from their words and their deeds. Unlike Plato, Thucydides never separated from its temporal manifestations what he believed was the eternal clarity he had attained, and he did not give his principles an existence independent of this world. Is it for this reason that Thucydides' work keeps, in Jaeger's fine phrase, "the charm of its imperishable actuality"?

6. *Human and nonhuman disasters* (1.23.1–3)

The technical character of the *History,* by which Thucydides separated general principles from the contingent, appears again in 1.23.1–3, where Thucydides makes a crucial distinction between sufferings of human and of nonhuman origin. Thucydides has previously argued that the Peloponnesian War was the largest war to date in terms of commitments of men and material resources. This was the point of the Archaeology (cf. 1.1.2–3 with 1.21.2). It was also the longest war (1.23.1). It also brought the greatest sufferings (1.23.1). Now appears the distinction just mentioned, between the two kinds of sufferings. The first consists of the desolation of cities, exile, and death in war or stasis. The second consists of earthquakes, eclipses of the sun, droughts, famines, and the plague. Of this second kind of suffering, Thucydides says: ταῦτα γὰρ πάντα μετὰ τοῦδε τοῦ πολέμου ἅμα ξυνεπέθετο. The language distinctly implies that Thucydides regarded this second class of sufferings as concomitant and contingent. In fact Thucydides generally takes a rationalistic view of natural phenomena. He gives no indication that he would agree with the Lacedaemonians that impiety could cause an earthquake (1.128.1). He says that he believes that eclipses of the sun can occur only at the time of the new moon (2.28), a point which he later corroborates (4.52.1), and he believes that a tidal wave was caused by an earthquake (3.89.5). Perhaps his use of the first person singular implies some dubiety (2.28; 3.89; cf. 1.22.2 οὐδ' ὡς ἐμοὶ δοκεῖ and my remarks on the fallibility of individual perspective). Yet he is confident enough of his naturalistic understanding of such phenomena to censure Nicias' scrupling over an eclipse of the moon (7.50), and he twice points out soldiers' mistaken fear of a thunderstorm (6.67.1, 7.79.3). In the second of these places Thucydides again observes that the event could be connected with the time of year. One can compare Thucydides' own naturalistic interpretation of such phenomena with, for example, the technical skill of the naval commander, Phormio, who, because he knew from experience that a breeze would come up at a certain time, was able to make this breeze a part of his tactics, whereas the same breeze appeared to the Spartans a matter of chance. The technical character of Thucydides' method, which separates the contingent from what is regular and thus to some degree predictable, finds an analogy in that rational calculation based on experience which we saw was the mark of technical skill.

Considering Thucydides' naturalistic observations on various meteorological phenomena, it is difficult to believe that he regarded the second kind of sufferings discussed above as anything but contingent upon the first. It has been said of 1.23.1–3 that "it is a poetic and dramatic statement," and "he deliberately removes all demarcation between political and natural destruction."[32] One should rather say that it was central to Thucydides' method to make this demarcation. Thucydides, who observes that the Lacedaemonians believed that an earthquake was caused by an act of impiety (1.128.1), refuses to make any such connections himself, and this refusal is eloquent of the rationalist's distinction between the human and divine. Thucydides does not believe that humans can cause earthquakes. Furthermore, he does not, like Herodotus, believe that earthquakes are portents. Herodotus says of the earthquakes which shook Delos for the first and last time in his lifetime, after Datis, one of Dareios' generals, had approached the island: "by this portent I think the god

---

32. Parry, λόγος *and* ἔργον, p. 116. This is a strengthened statement of Gomme's position: "Whether Thucydides himself thought that there might be some connection between such natural events and human actions is not clear," I, 151.

revealed the ills that would befall mankind" (6.98). For Thucydides, earthquakes and other natural disasters are only concomitants of the Peloponnesian War.

Parry was right, however, in his sense that Thucydides grants the eternal natural conditions of human life their force. While Thucydides, on the basis of his method can, so to speak, control the contingent and perceive the essential in the contingent, he also sees that the force of the contingent may, for certain men at certain times, be inevitable. In this respect, Thucydides could be compared with the author of the *De Arte* who moderately said that while he would not deprive tyche of its power, he believed that the good or bad luck of patients was generally the result of techne (*De Arte* 4).

7. *Causality:* prophasis *and* aitia[33]

The distinction between contingent particularity and general principle also applies to Thucydides' concept of

33. In this section, I am concerned with the distinction between *aitia* and *prophasis*, not with the problem of whether or not *prophasis* was a late addition to Book 1. For the latter problem, see A. Andrewes, "Thucydides on the Causes of the War," *CQ* NS 9 (1959), 223–239. The literature on *prophasis* and *aitia* is vast. See especially de Romilly, *Thucydides;* Luschnat, *RE* Supp. XII, cols. 1208–19 (critique of de Romilly and of Andrewes, *CQ* NS 9 (1959), 223–239, and Andrewes, "Thucydides and the Persians," *Historia* 10 (1961), 1–18); Gomme, I on 1.88; von Fritz, *Griech. Geschichtsschreibung*, Ia, 623ff.; Ib, 284ff.; L. Pearson, "Prophasis and Aitia," *TAPA* 83 (1952), 205ff. On αἰτίη and πρόφασις in Herodotus, see H. R. Immerwahr, "Aspects of Historical Causation in Herodotus," *TAPA* 87 (1956), 243–247: αἰτίη usually occurs in a human context and "nearly always in cases where blame is attached to an action" (244), whereas πρόφασις is a "professed motive" (246).

historical causality. Without going into the problems surrounding Thucydides' use of πρόφασις and αἰτία, one can
observe that Thucydides surely distinguishes between
cause in the sense of immediate cause, in particular,
charges brought by one party against another on particular grounds, and cause in the sense of fundamental,
underlying cause, whether or not stated by actors in the
History.[34] It appears from a valuable study that
Cochrane's interpretation of the meaning of prophasis in
Thucydides as "exciting cause"[35] was inaccurate, and "is
not borne out by the evidence, as this word has no such
meaning in the *History;* it acquires, however, the meaning
of 'real cause' by the apposition of ἀληθής and it is especially significant that Thucydides uses πρoφάσις in this
combination in two most important instances, i.e., Thuc.
I, 23, 6 and VI, 6, 1, where he is referring to the 'truest
cause' of the war in general and to the 'truest cause' of the
Sicilian expedition respectively."[36] In other words, aitia is
subjective, as against the relative objectivity of prophasis,
which can be translated, "reason that one can give," that
is, someone other than the actors concerned.[37]

34. This is the view of R. Sealey, "Thucydides, Herodotus, and the
Causes of War," *CQ* NS 7 (1957), 1–12.
35. C. N. Cochrane, *Thucydides and the Science of History* (Oxford
1929).
36. S. Schüller, "About Thucydides' Use of αἰτία and πρόφασις,"
Revue Belge 34 (1956), 976. This article contains a useful survey of the
words αἰτία and πρόφασις in the Hippocratic corpus.
37. Klaus Weidauer, *Thukydides und die Hippokratischen Schriften*
(Heidelberg, 1954), pp. 9, 11–14. Cf. G. Schäublin, "Wieder einmal
πρόφασις," *MH* 28 (1971), 144, who states that only in 2.49.1 does
Thucydides use *prophasis* as a medical term.

B. *Tyche in history*

1. *The problem*

A comparison of Thucydides' own use of tyche with its uses by speakers in the *History* gives promise of providing a test of the interpretation of Thucydides' method already advanced. Since Thucydides uses the word tyche in his own voice, it would seem that here if anywhere he has given a good index of what sort of thing or event ought to be attributed to tyche. Such a study of tyche, coupled with a study of Thucydides' use of the verb τυγχάνω, might suggest how chance works and to what extent.

In the present state of scholarship, it is no longer necessary either to deny Cornford's providential Tyche[38] or to affirm that tyche has some role. It is accepted that Thucydides "recognized an area of life which could never be subject to exact prediction and that his attitude in this is entirely Greek,"[39] but that Tyche ruled history is out of the question. Accordingly, recent scholarship has taken the paths of determining where Thucydides found chance and where he did not,[40] and of assessing the degree by which events fall short of plans.[41] Both of these approaches confuse, to some extent, Thucydides' historiographical methodology with his concept of history. Since the methodology is scientific, it

38. F. C. Cornford, *Thucydides Mythistoricus* (London, 1965).

39. Finley, *Thucydides*, p. 315.

40. H. Herter, "Freiheit und Gebundenheit des Staatsmannes bei Thukydides," *RM* 93 (1950), 133–153; repr. in *Thukydides* (Wege der Forschung XCVIII. Darmstadt 1968), ed. H. Herter, pp. 260–281.

41. Stahl, *Thukydides*.

is easy to think that Thucydides must have seen history unfolding according to discoverable laws at certain times and at other times affected by the unpredictable and irrational. Then one must discover which events Thucydides thought belonged to which category. Likewise, if in history reason is the norm, as in Thucydidean historiography, it is easy to think that Thucydides saw events solely in terms of the actors' plans. Then one must discover the degree by which events fall short of plans, and to this degree tyche will prevail and reason will be limited.

But Thucydides has taken care to distinguish between history and the sort of historiography attained by his methodology. This historiography achieves *to saphes,* which can hardly be achieved even in broad daylight by the actor in history. Only the great statesman or great general can approach the historian's grasp of *to saphes.* History, on the other hand, is a mixture of contingency and orderliness of varying proportions, though there is always an element of each. Reason or intelligence is not the norm in history but only the principle by which certain actors are guided, while for others tyche is the norm. The unexpected may be expected by some; for others, their confident plans miscarry. To attempt a statistical survey of such combinations of plans and events in Thucydides and to interpret his concept of history on this basis is to confuse this concept with his own methods and goals in writing history. Thucydidean historiography follows its own rules, which cannot be exactly the same rules that the actors in history follow. It is a great mistake to think that Thucydides demanded that history live up to the principles of Thucydidean historiography, and that he therefore felt grief or anger as he wrote each page, or that he thought history could live up to these principles, and that he had therefore learned optimism and hope from his violent teacher.

2. *Uses of tyche by Thucydides himself*

Of forty occurrences of tyche in the *History* only seven are in Thucydides' own voice. There are twenty-eight occurrences in speeches; two in indirect discourse (4.73.3, 5.16.1); one in a decretal formula (4.118.11); and two in which Thucydides is apparently stating a case from someone else's point of view (5.75.3, 7.33.6). Since they are so few, Thucydides' own uses of tyche are likely to be all the more significant.

Of these seven occurrences of tyche, four have the definite article, and of these four, in three the definite article has particular force. Demosthenes is described as τῇ τύχῃ ἐλπίσας (3.97.2). Smyth translated the phrase: "confident by reason of his good fortune."[42] With this use of tyche, one can compare the similar use of tyche in Thucydides' description of the Athenians at Pylos: βουλόμενοι τῇ παρούσῃ . . . ἐπεξελθεῖν (4.14.3; for the same phrase, cf. Pl. *Crit.* 43c3; *Phaed.* 84e1). The third place in which the definite article has particular force is also in the Pylos episode, where Thucydides remarks of the reversal of roles by which the Spartans attacked from the sea while the Athenians defended themselves on land: ἐς τοῦτό τε περιέστη ἡ τύχη (4.12.3). Here tyche is the

42. *Greek Grammar*, sec. 1517.

present situation. This is the neutral sense of tyche so common in Plato.[43]

In the fourth place in which tyche has the definite article, in the phrase τὰ τῆς τύχης (4.55.3), Thucydides is analyzing the Spartan state of mind after Sphacteria, and it is necessary to leave open the question whether this phrase expresses Thucydides' or the Spartans' view of the matter.

Such are the four occurrences of tyche with the definite article. In the three remaining places in which Thucydides uses tyche in his own voice, tyche occurs in the phrase *kata tychen* (by chance). Of these three, two refer to weather, and they occur in what are generally agreed to be important episodes.

After the Mytilene debate the Athenians, having changed their minds, send a second trireme to rescind the harsh orders carried by the first, and Thucydides observes that it was kata tychen that no wind prevented the second trireme from overtaking the first (3.49.4). In order to understand the irony of Thucydides' observation one must recall his description of the mood of the first meeting of the assembly concerning Mytilene: γνώμας ἐποιοῦντο, καὶ ὑπὸ ὀργῆς ἔδοξεν αὐτοῖς (3.36.2). This sentence recalls the distinction made in the prooemium to the first speech of Pericles between the gnome of Pericles and gnomai of the people, who are liable to passion and change. The constant, rational gnome of Pericles was antithetical in that prooemium to tyche.

43. Arnd Zimmerman, "Tyche bei Platon" (unpub. diss., Bonn, 1966), p. 103: "An einer sehr grossen Anzahl von Stellen meint "Tyche" nichts anderes als eine konkrete Situation, die sich irgendwie ergibt oder ergeben hat."

There was evidence that Thucydides understood the career of Pericles in terms of this antithesis. Now in the Mytilene episode, the same view of the Athenian assembly reappears. The Athenians made their first decision in anger. They showed better sense the next day, but through their anger they had already committed themselves to tyche. Thucydides observes that it was only by chance that they were able to rescind their original decision. The decision was thus contrary to what could have been surely planned.

The phrase kata tychen is used again of the storm which forced the Athenian fleet in at Pylos. Here it must be observed that of the seven uses of tyche by Thucydides in his own voice, four occur either in the Pylos episode (4.3.1, 12.3, 14.3) or in reference to Pylos (4.55.3); and Thucydides suggests that after Mantinea, the Greek world attributed the Spartan defeat on Sphacteria to tyche (5.75.3). The Lacedaemonian envoys who plead for their prisoners in Athens speak of the Athenian success as eutychia (4.17.4, 18.4) and tyche (4.18.3) and warn the Athenians about tyche (4.18.4–5). Since Cornford the role of tyche in the Pylos episode has been debated by scholars. Gomme reviews the evidence (the occurrences of tyche and τυγχάνω) and wishes to minimize the importance of chance.[44] But if the present interpretation of chance in Thucydides is correct—that which is, as everything must be to some extent, contrary to calculation—then chance has as large a role in the Pylos episode as in any in the *History*. In the same way that the decision of the Athenians to rescind their harsh decree concerning the Mytileneans carried weight finally

44. Gomme, III, 488–489.

only kata tychen, since no wind detained the trireme carrying the recision, so the conflicting recommendations of Eurymedon and Sophocles on the one hand and of Demosthenes on the other are finally decided kata tychen, when a storm forces the fleet to land at Pylos. When Gomme says that the Spartans' absorption in a festival, the arrival of the Messenian vessels, and the Spartans' omission to block the entrance to the harbor are matters of coincidence but not of chance, he misunderstands the Thucydidean concept of chance, which includes anything unforeseen or unforeseeable. If a coincidence was unforeseen or unforeseeable, it was a matter of tyche or chance. In any case, Gomme must admit that there were events which were "really accidental," the storm and the fire on the island. That the fortification of Pylos was due to an impulse (ὁρμὴ ἐνέπεσε 4.4.1) fits with the other indications of fortuitousness.[45]

There remains the third occurrence of the phrase kata tychen, in 5.37.3. Here Thucydides observes of the alliance proposed to the Boeotians by the Argives that it was kata tychen exactly what the Lacedaemonians had bidden the Boeotians seek from the Argives. One suspects that Thucydides is rather whimsical here, and one might connect this use of kata tychen with the frequent use of τυγχάνω in Book 5 of the presence or absence of ambassadors, which sometimes produces results which

---

45. Thucydides in his treatment of the Pylos episode reflects what may have been the common point of view. In Ar. *Clouds* 581–589, the chorus apparently refers to Cleon's success at Pylos when it says that there was *dysboulia* but the gods caused the plans to turn out for the better.

could not have been foreseen (5.22.1, 30.5, 44.1, 46.5, 50.5, 76.4). There may well be an undercurrent of irony in what has been called "the monotonous account of intrigues and counter-intrigues" in Book 5.[46]

The review of Thucydides' uses of tyche in his own voice shows that thrice he finds tyche—in the places where the phrase kata tychen appears—producing results which could not have been foreseen with any great certainty. Furthermore, in each of these three places, tyche produces a favorable result. In three other places, tyche refers to a concrete situation. Two of these situations (Demosthenes' before invading Aetolia and the Athenians' in the battle in the harbor at Pylos) are favorable to the subjects from whose point of view the situation is stated. Thus in four of seven places tyche wears a benign aspect, contrary to what one might have assumed would be true of Thucydides' own use of tyche.

The most significant uses of tyche by Thucydides in his own voice are in the phrase kata tychen with reference to the Mytilene debate and the Pylos episode. In both these places tyche has the negative sense that one would expect of an historian whose method is devoted to distinguishing the reasonable from the casual. In these two places tyche supervenes, with kindly effect either upon a decision made and then changed but changed, it might have been, too late, or upon a decision not yet finally made.

3. *Uses of tyche by speakers in the* History

Of a total of forty occurrences of tyche in the *History*, twenty-eight are in speeches. No single speaker's views

46. C. E. Graves, *The Fifth Book of Thucydides* (London and New York, 1891), p. 154.

can be identified with Thucydides', but Thucydides reveals his own view of tyche through the distribution of this word among the various speakers, the effect of events upon the views of tyche given by Thucydides to various speakers, and, finally, corroborative repetitions of one speaker's views by another speaker. The distribution of tyche among the speakers may be represented schematically as follows:

Rationalistic or disparaging view of tyche	Diffident, religious, or respectful view of tyche
(a) 1.140.1, 144.1 Pericles' first speech 2.42.4 Funeral Oration 2.62.5 Pericles' last speech	(a) 1.69.5 Corinthians at the allies' conference at Sparta 1.78.2 Reply of the Athenians 1.84.3 Archidamus
	(b) 2.87.2–3(*bis*) Peloponnesian commanders before second battle in Gulf of Corinth
(c) 3.45.5–6 (*bis*) Diodotus	(d) 4.18.3–5 (*ter*) Spartan envoys in Athens after Pylos
	(e) 4.64.1 Hermocrates at conference of Sicilian states at Gela 6.78.3 Hermocrates to the assembly at Camarina
	(f) 4.86.6 Brasidas to the citizens of Acanthus
(g) 5.111.4, 113 Athenians to Melians	(g) 5.102, 104 (*bis*), 112.2 the Melians

(h) 6.11.5 Nicias to Athenian assembly	(h) (5.16.1 Thucydides' analysis of Nicias' motives for seeking peace [not a speech])
	6.23.5 Nicias to Athenian assembly
	7.61.3 Nicias to the army before the last battle in the harbor at Syracuse
	(i) 7.67.4 Gylippus to the allies before the last battle in the harbor
	7.68.1 Gylippus (in the same speech)

This schematization corroborates the position of the present study that, in general, Athenians take a rationalistic view of tyche, and others, especially Spartans, are more diffident.

(a) Pericles' view of tyche is diametrically opposed to Archidamus' (see the first chapter of this study). The Corinthians' statement on tyche is primarily rhetorical. They warn the Spartans that by refusing to declare war now on the Athenians the Spartans run the risk of facing a stronger enemy and thus take greater chances. For present purposes, the most important point brought out by the schematization is that Pericles' views are opposed by those of his (anonymous) fellow-Athenians in Sparta, who remind the Spartans of the *paralogon* of war and that, protracted, war is wont to become a matter of chance. In the event, the war did bring with it the incalculable, first of all the plague, which even Pericles must refer to as *ta daimonia*. There is also the fact of Pericles' death and the dependence of his strategy upon his own persuasiveness and consistency, a strategy which was not maintained by his inferior successors, who ruined the city. One could venture to say that in practice the more diffident view of tyche proves to be the more appropriate one.

(b) The battles in the Gulf of Corinth have been analyzed in the second chapter of this study. The Peloponnesians conceive of their defeat in the first battle in terms of tyche, whereas they were really defeated by techne. In the second battle, chance does in fact intervene (n.b. ἔτυχε 2.91.3, which is emphatic by position), but in such a way that the Athenians convert it to their advantage and the Peloponnesians are again defeated. Only here can one say assuredly that the Peloponnesians' view of tyche is shown wrong by events.

(c) In his analysis of revolutionary psychology, Diodotus speaks with disdain of the passionate and unreasonable commitment to tyche; but ironically Thucydides converts this statement into a judgment on the Athenians themselves, who, having made their first decree passionately, in anger, were able to rescind it only kata tychen.

(d) The Spartan envoys use tyche thrice. Their use corresponds to, and thus seems to find corroboration in, Thucydides' own use of tyche (four times) in connection with the Pylos episode and his observation of the opinion of the Greek world after Mantinea that the Spartans had been defeated on Sphacteria by tyche. This makes a total of eight uses of tyche in connection with Pylos, out of a total of forty uses in the *History*. It would seem that

Thucydides did not admire the Pylos campaign as a piece
of strategy for the reason that it was not strategical: the
original decision was forced kata tychen by the storm. He
did not admire the tactics of the Athenian victory, either,
which began with an impulse on the part of the Athenian
soldiers and owed its success to an accidental fire.[47]
Thucydides' decision to include the anecdote concerning
the Spartan prisoner in Athens is noteworthy in connection with Thucydides' and the Spartan envoys' use of
tyche apropos of Pylos. These uses corroborate the interpretation of the anecdote in terms of the tyche-gnome
antithesis.

Finally, it should be noticed that the Spartan envoys'
warning to the Athenians concerning tyche (4.18.5) is
corroborated by Thucydides' notice of the fulfillment of
the warning (5.75.3; cf. 4.55.3). Unlike the historian, the
Athenians did not realize that they had good luck to
thank for their success.

(e) Hermocrates believes that gnome is subordinate to
tyche. Somewhat in the manner of the Spartan envoys in
Athens after Pylos, he argues from tyche for reasonable
concessions in his speech before the envoys of the Sicilian
states at Gela (4.64.1):

Καὶ ἐγὼ μέν, ἄπερ καὶ ἀρχόμενος εἶπον, πόλιν τε μεγίστην
παρεχόμενος καὶ ἐπιὼν τῳ μᾶλλον ἢ ἀμυνούμενος ἀξιῶ προιδόμενος
αὐτῶν ξυγχωρεῖν, καὶ μὴ τοὺς ἐναντίους οὕτω κακῶς δρᾶν ὥστε αὐτὸς
τὰ πλείω βλάπτεσθαι, μηδὲ μωρίᾳ φιλονικῶν ἡγεῖσθαι τῆς τε οἰκείας
γνώμης ὁμοίως αὐτοκράτωρ εἶναι καὶ ἧς οὐκ ἄρχω τύχης, ἀλλ' ὅσον
εἰκὸς ἡσσᾶσθαι.

47. Contempt for Cleon may be at work here. Plut. (*Mor.* 856B) says
that it is a sign of malignity in an historian when he describes a deed as
done μὴ φρονίμως ἀλλ' εὐτυχῶς.

And I, as I said at the beginning, though I represent the largest city and am one to attack someone else more than defend myself, foreseeing these [dangers], think that I should make concessions and not so harm my enemies that I myself am hurt more, nor, in foolish ambition, believe that I am complete master equally of my own mind and of chance, which I do not rule, but yield to a reasonable degree.

He uses the same argument and similar terms to the Camarinaeans in attempting to persuade them to abide by their alliance with Syracuse (6.78.3):

οὐ γὰρ οἷον τε ἅμα τῆς τε ἐπιθυμίας καὶ τῆς τύχης τὸν αὐτὸν ὁμοίως ταμίαν γενέσθαι· καὶ εἰ γνώμῃ ἁμάρτοι . . .

The same man cannot be controller equally of his desire and of chance. If his policy should err . . .

Thucydides apparently wanted to characterize the shrewd leader of democratic Syracuse, who was so Athenian in other ways (e.g., 7.21), as the opposite of "the first man" (2.65.10) of democratic Athens in the matter of tyche and gnome. Hermocrates is moderate in the traditional, pious way in recognizing and stressing essential limitations to human competence. We have seen how the figure of Nicias suggests an interpretation of the Sicilian disaster in terms of tyche. The figure of Hermocrates also serves to keep present in the mind of the reader the antithesis in which Pericles and Archidamus conceived of the war and to suggest the victory (from the actors' point of view) of the traditionally moderate understanding of tyche.

(f) The characteristic Spartan understanding of tyche shown in Brasidas' speech to the citizens of Acanthus has been discussed in Chapter I, section D.

(g) It has often been noticed that Thucydides jux-
taposes the Melian dialogue and the narrative of the
Sicilian expedition and that if we had the *History* in its
finished state the Melian dialogue would stand in the
center of the work. The arguments on both sides in the
Melian dialogue are tested, as it were, in action, and
the Melians' belief in tyche is in a way vindicated by the
Athenians' misfortunes, even if what the Melians believed did not hold good for themselves. The Athenians
who speak to the Melians recall Pericles in their disdain
of tyche, when they speak of "disgrace more disgraceful
since from foolishness (*anoia*) not from chance (tyche)."
In the same way that reason ought to be able to control
tyche, as in the thought of the prooemium to the first
speech of Pericles, so want of reason can inflict a greater
disgrace than tyche can. In the Melian dialogue the mod-
ernity of the Athenians as opposed to the conservatism of
the Melians, the kinsmen of the Spartans, emerges in the
conflicting views of tyche.[48] The Athenians see mere
chance, which they connect with hope, as Pericles and
Diodotus did. The Melians believe that tyche is an expression of the gods' will and that the gods are just: thus
the Melians' reliance on tyche.[49] The Melians are the only
ones in the *History* who speak of τύχη ἐκ τοῦ θείου (cf. Hom.
Il. 20.434–5). One cannot argue that the fact of the Athenian disaster and the interpretation of the disaster in
terms of tyche by Nicias and Gylippus (in such a way as to
recall the Melians' position) confirm the Melians' belief in

48. F. M. Wasserman, "The Melian Dialogue," *TAPA* 78 (1947), 29.
49. In Euripides *Bellerophon* (fr. 286N³), that small god-fearing
cities are defeated by larger, wicked ones is an example to show that
there are no gods.

a divine tyche, but Thucydides clearly wished to develop an interpretation of the Sicilian expedition by the actors in terms of tyche in the sense of chance. Chance in Thucydides is that which is contrary to calculation, and great indeed was the *paralogos* experienced by the Athenians (7.55). Thucydides observes the fact that Gylippus reached the Heights just a moment before the Athenians finished their walling operations: παρὰ τοσοῦτον μέν Συράκουσαι ἦλθον κινδύνου (7.2). As Churchill said, "Thus on small agate points do the balances of the world turn." There is also the fact that Syracuse is the Athenians' Pylos (7.71.7),[50] and an interpretation of Pylos in terms of tyche is inescapable (see sec. B.3.d above).

(h) Further evidence of the complexity of the character of Nicias is that his statements concerning tyche are both Lacedaemonian in spirit and, in one case, Athenian. In counseling the Athenians against undertaking the Sicilian expedition, he warns them not to be aroused by the misfortunes of their enemies but "to get the better of them *in planning* (τὰς διανοίας)." But it would have to be conceded that Nicias' statement, despite its apparent affinities with the Periclean concept of the tyche-gnome antithesis, serves, like Artabanus' strictures on good planning (see Chap. I, sec. A), the negative purpose of dissuasion and is really an expression of his diffidence before tyche. Nicias' other statements concerning tyche have already been discussed in the preceding chapter, where it was argued *inter alia* that the figure of Nicias contributed to an interpretation of the Sicilian disaster in terms of tyche.

50. Cf. Finley, *Three Essays*, pp. 146–147.

(i) The words of Gylippus seem to sum up the theme of tyche in the Sicilian episode. Nicias had said ὅτι ἐλάχιστα τῇ τύχῃ παραδοὺς ἐμαυτὸν βούλομαι ἐκπλεῖν, παρασκευῇ δὲ . . . (6.23.5). But before the last battle in the harbor at Syracuse, Gylippus observes that the Athenians must now run their risks οὐ παρασκευῆς πίστει μᾶλλον ἢ τύχης (7.67.4). Gylippus' τύχην ἀνδρῶν ἑαυτὴν παραδεδωκυῖαν (7.68.1) sums up the matter.

This review of the uses of tyche by various speakers in the *History* shows that in only one instance, the naval conflict in the Gulf of Corinth (b), does the Lacedaemonian concept of tyche prove incorrect. For the most part, the Athenians' rationalism and pride meet practical defeat. Diodotus even seems to damn the Athenians out of his own mouth, in his strictures on tyche. The contrast between Hermocrates' and Pericles' concepts of the tyche-gnome antithesis appears to be intentional and to provide terms in which to understand Hermocrates' success and the Athenian defeat. Furthermore, there is a chain of responsions which begins with Thucydides' analysis in terms of tyche of Nicias' desire for peace (5.16.1) to Nicias' almost exact repetition of the same point in a speech to the Athenian assembly (6.23.5), to Nicias' tacit recognition of the defeat of his principle (7.61.3), to Gylippus' corroboration of this recognition (7.67.4). Nicias' recognition that in the final battle in the harbor at Syracuse the Athenians' hopes rest with tyche also corresponds to the position of the Melians (5.102), a position which the Athenians had scorned. Thucydides shows how the actors in the *History* understand events in terms of tyche; whether Thucydides himself agreed is another question.

4. *Thucydides' use of* τυγχάνω

There are several quite clearly definable categories of Thucydides' use of τυγχάνω, and in general use of this verb supports the interpretation of his method and of his use of tyche already proposed. One of these categories, ambassadorial τυγχάνω, has already been mentioned. LSJ give as the first meaning of this verb: "happen to be at a place." This meaning clearly applies to ambassadors, whose presence or absence cannot always be foreseen by others concerned. Thus the ambassadorial τυγχάνω can be subsumed under a broader category, that of coincidence, in which τυγχάνω is joined with the participle of another verb. The categories of τυγχάνω that interest us here are (a) coincidence; (b) τυγχάνω of ships; (c) τυγχάνω with the genitive of attaining some end not through calculation, and so on (LSJ B.I.1), but through luck (LSJ B.II.2. N.b. that LSJ implicitly distinguish between these two meanings); (d) τυγχάνω in the vicinity of πίπτω and compounds; (e) randomness.

(a) τυγχάνω of coincidence is by far the most common use of this verb in Thucydides. The verb picks out of all the possibilities the one which actually happened in concurrence with something else (2.49.1):

τὸ μὲν γὰρ ἔτος, ὡς ὡμολογεῖτο, ἐκ πάντων μάλιστα δὴ ἐκεῖνο ἄνοσον ἐς τὰς ἄλλας ἀσθενείας ἐτύγχανεν ὄν.

Of all years that one, it was agreed, happened to be freest of other illnesses.

This idiom may also express a coincidence that might have occurred but did not in fact occur (1.136.3, 4.13.4).

It is a truism that τυγχάνω with a participle has often a neutral sense and should not be translated. What is not so well known is that τυγχάνω with the participle often means "to happen *by chance* to . . . ." For this sense, see Aristotle, *Phys.* 196a22 (ὅπως ἂν τύχῃ) and context. At crucial points in the action a coincidence may have the force of sheer, irrational chance, and in such places the verb could almost be replaced by the stronger κατὰ τύχην.[51] One of these places is the arrival of Gylippus on the Heights at Syracuse just in time to prevent the Athenians from walling off the city.[52] Two other such places are the eclipse of the moon which caused the fatal delay (7.50.4) and the storm which so dispirited the retreating Athenian army (7.79.3). Probably Thucydides does not use the phrase κατὰ τύχην of these events because he observes that they could have been expected because of the time of the year. But the absence of a wind to prevent the second trireme and the wind which forced the Athenian fleet in at Pylos could in no way have been expected, and thus the phrase κατὰ τύχην applies in these places.

In one place, in which Thucydides states a coincidence from the point of view of Brasidas, there seems to be θεία τύχη lurking in τυγχάνω. Thucydides says that Brasidas believed the capture of Lekythos to have occurred "in other than mortal fashion," since there was a shrine of

---

51. That τυγχάνειν with the participle can have this force is shown clearly by Pl. *Phaedr.* 58a6–7: τύχη τις αὐτῷ . . . συνέβη. ἔτυχεν γὰρ . . . Cf. Thuc. 4.73.3, where τύχη and τυγχάνω occur in the same context.

52. Cf. J. R. Wheeler, "The Participial Construction with τυγχάνειν and κυρεῖν," *HSCP* 2 (1891), 156.

Athena there and Brasidas had happened (ἔτυχε) to announce a reward to the first man on the wall (4.116.2).

(b) The very common use of τυγχάνω of ships in Thucydides (1.57.6; 104.2, 116.1(*bis*); 2.31.1, 93.2; 3.3.4, 33.1, 105.3; 4.9.1, 104.5; 8.61.2, 79.2, 91.2) perhaps should be understood as a subcategory of coincidence.[53] The conditions of sailing were such that one could not be sure where a ship or a fleet would appear at a certain time, and thus the appearance would always be to some degree a coincidence.

(c) Therefore, to catch a ship in a certain place is a matter of coincidence, and τυγχάνω with the genitive may connote good luck, as when Themistocles is described as ὁλκάδος τυχών (1.137.2), with which can be compared the similar ὁλκάγος . . . ἐπιτυχών (3.3.4; cf. 3.42.5). Lamberton observes that "ἐπιτυχεῖν usually takes the dat. and the sense is *to meet* or *to catch* . . . ; but where the notion of good luck appears we find the gen., cp. Xen. *Oec.* 12.20 . . . , Thuc. 7.25.2."[54]

(d) From the point of view of most Greek literature prior to Thucydides tyche is objective and is connected with the divine. Tyche comes from outside and is what befalls one. Thus Plato, who to some extent preserves the

53. Meillet, *Traité*, p. 614, cites *Od.* 14.334 (τύχησε γὰρ ἐρχομένη ναῦς) as an example of complete degradation of the sense of the main verb. Thucydides' use of naval τυγχάνω makes one suspicious of Meillet's claim.

54. W. A. Lamberton, *Thucydides: Books II and III* (New York, 1905), p. 222. When Pindar uses τυγχάνειν of his own poetic activity—of hoping "to hit the mark" (e.g., *N.* 6.26ff.)—he places himself along with the laudandus in the world of tyche. See Hans Strohm, *Tyche: zur Schicksalsauffassung bei Pindar und den frühgriechischen Dichtern* (Stuttgart, 1944), p. 39.

earlier religious view,[55] can speak of τύχαι . . . καὶ ξυμφοραὶ παντοῖαι πίπτουσαι (*Laws* 709a2; cf. 747c7, 873c6; *Epist.* VII 324c1). Or the matter could be stated from the opposite point of view: οὗτοι μέν νυν τοιαύτῃσι περιέπιπτον τύχῃσι (Hdt. 6.16.2). Considering this relation of the notion of falling and tyche, it is not surprising that συμπίπτω can be used by itself to express coincidence (Hdt. 5.36; Thuc. 4.68.3).

This same poetic and religious association of tyche and falling (cf. Empedocles B 104 and 59, where συγκυρεῖν = τυγχάνειν: Simpl. *Phys.* 327; cf. Soph. *OC* 1404; Hdt. 8.87.3) leaves a trace in Thucydides. He says of the slaughter at Mykalessus: ξυμφορὰ . . . ἐπέπεσεν (7.29; cf. 5.14). But for the most part Thucydides uses πίπτω and its compounds with human subjects in the vicinity of τυγχάνω with the participle, often expressing something undesirable coincident upon the "falling" (1.106.1; 2.4.5, 25.2; 3.30.2, 98.1; 4.12.2; 7.29 [three times of persons], 70.4; 8.41.2). In fact there is only one place in which a compound of πίπτω in the vicinity of τυγχάνω has a nonhuman subject. In 2.91.3, in describing the second battle in the Gulf of Corinth, Thucydides observes of the effect upon the Peloponnesians of the unexpected turn of events: γενομένου τούτου ἀπροσδοκήτου τε καὶ παρὰ λόγον φόβος ἐμπίπτει. One could say that fear is the subjective correlative of the objective fact which was expressed by τυγχάνω (ἔτυχε δὲ ὁλκὰς ὁρμοῦσα 2.91.3).

This analysis of a chance or coincidental event in terms

55. E. G. Berry, *The History and Development of the Concept of* θεία μοῖρα *and* θεία τύχη *Down to and Including Plato* (Chicago, 1940), pp. 49ff.

of its subjective effect is in keeping with the implicit
Periclean doctrine of tyche, according to which the
statesman is seriously affected by tyche only in its effect
upon the gnomai of the people, which he must know how
to control. One recalls that in Diodotus' analysis of revolutionary psychology, tyche was connected with the passions. But Thucydides' and Pericles' views are not really
the same in this matter. Pericles believed that the control,
perhaps even the self-control, of the people under the
democracy was possible, and, in his own time, he was
proven right. Thucydides, however, who outlived Pericles, saw the passional, tychistic nature of political life
reassert itself in the course of the war. The Periclean
principle of gnome was to endure only in Thucydides'
own work.

(e) It was observed in the discussion of Thucydides'
methodological statements that τυγχάνω expressed the
random or contingent from which Thucydides intended
to separate the *idea* (especially 2.51.1, 5.20.2). This use of
τυγχάνω to express mere randomness has several parallels in Thucydides (1.142.9; 3.43.5; 4.25.2, 26.6, 93.5;
5.64.4). One of these places calls for attention. Diodotus
rebukes the Athenians with these words (3.43.5):

νῦν δὲ πρὸς ὀργὴν ἥντιν' ἂν τύχητε ἔστιν ὅτε σφαλέντες τὴν τοῦ
πείσαντος μίαν γνώμην ξημιοῦτε.

Gomme well translated the first words: "according to
your feelings at the moment."[56] This is precisely the
reduction of chance or the random to the subjective
which was the basis of Pericles' thought.

56. Gomme, II, 316.

5. δυστυχία, δυστυχής, εὐτυχία, εὐτυχής, ξυντυχία, *compounds of* τυγχάνω

In general, Thucydides' use of these words (δυστυχία, κτλ.) is just what the discussions of τύχη and of τυγχάνω would lead one to expect. Of twenty-eight occurrences of εὐτυχία, εὐτυχής, and εὐτυγχάνω, for example, nineteen are in speeches and most of the others describe or analyze states of mind.[57] Again, compounds of τυγχάνω are used eleven times of ships or of sailing (cf. sec. B.4.b above).[58] δυστυχία and the rest will be discussed, however, not with a view to repeating what the discussion of τύχη and of τυγχάνω has already shown or suggested but in order to draw out important implications and reach certain conclusions.

Thucydides' understanding of tyche as originating in the passions or as decisive mainly in its effect on the passions is revealed quite clearly in his accounts of the assassination of Hipparchus by Harmodius and Aristogeiton. Thucydides mentions this event first in 1.20.2 to illustrate how uncritically men receive reports of the past, even of their own city's past. Hippias, not Hipparchus, was tyrant. The assassins, having given up hope of killing Hippias, "chanced upon" Hipparchus (περιτυχόντες 1.20.2) and killed him instead. In narrating the event in much greater detail in 6.54–59, Thucydides uses

57. εὐτυχία in speeches: 1.120.3, 4, 2.44.2, 4.17.4, 7.77.2; εὐτυχής in speeches: 2.44.1, 4, 6.17.1; εὐτυγχάνω in speeches: 2.44.4, 60.3, 61.1, 3.39.4, 4.17.4, 18.4, 62.4, 6.23.3, 7.63.4, 68.3, 77.3.

58. ἐντυγχάνω: 5.5.1, 2; ἐπιτυγχάνω: 3.3.5, 7.25.2, 8.14.1, 34.1; περιτυγχάνω: 3.33.3, 4.120.2, 8.23.4, 39.3, 101.1. παρατυγχάνω is used of ambassadors (2.67.2; cf. the discussion of the phrase *kata tychen* in 5.37.3, sec. B.2 above).

the same verb (6.57.3).[59] Indeed, at the beginning of this second narrative Thucydides refers to the event as a whole as having come about δι' ἐρωτικὴν ξυντυχίαν (through the mishap of a love affair) (6.54.1). In conclusion he uses the phrase τοῦ παθοῦς τῇ δυστυχίᾳ (by the mischance of the passion) (6.55.4). The mischance consists in the passion. Elsewhere Thucydides says δι' ἐρωτικὴν λύπην (through a lover's wound) (6.59.1) and δι' ὀργῆς . . . ἐρωτικῆς (with a lover's fury) (6.57.3). Thus the "enterprise" (τόλμημα 6.54.1) of Harmodius and Aristogeiton is in reality "an unthinking act" (ἀλόγιστος τόλμα 6.59.1).

Thucydides mentions this chance event first in connection with his own carefulness as an investigator of history and second in connection with the effect of the same event, misremembered in popular history, on the course of the war. The Athenians' misrecollection determined the manner of their investigation of the mutilation of the herms and of the profanation of the mysteries. With regard to the latter, the Athenians were led to recall Alcibiades, who consequently defected to the Spartans. Thus the Athenians lost their best hope[60] and unwittingly prepared the Sicilian disaster. A chance event, through misrecollection, preserves its force and, over a century later, contributes to an outcome that Thucydides calls δυστυχέστατον (most disastrous) (7.87.5). If the Athenians had been more careful historians, they might have fared better. Here is an argument both for the power of tyche in history and for Thucydidean his-

59. περιέτυχον. προσπεσόντες occurs in the immediate context: sec. B.4.d above.
60. 6.15.4. See Chap. II, n. 71.

Chance and Intelligence in Thucydides

toriography, which rests on principles opposed to tyche. Examination of δυστυχία κτλ. shows again the habit of mind which discriminates between the orderly and its opposite. Introducing the catalogue of Athenian allies that fought in Sicily (7.57.1), Thucydides says that they did not join the campaign with just cause (κατὰ δίκην) or according to kinship with one another, but as each nation, either through self-interest or necessity, stood in relation to the event (ξυντυχίας).[61] In other words, the alliances that form the Athenian army have a coincidental character, which appears in contrast to what might have been expected, the cause of justice or kinship. The Sicilian expedition as a whole is called a ξυντυχία, a coincidence, a conjuncture of each individual nation's position with the requirements of the Athenian campaign.[62]

Another example of ξυντυχία in this sense indicates Thucydides' methodical discrimination between a normal order and an actual, disruptive contingency. Thucydides says of the Athenian defeat at Amphipolis, "On the Athenian side, there fell about six hundred, on the side of the enemy, only seven, since the fighting did not take place in regular battle order (ἐκ παρατάξεως) but developed out of that particular conjuncture and with

61. Concerning the text, see Dover, in Gomme, IV, 436. The ὡς ἕκαστος idiom occurs in the same context with ξυντυχία (see sec. A.3 above), as in 3.45.4 (Diodotus). This idiom occurs in the same context with προστυγχάνω in 1.97.1. For the relation of necessity and ξυντυχία, see 7.70.6 (the great battle in the harbor at Syracuse).

62. The sense of coincidence or conjuncture in ξυντυχία is shown in the phrase ἅμα τοῦ ἔργου τῇ ξυντυχίᾳ (3.112.7), used of the Athenian ships that come sailing along just as the Ampraciots are being driven into the sea by Demosthenes, i.e. "just at the same time as this action." Classen-Steup, *Thukydides,* III, 224, comment: "Th. hätte auch einfach ἅμα τῷ ἔργῳ sagen können."

196

the Athenians already in panic (ἀπὸ . . . τοιαύτης ξυντυχίας καὶ προεκφοβήσεως)" (5.11.2). The particular conjuncture is the unexpected attack from both sides on the Athenian column withdrawing to Eion. Thucydides contrasts this situation with "regular battle order." Furthermore, he couples in one phrase the emotional concomitant of this situation, the Athenians' panic, with the term (ξυντυχία) that describes the situation. The effect of situation upon mental state is crucial, since it is thus that chance has its power.

The Athenian general at Amphipolis was Cleon. His decision to withdraw followed from his general strategy, to which Thucydides refers in an almost satirical chapter as τῷ τρόπῳ ᾧπερ καὶ ἐς τὴν Πύλον εὐτυχήσας ἐπίστευσέ τι φρονεῖν (in the same way in which he had been lucky at Pylos and thus believed in his wisdom) (5.7.3).[63] From Thucydides' point of view, Cleon was only lucky (εὐτυχήσας) at Pylos. This passage corroborates the previous discussion of Thucydidean uses of τύχη apropos of Pylos (sec. B.2 above). In the same way that the Athenians later do themselves harm through their misrecollection of Athenian history, so here Cleon brings about his own death and the destruction of an Athenian army through his misunderstanding of his success at Pylos. In both cases, the passions are the element in which chance works itself out, for better and worse, from beginning to end.

But these events, while contrary to logos (cf. ἀλόγιστος τόλμα 6.59.1), find their place in Thucydides' logos. In

63. It is not clear exactly what Thucydides understood Cleon's strategy to be: see Gomme, III, 639.

fact, it is only here that they appear as what they are. The exceptions, no matter how numerous or striking, prove the rule. Archidamus' apothegm, "the chances that befall us cannot be analyzed in words" (1.84.4; cf. Chap. II. sec. B), is shown to be false. Events can be analyzed, and it is the project of the *History* to analyze them. The main difference between Thucydides and Archidamus would seem to be that Thucydides does not regard chance events as "befalling" men, as coming from outside, but as originating in men's passions. These passions, further-more, are not simply random, but work themselves out in an orderly way.[64] Though any given event may defy reason from the point of view of both the historian and those who participated in the event, this event will be found to belong to a pattern, and the pattern is demon-strable. Though it may be true of individual battles that even in broad daylight the individual participant can hardly understand what is happening right in front of him,[65] the war as a whole yields clarity.

The pattern is not merely analytical and after the fact but is experienced, even if only partially, without com-plete comprehension, by the actors in the *History*. Thus Thucydides can let the actors speak for themselves and can adopt their terms and principles for his own analysis. For example, the Corinthians speak of the danger of elation inspired by good luck in war (1.120.3, 4). Cleon (3.39.4) and of course the Spartans (4.17.4) enunciate the

64. See Finley, *Thucydides*, 46–60, 98–100.

65. 7.44.1, quoted in sec. A.3 above. Compounds of τυγχάνω often occur in accounts of battles, raids, and other violence. ξυντυγχάνω: 7.70.6; ἐντυγχάνω: 4.40.2, 127.2, 7.29.4 (Mycalessus), 43.5, 44.5; παρατυγχάνω: 3.82.7 (stasis); περιτυγχάνω: 5.59.1, 66.1, 94.2; ἐπιτυγχάνω: 3.75.4.

same principle. Thucydides himself in describing the Athenian state of mind in the year 424 says: "In their present prosperity (τῇ . . . παρούσῃ εὐτυχίᾳ) the Athenians expected to be opposed in nothing, but rather to achieve both possible and impossible goals with great or equally with deficient preparation. The cause of this attitude was the unexpected success of most of their enterprises, which was a support for their hopes" (4.65.4).[66] Here Thucydides takes over a principle that is nearly proverbial in the speeches just cited, and he uses the same main term, εὐτυχία, that the others use.[67] Just as the Sicilian expedition and its disastrous end were consistently interpreted in terms of τύχη by various speakers, so also the words εὐτυχία, εὐτυχής, δυστυχία, and δυστυχής, as they are used especially by the Spartans and Nicias and occasionally by Thucydides himself, form a consistent interpretation of that event.[68] In the case of these latter words Thucydides' own usage of them would seem to corroborate the speakers' views of events. In the same way, Thucydides' use of ξυντυχία would seem to corroborate Diodotus' (cf. 7.57.1 with 3.45.4). And when Thucydides speaks of δυστυχία in his final estimate of Nicias (7.86.5), he seems implicitly to corroborate Nicias' view that human life is subject to tyche.[69]

But as for Nicias, it has already been suggested that the

66. See Gomme, III, 525–526, for a valuable discussion of this passage.

67. His estimate of the Athenian mood at this point in the war is repeated in 5.14.1, where he again uses the phrase τῇ παρούσῃ εὐτυχίᾳ.

68. For the speakers' interpretation of the Sicilian expedition and its disastrous end, see the conclusion of sec. B.3 above.

69. For Nicias' view of tyche, see especially 6.23.3, quoted in Chap. 2, sec. D.1.

word δυστυχία states the matter from Nicias', not Thucydides', point of view.[70] The word has, in fact, a double meaning, an ambiguity that arises from Thucydides' pervasive agreement with and detachment from the actors' points of view. First, the death of Nicias is the bad luck, the mischance that disrupts the prosperity that he had hoped to preserve to the end. Second, in the context of Thucydides' purview of the Sicilian expedition and its defeat, the mischance of Nicias' death is simply a fact, a reversal that can be explained. This reversal is not altogether unpredictable and does not "befall" Nicias from some superhuman realm, as the pious Nicias doubtless believed. Rather it belongs to a discernible human order of success and failure and in this order is simply a fact.

Even in the speeches, Thucydides brings it about that the words under discussion are ambiguous. A good example of Nicias' use of the participle of εὐτυγχάνω in his hortatory speech to the Athenian and allied troops before the battle in the harbor at Syracuse (7.63.4): "Show that . . . your knowledge (ἐπιστήμη) is stronger than the other's lucky (εὐτυχούσης) strength." The success of the Syracusans up to this point is attributed by Nicias to luck. In the same way, in his last words in the *History*, when the situation is even more desperate, he says (7.77.3): "The enemy has had enough good luck (ηὐτύχηται), and if some god felt enmity against our campaign, we have now been sufficiently punished." From this sentence, and from 7.77.1–2, which has already been discussed (Chap. 2, sec. D.3), it is clear that Nicias regards the fortunes of

70. See Chap. II, sec. D.4, toward the end.

war as god-sent. Thus in 7.63.4 Nicias contrasts the sure, undiminished naval skill (ἐπιστήμη) of the Athenians and their allies with the temporary grace that the enemy has enjoyed. But in the context of all of Nicias' previous statements concerning tyche and in the context of his strategic mistakes, especially the biggest mistake, which was caused by pious superstition (7.50.4), his use of εὐτυχούσης has quite another sense. It means the factual success of the Syracusans, which is more than lucky. The Athenian naval skill, furthermore, has, as the reader has already been told, no more scope (7.62.2). Thucydides clearly does not share Nicias' point of view.

In one of the speeches of Alcibiades, Thucydides has even contrived something akin to "tragic irony." Alcibiades says (6.17.1): ὁ Νικίας εὐτυχὴς δοκεῖ εἶναι. In the immediate context, this statement can only mean: "Nicias has the reputation of being prosperous." Alcibiades is trying to persuade the Athenians to undertake the expedition against Sicily and to capitalize on this prosperity or luckiness of Nicias. But in the wider context of the reader's knowledge of the defeat of the expedition and the death of Nicias, the ambiguous verb that Alcibiades uses (δοκεῖ) gives his statement quite a different implication: "Nicias seems to be prosperous [but in fact is not, or will not be in the future]."

So both in speeches and in his own usage of such words as εὐτυχία and δυστυχία, Thucydides maintains a strict ambiguity. These words mean one thing from the speaker's or actor's point of view and another from Thucydides'. The only exceptions to this rule are Pericles, for whom gnome is the norm and who is thus in fundamental accord with Thucydides' own practice in writing the *History*, and those speakers who make general statements concerning the effect of good or bad luck on the passions. To the latter group belong the Corinthians (1.120.3, 4), Diodotus (3.45.4), Cleon (3.39.4), and the Spartans (4.17.4). But none of these maintains gnome or logos as a superior principle. In fact the Spartans interpret their failures in the Archidamian war as bad luck incurred through their having broken treaties with the Athenians (7.18.2; cf. 4.55.3). Thus, of all speakers and actors in the *History*, it is really only Pericles whose views resemble Thucydides' own. Pericles' statement that "all things are born to be diminished" (2.64.3) is perhaps the statesman's version of the cycle of greatness and decline which the historian says will be repeated (1.22.4). Paradoxically, it is the statesman who trusts to gnome as against tyche who accepts such an alternation in human affairs, while an Archidamus or a Nicias, with his deference to tyche, hopes to preserve prosperity to the end.

Yet the detachment of Thucydides from the events that he narrates is perhaps not so great as Pericles' superiority to other Athenians of his era. Thucydides lets the speakers give an account of things, an account which he at least partly corroborates, in terms of tyche. The ultimate irony is not Thucydides' irony with respect to this or that view, but that all the winding ways of tyche follow a single cyclical way, and this single way can be traced more or less exactly in a historical work (1.22.4). The truth of this work is not simply an intellectual construction but is the clarity of the events themselves, which is at least partly accessible to the actors and speakers concerned. For this reason, Thucydides shares with them certain important analytical and descriptive terms.

In their experience of what they call chance or good luck
or bad luck, they partially experience the order that is
more fully exposed in the *History* as a whole. That the
actors do not experience the truth more fully, cannot
make better predictions, act more prudently, is not due
so much to intellectual or perspectival limitations as to
the human situation that is implied in the cyclical concept
of human life.

In *Problemata* 17.3 (916a18–39) Aristotle, discussing
the question of the meaning of "earlier" and "later,"
shows that the saying that mortal things are a cycle
(916a28: cf. *Phys.* 223b24–26; Hdt. 1.207.2) is reasonable
on the hypothesis that there is no fixed series of events
extending back from the present but rather a beginning,
middle, and end. On this hypothesis, to grow old is to
reach the end and turn back toward the beginning, and
what perishes will come again, at least in some general
sense. In illustration of this argument Aristotle quotes
the clever saying of Alcmaeon that "men perish because
they cannot connect the beginning to the end"
(916a34–35 = D.-K. B2). Human affairs are a cycle, but
humans may not live through a whole cycle, and, if they
do, their perception of the cycle comes after the fact.
Human ignorance is thus an objective condition. Humans are doomed to partial knowledge.

In the *History* the actors and speakers experience only
some one arc of the cycle, whereas experience reflected
in the *History* is a whole cycle (cf. 5.26.5 ἐπεβίων . . . διὰ
παντὸς αὐτοῦ). Thucydides' truth is the same as the truth
of the actors and speakers, however, in that it is essentially limited to the revelations that come in and only in
historical experience. Just as in Pericles' theory, techne

comes from ἐμπειρία (experience) and μελέτη (practice), so in the *History* truth comes from the events themselves, and Thucydides refrains from general lessons. He did not write the technical treatise that must be expected if interpretations of Thucydides as political scientist or the like are true. If what had happened was to happen again, then it was enough for Thucydides to state exactly what had happened. Indeed the requirement of ἀκρίβεια (factual exactness) follows from the presupposition of recurrence.

The truth of the events as the truth of the *History* is the basis for Thucydides' agreement and disagreement with the views of the speakers and actors, the basis for the ambiguity already discussed. It is thus in the nature of Thucydidean narrative to confer a certain validity on particular points of view even as these are transcended in the forward movement of the work. If tyche is, as in Pericles' view, "whatever turns out contrary to logos" (1.140.1), then one could even say that it is Thucydides' logos itself that constitutes and defines the casualness of events which the participants attribute to chance for reasons of their own. The Thucydidean logos, gathering events into a clarity, moves past the separate views of the moment toward a future that will be the same as the past. The *History* itself is a complete cycle and, as such, will be "a possession forever." Thucydides asserts the immortality of his work in connection with the recurrence of the events described (1.22.4).

Conclusion

The gnome- and techne-tyche antitheses have different implications for historiography and for history. The
historian, with his hindsight, can separate the merely
contingent elements from the main trends of a certain
period of history. A great statesman may perceive the
main trends and may base his plans on his perception,
but the unknown future sets limits to the efficacy of his
foresight. The difference between historiography and
history is illustrated by the difference between the
historian's and the statesman's concept of his work. Pericles, no matter how self-confident in his strategy, sees an
ultimate futility in human affairs: πάντα γὰρ πέφυκε καὶ
ἐλασσοῦσθαι (2.64.3). The compensation for this futility
is immortal fame. Thucydides' work, on the other hand,
is in itself a κτῆμα ἐς αἰεί (1.22.4). It is not subject to the
law of decay that ultimately governs political life.

Still greater is the difference between the historian's
understanding of historical events and that of the persons concerned in these events. Most men are lazy in the
search for truth (1.20.3). In the matter of causality, for

example, Thucydides' scorn of the common man's understanding, which attributed such importance to the Megarean decree,[1] is implicit. In his correction of the common opinion of the tyrants and of the tyrannicides, it is explicit (6.54). No doubt it is pervasive, in ways no longer easily sensed. The numbering of the years of the war in accordance with the annalistic method betrays a perspective quite different from that of the citizen, for whom each year had a name, not a number.

The quest for *to saphes* carries Thucydides beyond the common understanding, even if he narrates events from the actors' point of view, and gives the *History* a character different from Herodotus' memorial to the glorious deeds of Greeks and barbarians. Unlike Herodotus, Thucydides does not put his work at the service of memory but rather puts historical events at the service of analysis and clarification. Thucydides' perception derives from his own investigations (1.22). Traditionally, knowledge of the past, the present, and the future came to men as revelations from the Muses (Hes. *Theog.* 32; cf. M. L. West, *Hesiod: Theogony,* p. 166 on 32). Thucydides, who consciously breaks with the poetic tradition (1.21.1), is rightly seen as a figure of the fifth-century enlightenment. In particular, he expresses the technical spirit of this period: in the strictness of his method, in his confidence in his method, and in the conception of method as eliminating the merely contingent and aiming at the idea, he especially resembles the author of the Hippocratic *De Arte,* who defended "the art" against those who attributed its successes to tyche. One might

1. Cf. de Romilly, *Thucydides,* p. 17 and nn. 1–6.

venture to say that the first of the Hippocratic *Aphorisms* sums up Thucydides' view of the relation of history and historiography: ὁ βίος βραχύς, ἡ δὲ τέχνη μακρή (life is short, art long) (Littré IV, 458).

This technical character of Thucydides' work presupposes or exemplifies a break with the earlier point of view which made chance primary and human competence subordinate to chance: πάντα τύχη καὶ μοῖρα . . . ἀνδρὶ δίδωσι (Archil. 5D; cf. Theog. 129–130; Hdt. 1.32.4). Roughly speaking, the earlier Greeks, from what was essentially a religious point of view,[2] saw mortal affairs in terms of tyche. Thucydides reverses this situation and sees tyche in terms of human affairs, as that which is unexpected or contrary to calculation.[3] τὸ παράλογον τοῦ πολέμου, a notion well known to actors in the *History*, epitomizes Thucydides' own procedure. Through the *logoi* (speeches) of the actors, with their various and often contradictory points of view, he shows what the prospects are, and then, in the narrative, what results from, or in spite of, these logoi.[4] Thucydides makes this comparison of words and deeds both apropos of the war as a whole, especially through the speeches of the Corinthians, Archidamus, and Pericles before the outbreak of the war, and also apropos of many particular situations during the war. Tyche is then the degree by which the outcome differs from the expectation.[5]

No matter what Thucydides considered the role of

2. H. Strohm, *Tyche,* p. 99; A. A. Buriks, περὶ τύχης, p. 118 (résumé in French); Berry, *History and Development,* pp. 34ff.

3. Cf. Herter, *Thukydides,* p. 262.

4. Raymond Aron, *Dimensions de la conscience historique* (Paris, 1961), p. 137.

5. de Romilly, *Histoire et raison,* p. 176.

tyche in history, for historiographical purposes he sys-
tematically excluded tyche as a principle. The religious
Herodotus takes the divine as his principle,[6] and the
divine is the source of chance.[7] Thus Herodotus' own
logos becomes casual, seeking for digressions from beginning to end (4.30.1), with a compelling force of its
own (e.g. 2.3; 4.195.2; 7.152.3, 239.1). Herodotus is to
some degree subject to his logos, whereas in Thucydides,
as the methodological statements clearly show (cf.
3.90.1), a consistent intention has been imposed upon
the narrative.

Although logos has become the function of method in
Thucydides, the actors in history are far from being able
to employ logos in the same fashion. Thucydides narrates events from the point of view of the actors, and in
this way he gives tyche importance. The logoi of the
actors, the speeches, contain statements about tyche
which are proven true. To the actors historical events
must present themselves as a combination of the rational
and the irrational. Though Thucydides scorns the common man's capacity for truth, he does not seem to expect
that history should be as orderly as historiography. Thus
the compassion that he occasionally expresses,[8] and thus
his reservations as regards the usefulness of his work.[9]
Thucydides may have thought that his own understanding of events was possible only in retrospect, though he
says that he foresaw how great the war would be (1.1).

If the historian's truth can never be realized in action,

6. How and Wells, *Commentary*, I, 48–50.

7. Berry, *History and Development*, p. 35.

8. G. Bowersock, "The Personality of Thucydides," *The Antioch Review* 25 (1965), 135–146.

9. Cf. the extravagant claims of Polybius: 9.2.5.

which is doomed to a certain irrationality, then a crucial step has been taken. As Cornford observed, "The death of Pericles and the Peloponnesian war mark the moment when the men of thought and the men of action began to take different paths,"[10] and Thucydides, having been a man of action, will have found in exile the separate path of thought. The repudiation of Pericles' achievement in Plato's *Gorgias* is the consummation of this divergence.[11] Socrates separates techne from empeiria, and puts techne, which now has a logical dimension, on another plane (500e4–501b1; cf. *Phaedr.* 260e, 271a–c). On these grounds, techne is denied Pericles (503b6ff., 515e2ff.; cf. Arist. *EN* 1140b7ff.).

Such conclusions could have been reached only after philosophy had established itself as a separate way of life. The world of Thucydides' *History* and the *History* itself plainly antedate this distinction between the political and the philosophical life,[12] even if Thucydides has taken the crucial step in the direction of the latter. Unlike Socrates, Thucydides admired Pericles and for the very reasons for which Socrates refused to admire him. In the *History*, Pericles more than anyone else is the spokesman of gnome and techne; and the *History* itself bears the stamp

10. F. M. Cornford, *The Unwritten Philosophy and Other Essays* (Cambridge, 1950), p. 54. Cf. Strauss, *The City and Man*, pp. 159–60.

11. On connections between Plato and Thucydides, see Luschnat, *RE* Supp. XII, cols. 1276–84.

12. For this distinction, see Pl. *Gorg.* 500c. W. Jaeger, *Aristotle: Fundamentals of the History of his Development*,[2] trans. Richard Robinson (Oxford, 1950), pp. 426ff., argues that the various anecdotes (preserved mainly by Diogenes Laertius) that imply a deliberate "theoretic life" on the part of some of the pre-Socratic philosophers stem from Plato's school or are formed later on the model of the Platonic ideal of the philosophic life.

of these principles. In the same way that techne is connected with empeiria in Pericles' view, so for Thucydides *to saphes* must be embodied in historical experience, and general laws or rules cannot be stated. Techne has not yet become logical. Furthermore, Pericles is the historian in the *History*. His analysis of the Greek world at the time of the Peloponnesian War echoes Thucydides' own.

But in the career of Pericles himself tyche was to find a place. Night began to fall as soon as the sun had passed its zenith, and already in the Funeral Oration a change from the mood of the first speech is discernible. In the sequence of the speeches of Pericles Thucydides traces a change or a decline from exhortation in the name of gnome or techne (the navy) in the first speech and the speech in *oratio obliqua* to a rather moral exhortation in the two latter speeches, though even in the last Pericles does not abandon gnome but makes it the source of the disdain the Athenians should feel for their enemy (2.62.4). In the first speech and the speech in *oratio obliqua,* before the war has begun, little or nothing of moral exhortation is heard. The Funeral Oration, the first speech after the war has begun, faces the rhetorical challenge of making acceptable the inevitable failure (in the terms in which Pericles at first presented it) of the Athenian principle of chremata. In war men must use, and lose, their *somata* (bodies) (2.43.2) as well as their chremata. The conventions of the epitaphios are admirably suited to the necessary change in emphasis, since such a speech had traditionally called for praise of the city. In this way Pericles found it possible to set forth the primacy of the polis as the grounds for self-sacrifice, as he later sets forth the same grounds for sacrifice of

chremata (2.62.2–3). The optimism of the first speech
and of the speech in *oratio obliqua* is controverted in a
strict demand for the subordination of the individual to
the city.[13] The fallen soldiers "knew their duty" (*ta deonta*)
(2.43.1).

In the Funeral Oration Pericles implicitly recognizes
that power rests ultimately not with man as technician
and planner but with man as mortal and citizen. Here
one detects an unexpected kinship with the thought of
Solon. But man's mortality, which in Solon's thought is
the same as frailty and abjectness, becomes paradoxically
in the Funeral Oration his greatness, since dedication to
the polis is a redemption of individual limitations. The
city can be the author of such a redemption only when
the citizen is free (2.37.2) to do otherwise but sets the
city's ends above his own, since the city is the embodiment
of his own character (2.41.2); and in the preservation of
the city he finds his own immortality. The universality of
Athenian power and fame assures individual bravery of
immortality (2.43.2–3; with πᾶσα γῆ cf. 2.41.4 πᾶσαν . . .
θάλασσαν καὶ γῆν and 2.38.2 ἐκ πάσης γῆς τὰ πάντα).

But there underlies this difference between Solon and
Pericles a more fundamental similarity, in that Pericles in
the Funeral Oration tacitly recognizes that man as mortal
and man as citizen are really one and the same, whereas
the first speech and the speech in *oratio obliqua,* with their
proud rationalism, surely implied that Athenian policy
had gone a step beyond the old-fashioned, Spartan risk
of life (1.141.5; cf. 1.123.1). The occasions of the two

13. Cf. Flashar, *Der Epitaphios,* p. 31.

latter speeches are loss of life. In the last speech, Pericles is forced to state a moral principle of endurance (φέρειν χρὴ κτλ. 2.64.2) that utterly controverts the prooemium to the first speech, where even the possibility of reversals was conceived of in terms of an active, not a passive, response (n.b. βοηθεῖν 1.140.1). The implications for Thucydides' interpretation of Pericles are profound. "If even the wisest and most disinterested leader had not foreseen the epidemic that would attend the crowding of the population within the walls and if what was to be his famous Thucydidean attribute of *prognosis* had proved incomplete, what final trust could be placed in human foresight?"[14] Thucydides himself, though he does not raise the question in so many words, implies even in his undeniably laudatory (and perhaps apologetic) portrait of Pericles that it was a question for him, too.[15]

Even the career of Pericles might, then, be taken as an expression of the interaction of gnome or techne and tyche, of their mutual limitations, which Thucydides found everywhere. The work of Luschnat, de Romilly, Aron, and Stahl have made it sufficiently clear that Thucydides designed the *History* in such a way as to bring out the relation of plans and events.[16] But these studies did not solve the problem of Thucydides' own position. Thus those who agree on the fundamental design dis-

14. J. H. Finley, Jr., "Politics and Early Greek Tragedy," *HSCP* 71 (1966), 10.

15. Cf. Herter, *Thukydides*, pp. 268–269; Flashar, *Der Epitaphios*, pp. 42–43.

16. Luschnat, *Die Feldherrnreden;* de Romilly, *Histoire et raison;* Aron, *Dimensions;* Stahl, *Thukydides.* See also V. J. Hunter, "Thucydides and the Historical Facts," *CJ* 67 (1971), 14–19.

agree as to whether Thucydides was a pessimist or an optimist.[17] Those who place more emphasis on Thucydides' methodology and his admiration for the rational Pericles will conclude that Thucydides was an optimist. Those who amass examples of rational plans that miscarried and irrational plans that succeeded will conclude that he was a pessimist. Both approaches take the half for the whole. Thucydides is neither Euripides nor Plato. His world is not simply casual, with everything turning out contrary to expectation, as in the late plays of Euripides, nor is it perfectly orderly and logical but therefore problematically related to practical life. *To saphes* emerges from the events, no matter how contrary they may be to the principles guiding the narrative; the rationalism of Thucydides is undismayed. "It is reason itself which recognizes that chance, contradiction and appearance, has its sphere, *though a limited one,* and its right, but does not bother to settle contradictions of this sort . . ."[18] The *History,* however, has not reached, but only points to, the distinction between the theoretical and

17. For Thucydides the pessimist, see especially Stahl, *Thukydides;* H. Strasburger, *Die Wesensbestimmung der Geschichte durch die antike Geschichtsschreibung* (Wiesbaden, 1966), p. 23. For Thucydides the optimist, see Herter, *Thukydides,* pp. 280–281, against Stahl, and de Romilly, "L'optimisme de Thucydide et le jugement de l'historien sur Périclès," *REG* 78 (1965), 557ff.

18. "Die Vernunft ist es selbst, welche anerkennt, dass die Zufälligkeit, der Widerspruch und Schein ihre, *aber beschränkte* Sphäre und Recht hat und sich nicht bemüht, dergleichen Widersprüche ins Gleiche und Gerechte zu bringen . . . " G. W. F. Hegel, *Grundlinien der Philosophie des Rechts oder Naturrecht und Staatswissenschaft im Grundrisse,* ed. E. Moldenhauer and K. M. Michel (Frankfurt, 1970), sec. 214.

the active life which Socrates was elaborating and to some degree personifying even as the Peloponnesian War went on. With all his rationalism, Thucydides is equally on the side of the active life, no matter what its disappointments, and in the active life the prize is not truth, though there may be truth, but immortality (1.22.4; cf. 2.41.4, 43.2).

Appendix, Works Cited, and Index

Appendix

Interpretation of 2.42.4

Gomme has summarized and criticized previous interpretations and has given his own, which, however, has the disadvantage of requiring alteration of the text. The present interpretation differs from all the preceding in establishing the semantics of one key term (δέος) before determining the syntax of the clause in which it appears. This procedure has been prompted by the evident inadequacy of all previous interpretations, which have differed from one another mainly in the determination of the phraseology.[1] On the basis of the semantics of *deos* to be suggested, the last clause of 2.42.4 can be construed so as to satisfy both the stylistic requirements of the immediate context, that this clause provide a climax to the five preceding antitheses of the period and do so in a rhythmically effective fashion, and also the rhetorical requirements of the broader context of the *laudatio funebris:* namely, that this clause be epaenetic, that it be consolatory, and that it express a thought consonant with

1. With the exception of L. Pearson, *AJP* 64 (1943), 399–404. Cf. Gomme, II, 135.

the Thucydidean Pericles' concept of the polis as it emerges not only in the Funeral Oration but also in his other speeches.

All preceding interpretations of this passage have taken deos to mean "fear," apprehension in the face of danger. But in several places in Greek literature in which military bravery and civic duty are the subjects, deos has the positive meaning of "shame." This positive meaning emerges from the association of deos in these places with *aidos* or *aischyne*. The most striking of these places is Sophocles, *Ajax* 1073–80:

οὐ γάρ ποτ᾽ οὔτ᾽ ἂν ἐν πόλει νόμοι καλῶς
φέροιντ᾽ ἄν, ἔνθα μὴ καθεστήκῃ δέος,
οὔτ᾽ ἂν στρατός γε σωφρόνως ἄρχοιτ᾽ ἔτι,
μηδὲν φόβου πρόβλημα μηδ᾽ αἰδοῦς ἔχων . . .
δέος γὰρ ᾧ πρόσεστιν αἰσχύνη θ᾽ ὁμοῦ,
σωτηρίαν ἔχοντα τόνδ᾽ ἐπίστασο.

Deos supports military and civic virtue. For the same notion of deos as a source of civic virtue one can compare Hdt. 7.104; Aesch.*Eum.* 520–528, 693–709 (esp. 702); Pl. *Rep.* 465a11 and context. For deos as a source of military virtue, see *Il.* 15.656–658 (cf. Archidamus' use of δείδω in a positive sense of an army: 2.11.4; Thucydides once uses this verb in this sense of Athenian generals: 1.49). In fact, the connection of deos and aidos is formulaic in Homer. This connection occurs once apropos of religious feeling (*Hymn Dem.* 190); but thrice these words are used by humans of humans (Odysseus to Alcinous, 7.305; Eumaeus to Odysseus, of his master, 17.188; Hermes, whom Priam takes to be a mortal, to Priam, 24.435). ἵνα γὰρ δέος ἔνθα καὶ αἰδώς (Epicharmus, fr. 221K) was probably proverbial in the fifth century. The same expression appears in a pair of hexameters quoted by Socrates in *Euthyphro* 12a (schol. Soph. *Ajax* 1074, quoted above, assigns these lines to the *Cypria*). Cf. Hdt. 3.27.3; Pl. *Phaedr.* 250e5, 254e9. Pericles is using deos in 2.42.4 in just the same sense in which he has already used this term previously in the Funeral Oration, the sense of "proper fear," as Gomme translated the word in his note on that place (2.37.3).[2]

If this is the correct sense of deos in 2.42.4, one might wonder why it has not occurred to any of the commentators. Probably the reason is that Pericles is speaking of men who died on the battlefield, and in this context deos seems as if it ought to mean "fear of the enemy." But throughout this long sentence Pericles has in mind not the actual scene of their death nor even their deeds as such, but rather the choice preceding the deeds, the moral disposition of these men: thus the various words describing mental action: τιμωρίαν . . . ποθεινοτέραν λαβόντες; νομίσαντες; ἐβουλήθησαν; ἀξιοῦντες; ἡγησάμενοι. And when Pericles draws a lesson from these observations for posterity, he speaks of the *dianoia* of the fallen soldiers (2.43.1). The focus on the spirit rather than the fact in this portion of the Funeral Oration epitomizes the speech as a whole, which concentrates not on the deeds of the ancestors nor on the material acquisitions of the city, but on the ways of the people and the quality of the Athenian constitution and character.

2. Gomme, II, 112. Concerning fear as a virtue, cf. *The New York Times,* July 29, 1972, p. 29, of the trainees at the Marine base on Parris Island, S.C.: "Their 11-week course, emphasizing physical toughness, *unquestioning obedience and fear,* is planned to shock them out of civilian patterns and mould them into disciplined fighting machines" (my italics).

Appendix

Deos in the sense of "proper fear" or "shame"—that is, a fear of disgracing oneself in the eyes of one's fellows—is required in 2.42.2 in order to remove what was always the main obstacle to a satisfactory interpretation of the last clause: namely, the awkward contrast between deos and *doxa* drawn by what seemed to be the only two possibilities of the syntax. One of these possibilities, followed by most commentators, is to construe the genitives δόξης and δέους as depending upon ἀκμῆ and to take ἀπηλλάγησαν as absolute: "at the peak of their fame rather than the peak of their fear, they were taken away."[3] The

3. So. J. Classen, *Thukydides* (Berlin, 1879), II, 71: "'da ihre Seele nicht von Furcht, sondern im höchsten Grade (ἀκμῆ) von dem Gedanken des zu erringenden Ruhmes erfüllt war'." Classen remarks—quizzically?—: "Beide Genetive hängen grammatisch von ἀκμῆ ab, doch hat dieser Ausdruck nur für den ersteren (δόξης) seine volle Bedeutung." For the most part, translators have followed Classen's interpretation. Rex Warner, *Thucydides: History of the Peloponnesian War* (Baltimore, 1954), p. 121: "and, in a small moment of time, the climax of their lives, a culmination of glory, not of fear, were swept away from us." E.-A. Bétant, *Histoire de la Guerre du Péloponèse de Thucydide* (Paris, 1869), p. 97: "et dans un rapide moment, ils sont sortis de la vie, au plus fort de la gloire, non à l'instant de la crainte." Bétant faced the difficulty later noted by Classen and translated ἀκμῆ in two different ways. C. F. Smith, *Thucydides* (Cambridge, Mass., and London, 1951), p. 335: "and in the brief instant ordained by fate, at the crowning moment not of fear but of glory, they passed away." Thomas Hobbes, *Thucydides: the Peloponnesian War*, ed. David Grene (Ann Arbor, 1959) I, 113: "and so in a moment, while fortune inclineth neither way, left their lives not in fear but in opinion of victory." Otto Regenbogen, *Thukydides Politische Reden* (Leipzig, 1949), p. 121: "und im kurzen Augenblick der Entscheidung wurden sie auf der Höhe des Ruhmes mehr als der Angst, der Macht des blinden Ungefährs enthroben." Regenbogen's is one of only two translations I have encountered which take τύχης as governed by the verb—which I believe is the correct interpretation. Regenbogen is like the others, however, in his understanding of the

objection to this interpretation is that it leaves the obscure phrase δι᾽ ἐλαχίστου καιροῦ τύχης—what is the point of tyche here?—and a rhetorical infelicity that Gomme described as follows: "It is a very poor compliment to a man who has chosen to stand against the enemy, who trusts to his own valour in the moment of fighting, who prefers death to surrender and has 'run away from τὸ αἰσχρὸν τοῦ λόγου', to say that he was not at the extreme point of fear when he died."[4]

The other possibility is to construe τύχης with ἀκμῇ and

---

phrase involving *deos* and *doxa*. Flashar, *Der Epitaphios*, p. 29, n. 59, follows Regenbogen. Flashar records and rejects Schadewalt's translation of δέος as *Ehre*. J. H. Oliver, in a review of Kakridis, *Der thuk. Epitaphios, AJP* 85 (1964), 107, construes τύχης as governed both by δόξης and δέους and also by the verb, and translates: "and in a very brief moment of time, simultaneously at a peak of their expectation rather than their fear of fortune, they were quit of her." It is doubtful, however, that τύχης could fill the two syntactical roles assigned it by Oliver. Oliver's interpretation of τύχης through δέους as a single phrase goes back to Classen-Steup, *Thukydides*,[5] II (Berlin, 1914), 114–115. Steup, including καιροῦ in this phrase, translates: " 'mit dem höchsten Grade nicht sowohl der Befürchtung als der Erwartung eines entscheidenden Eingreifens des Geschicks'. " (Steup sees that the verb must then be absolute.) Whether *kairou* is included in the phrase (Steup) or not (Oliver), there are two objections to this interpretation. First, tyche without further specification would not have the precisely negative meaning required, since one's expectations of tyche may be optimistic (3.45.6; 4.18.3 and 5.73.3, 86.6). Second, what is the point of saying that they were *at the peak* of their expectations rather than their fear," i.e., rather than at the peak of their fear? The phrase ἅμα ἀκμῇ becomes otiose. Furthermore, as I have shown in the text of this study, the whole sentence is built on a single, main antithesis which is stated in various ways, and the function of the key terms of the final clause is to sum up the various statements of the main antithesis. This these terms cannot do in Oliver's and Steup's interpretation.

4. Gomme, II, 134.

to take δόξης and δέους as depending on ἀπηλλάγησαν.[5] This interpretation leaves the still greater rhetorical infelicity of brave men quit of glory but not of fear. And again there is a difficult phrase involving tyche. Furthermore, "ἀπαλλαγῆναι is consistently used with a genitive by Thucydides in the sense 'get quit of' something undesirable,"[6] so that one would not expect this verb to govern *doxas.*

But if deos is a virtue, as the semantics of the word clearly allow, then the contrast of deos and doxa, also something positive, is dissolved and a more appropriate contrast with tyche emerges. The two genitives, τύχης and δέους, depend upon the verb ἀπηλλάγησαν, and thus the meaning of the verb as Thucydides consistently uses it is also salvaged. The meaning of the clause is : "they were freed from tyche [i.e., the whims of fortune] rather than from proper fear [i.e., their sense of duty]." In effect, Pericles praises the fallen soldiers for the bravery that was the result of their deos. For as Plutarch said (*Cleom.* 9): τὴν ἀνδρείαν δέ μοι δοκοῦσιν οὐκ ἀφοβίαν ἀλλὰ φόβον ψόγου καὶ δέος ἀδοξίας οἱ παλαιοὶ νομίζειν. It is precisely this

5. So [Crawley], *The Complete Writings of Thucydides: The Peloponnesian War* (New York, 1951), p. 107: "And after one brief moment, while at the summit of their fortune, escaped, not from their fear, but from their glory." H. M. Wilkins, *Speeches from Thucydides Translated into English* (London, 1873), p. 73: "and, in a moment, at the very crisis of victory, were carried away from a scene, not of terror, but of glory." B. Jowett, *Thucydides Translated into English* (Oxford, 1881), p. 121: "and in an instant, at the height of their fortune, they passed away from the scene, not of their fear, but of their glory." In a footnote, Jowett adds: "Or, taking τύχης with καιροῦ: 'while for a moment they were in the hands of fortune, at the height, not of terror but of glory, they passed away'."

6. Gomme, II, 134; L. Pearson, *AJP* 64 (1943), 401.

deos adoxias in the Athenian soldiers, this "proper fear" of losing face, which Pericles is praising, and that is why they reached a peak of doxa in retaining their deos. The clause under discussion proves, then, to be fittingly epaenetic.

Now that tyche depends upon the verb, and not, as was usually thought, on *kairou*, it is possible to see the meaning of the phrase δι᾽ ἐλαχίστου καιροῦ. The phrase is consolatory. Death was instantaneous. As Pericles later says, ἀναίσθητος θάνατος (2.43.6).[7] In δι᾽ ἐλαχίστου καιροῦ, Pericles has put in the superlative degree the thought of Euripides, *Helen*, 302: [σμικρὸν δ᾽ ὁ καιρὸς σάρκ᾽ ἀπαλλάξαι βίου]. "A brief thing is the moment in which to free the flesh from life." One notes in passing that Pericles, partly no doubt for the sake of consolation, has varied the familiar βίου ἀπαλλάσσεσθαι[8] so that the fallen soldiers are freed of something unpleasant.

The present interpretation of the last clause of 2.42.4 also demonstrates that this clause provides a rhythmically effective and a logical climax to the five preceding antitheses of this long sentence. ἅμα ἀκμῇ τῆς δόξης,

7. LSJ translate *anaisthetos* "unfelt," but their entry suggests that the active sense was much more common, as one would expect (cf. Smyth, *Greek Grammar*, sec. 472b). This sense of *anaisthetos* finds a close parallel in Epicurus, *K.D.* II: ὁ θάνατος οὐδὲν πρὸς ἡμᾶς· τὸ γὰρ διαλυθὲν ἀναισθητεῖ· τὸ δ᾽ ἀναισθητοῦν οὐδὲν πρὸς ἡμᾶς. Epicurus' borrowings from Democritus are well known. Much of Epicurus' physical doctrine comes from Democritus. Their views of death were similar (W. K. C. Guthrie, *A History*, II, 434–435). P. von der Mühll, "Epikurs Κύριαι Δόξαι und Demokrit," *Festgabe Adolf Kaegi* (Frauenfeld, 1919), pp. 172–178, has shown similarities in literary form, style, and content between the *Kuriai Doxai* and the ethical *Hypothekai* of Democritus. Perhaps in *anaisthetos* we have a Democritean allusion in the Funeral Oration.

8. LSJ s.v. ἀπαλ. B.II.2.

which means "at the peak of their reputation," forms a rough antithesis with the other prepositional phrase of the clause (δι' ἐλαχίστου καιροῦ)—the *briefest* moment of death as against the *highest* point of fame. At the same time the two prepositional phrases are rhythmically balanced, since each contains seven syllables. This use of syntactically and rhythmically corresponding units which are at the same time antithetical in sense is quite characteristic of the style of the Funeral Oration, as Kakridis has well shown in his commentary.[9]

Schematically, then, the structure of the clause is as follows: (A) prepositional phrase—(B) genitive governed by verb—(A) prepositional phrase—(B) genitive governed by verb. There is balance and antithesis not only between the A elements but also between the B elements. The latter are in balance as parisyllabics and paroxytones. But here there is a slight inconcinnity in that δέους has the definite article while τύχης does not. As regards meaning, there is no reason to be disturbed by the absence of the definite article. Of thirty-three examples of tyche in the singular in Thucydides, eighteen have the definite article and fifteen do not. The definite article with tyche is either particular or generic, depending upon the context.[10] What Smyth observed of the generic article is true of Thucydides' treatment of the generic article with tyche: "The generic article is frequently omitted, especially with abstracts . . . , without

9. Kakridis, *Der thuk. Epitaphios*, pp. 43–45.
10. τῇ τύχῃ ἐλπίσας (3.97.2) is a good example of the particular definite article with tyche. Smyth, *Greek Grammar*, sec. 1517, translates this phrase: "confident by reason of his good fortune."

appreciable difference in meaning."[11] One example will illustrate this point very clearly. Nicias describes himself as ἐλάχιστα τῇ τύχῃ παραδοὺς ἐμαυτόν (6.23.3). Here Nicias echoes a clause from the description of Nicias already given by Thucydides: ὅστις ἐλάχιστα τύχῃ αὐτὸν παραδίδωσι (5.16.1). The occurrence of the definite article in one place but not in the other is a matter of indifference. The absence of the definite article in 2.42.4 is, then, no cause for alarm.

It might be objected against the present interpretation that the definite article with δόξης still causes the reader to contrast this word with τοῦ δέους. But it is precisely the reader, with his visual approach to the text, whose interpretation will go astray. The speaking voice could easily mark the phrases for a listening audience. As K. J. Dover said of another passage: "The hearer is more important than the reader; the spoken word can make quite clear what is parenthetic and what is not, and if we assume that Thucydides thought of what he wrote as sounds, not as marks on papyrus, we need not have recourse to the hypothesis . . . " etc.[12]

11. Smyth, *Greek Grammar*, sec. 1126.
12. K. J. Dover in Gomme, IV, 408.

Works Cited

Andrewes, A. "The Mytilene Debate," *Phoenix* 16 (1962), 64–85.

—— "Thucydides and the Persians," *Historia* 10 (1961), 1–18.

—— "Thucydides on the Causes of the War," *CQ* NS 9 (1959), 223–239.

Aron, Raymond. *Dimensions de la conscience historique.* Paris, 1961.

Barrett, W. S. *Euripides: Hippolytus.* Oxford, 1964.

Benardete, Scth. "The Aristeia of Diomedes and the Plot of the Iliad," ΑΓΩΝ No. 2 (1968), 10–38.

—— "χρή and δεῖ in Plato and Others," *Glotta* 43 (1965), 285–298.

Bender, G. F. *Der Begriff des Staatsmannes bei Thukydides.* Würzburg, 1938.

Benveniste, Emil. *Le Vocabulaire des institutions Indo-Européenes.* Paris, 1969.

Berry, E. G. *The History and Development of the Concept of θεία μοῖρα and θεία τύχη down to and including Plato.* Chicago, 1940.

Bill, C. P. "τὰ κοινὰ τοῦ πολέμου," *CP* 32 (1937), 160.

Bischoff, Heinrich. *Der Warner bei Herodot.* Marburg, 1932.

Bodin, Louis. "Thucydide I.84," in *Mélanges Desrousseaux* (Paris, 1937), 19–25.

Bowersock, Glen W. "The Personality of Thucydides," *The Antioch Review* 25 (1965), 135–146.

—— *Pseudo-Xenophon: Constitution of the Athenians.* Cambridge, Mass., and London, 1968.

Bowra, Sir Maurice. *Early Greek Elegists.* Cambridge, Mass., 1938.

—— *Sophoclean Tragedy.* Oxford, 1944.

Bradeen, D. W. "The Popularity of the Athenian Empire," *Historia* 9 (1960), 257–269.

Browne, G. M., and Koenen, Ludwig. "Zu der griechischen-koptischen Rezension der Menandersentenzen," *ZPE* 8 (1971), 105–108.

Bruns, Ivo. *Das Literarische Porträt der Griechen.* Berlin, 1898.

Buriks, A. A. περὶ τύχης: *De ontwikkeling van het begrip tyche tot ann de Romeinse tijd, hoofdzakelijk in de philosophie.* Leiden, n.d.

Busch, Gerda. *Untersuchungen zum Wesen der* τύχη *in den Tragödien des Euripides.* Heidelberg, 1937.

Camerer, L. *Praktische Klugheit bei Herodot: Untersuchungen zu den Begriffen* μηχανή, τέχνη, σοφία. Cologne, 1965.

Chambers, Mortimer. "Studies on Thucydides," *CW* 62 (1969), 245–254.

Chroust, A. -H. "Treason and Patriotism in Ancient Greece," *Journal of the History of Ideas* 15 (1954), 280–288.

Cochrane, C. N. *Thucydides and the Science of History.* Oxford, 1929.

Cole, Thomas. *Democritus and the Sources of Greek Anthropology.* 1967.

Cornford, Francis. *From Religion to Philosophy.* London, 1912.

—— *Thucydides Mythistoricus.* London, 1965.

—— *The Unwritten Philosophy and Other Essays.* Cambridge, 1950.

Denniston, J. D. *The Greek Particles*[2]. Oxford, 1959.

Deubner, Ludwig. "Personifikation," in W. H. Roscher, *Ausführliches Lexikon der griechischen und römischen Mythologie* (Leipzig 1916–1924). V, 2142–45 (on Tyche).

Diels, Hermann, and Walther Kranz. *Die Fragmente der Vorsokratiker*[11]. Zurich and Berlin, 1964.

Diller, Hans. "Freiheit bei Thukydides als Schlagwort und als Wirklichkeit," *Gymn.* 69 (1962), 189–204.

Dodds, E. R. *Euripides: Bacchae.* Oxford, 1960.

—— *Plato: Gorgias.* Oxford, 1959.

Donini, Guido. "The Attitude of Thucydides to the Government of the Five Thousand." Unpub. diss., Harvard University, 1966.

—— *La Posizione di Tucidide verso il governo dei cinquemilia.* Turin, 1969.

—— "Thuc. 7,42,3: Does Thucydides Agree with Demosthenes' View?," *Hermes* 92 (1964), 116–119.

Dumézil, George. *L'Idéologie tripartite des Indo-Européens.* Brussels, 1958.

Edmunds, Lowell. "Necessity, Chance, and Freedom in the Early Atomists," *Phoenix* 26 (1972), 342–357.

Works Cited

Ehrenberg, Victor. "Polypragmosyne: A Study in Greek Politics," *JHS* 67 (1947), 46–67.

——— *Sophocles and Pericles.* Oxford, 1954.

Erfa, C. E. von "αἰδώς und verwandte Begriffe in ihrer Entwicklung von Homer bis Demokrit," *Philologus* Supp. 30 (1937).

Ferguson, W. S. *The Treasurers of Athena.* Cambridge, Mass., 1932.

Finley, John H., Jr. "Politics and Early Greek Tragedy," *HSCP* 71 (1966), 1–13.

——— *Three Essays on Thucydides.* Cambridge, Mass., 1967.

——— *Thucydides.* Cambridge, Mass., 1942.

Flashar, Hellmut. *Der Epitaphios des Perikles: Seine Funktion im Geschichtswerk des Thukydides* (Sitzungsberichte der Heidelberger Akademie der Wissentschaft, Philologische-Historische Klasse, 1969, 1). Heidelberg, 1969.

Freeman, Kathleen. *Ancilla to the Pre-Socratic Philosophers.* Cambridge, Mass., 1948.

——— *The Work and Life of Solon with a Translation of His Poems.* Cardiff, 1926.

Frischauer, Willi. *Onassis.* New York, 1968.

Fritz, Kurt von. *Die Griechische Geschichtsschreibung*, vol. I. Berlin, 1967.

Fuhrmann, Manfred. *Anaximenis Ars Rhetorica.* Berlin, 1966.

Gardiner, Tudor. "Terms for Power in Thucydides." Unpub. diss., Harvard University, 1968.

Gildersleeve, B. L. "Brief Mention," *AJP* 33 (1912), 239–240; repr. in *Selections from the Brief Mention of*

Basil Lanneau Gildersleeve, ed. C. W. E. Miller (Baltimore: Johns Hopkins Press, 1930), 256.

Gomme, A. W. "Four Passages in Thucydides," *JHS* 71 (1951), 70–80.

—— "The Interpretation of καλοὶ κἀγαθοί in Thucydides 4.40.2," *CQ* NS 3 (1953), 65–68.

—— "Thucydides Notes," *CQ* 42 (1948), 10–14.

Gomperz, Theodor. *Die Apologie der Heilkunst*. Leipzig, 1910.

Grosskinsky, August. *Das Programm des Thukydides*. Berlin, 1936.

Guthrie, W. K. C. *A History of Greek Philosophy*, vols. II–III. Cambridge, 1965.

Hegel, G. W. F. *Grundlinien der Philosophie des Rechts oder Naturrecht und Staatswissenschaft im Grundrisse*, ed. E. Moldenhauer and K. M. Michel. Frankfurt, 1970.

—— *Lectures on the History of Philosophy*, I, trans. E. S. Haldane. London, 1892.

—— *The Philosophy of History*, trans. J. Sibree. New York, 1944.

Heinimann, Felix. "Ein vorplatonische Theorie der τέχνη," *MH* 18 (1961), 105–130.

Herter, Hans. "Freiheit und Gebundenheit des Staatsmannes bei Thukydides," *RM* 93 (1950), 133–153; repr. in *Thukydides* (Wege der Forschung XCVIII. Darmstadt, 1968), 260–281.

—— *Glück und Verhängnis. Über die altgriechische Tyche. Hellas* (Bonn) IV, 1–2 (1963), 1–16.

—— "Das Königsritual der Atlantis," *RM* 109 (1966), 236–259.

—— "Theseus der Athener," *RM* 88 (1939), 311–322.

———, ed. *Thukydides* (Wege der Forschung XCVIII). Darmstadt, 1968.

——— "Zur ersten Periklesrede des Thukydides," in *Studies Presented to D. M. Robinson,* II, ed. G. E. Mylonas and Doris Raymond (St. Louis, 1953), 613–623.

Herzog-Hauser, Gertrud. "Tyche," in *RE* 14, 1643–89.

How, W. W., and J. Wells. *A Commentary on Herodotus.* Oxford, 1928.

Huart, Pierre. *Le Vocabulaire de l'analyse psychologique dans l'oeuvre de Thucydide.* Paris, 1968.

Hunter, V. J. "Thucydides and the Historical Facts," *CJ* 67 (1971), 14–19.

Immerwahr, H. R. "Aspects of Historical Causation in Herodotus," *TAPA* 87 (1956), 241–280.

——— "*Ergon:* History as Monument in Herodotus and Thucydides," *AJP* 81 (1960), 261–290.

——— *Form and Thought in Herodotus.* Cleveland, 1966.

——— "Historical Action in Herodotus," *TAPA* 85 (1954), 16–45.

Jaeger, Werner. *Aristotle: Fundamentals of the History of His Development²,* trans. Richard Robinson. Oxford, 1950.

——— *Paideia: The Ideals of Greek Culture,* trans. Gilbert Highet. Oxford, 1946.

——— *The Theology of the Early Greek Philosophers.* Oxford, 1967.

Jones, A. H. M. "Athenian Democracy and Its Critics," *The Cambridge Historical Journal* 11 (1952), 1–26.

Kagan, Donald. *The Great Dialogue.* New York, 1965.

Kern, Otto. *Die Religion der Griechen,* vol. III. Berlin, 1938.

Knox, B. M. W. *Oedipus at Thebes*. London and New Haven, 1957.

Lesky, Albin. *A History of Greek Literature*, trans. James Willis and Cornelis de Heer. New York, 1966.

——— *Thalatta*. Vienna, 1947.

Luschnat, Otto. *Die Feldherrnreden im Geschichtswerk des Thukydides. Philol.* Supp. 34 (1942).

——— "Thukydides," in *RE* Supp. 12 (1971), 1085–1354.

Luther, Wilhelm. *"Wahrheit" und "Lüge" im Ältesten Griechentum*. Leipzig, 1935.

Meillet, Antoine, and Joseph Vendryes. *Traité de grammaire comparée des langues classiques*. Paris: H. Champion, 1963.

Meyer, G. *Laudes Inopiae*. Göttingen, 1915.

Momigliano, A. D. *Studies in Historiography*. New York and Evanston, 1966.

Mossé, Claude. "Armée et cité grecque," *REA* 65 (1963), 290–297.

Mugler, Charles. "Sur la méthode de Thucydide," *Lettres d'humanité* 10 (1951), 20–51.

Mühll, Peter von der. "Epikurs κύριαι δόξαι und Demokrit," in *Festgabe Adolf Kaegi* (Frauenfeld, 1919), 172–178.

Müri, Walter. "Beitrag zum Verständnis des Thukydides," *MH* 4 (1947), 251–275.

Murray, H. A. "Two Notes on the Evaluation of Nicias in Thucydides," *BICS* No. 8 (1961), 33–46.

Neil, R. A. *Aristophanes: Knights*. Cambridge, 1901.

Nietzsche, Friedrich. *The Genealogy of Morals*, trans. F. Golffing. New York, 1965.

——— *Werke*, vol. II, ed. K. Schlechta. Munich, 1966.

Works Cited

Nilsson, Martin. *Geschichte der griechischen Religion²*, vol. II. Munich, 1961.

North, Helen. *Sophrosyne: Self-Knowledge and Self-Restraint in Greek Literature*. Ithaca, N.Y., 1966.

Oliver, J. H. Review of J. Kakridis, *Der thukydideische Epitaphios*, in *AJP* 85 (1964), 105–107.

Page, D. L. *Poetae Melici Graeci*. Oxford, 1962.

Parry, A. M. "λόγος and ἔργον in Thucydides." Unpub. diss., Harvard University, 1957.

––––––– "The Language of Thucydides' Description of the Plague," *BICS* No. 16 (1969), 106–118.

––––––– "Thucydides' Use of Abstract Language," *Yale French Studies* No. 45 (1970), 3–20.

Patzer, Harald. *Das Problem der Geschichtsschreibung des Thukydides und die thukydideische Frage*. Berlin, 1937.

Pearson, Lionel. "Prophasis and Aitia," *TAPA* 83 (1952), 205–223.

––––––– "Three Notes on the Funeral Oration of Pericles," *AJP* 64 (1943), 399–407.

Peremans, Willy. "Thucydide, Alcibiade et l'expedition de Sicile en 415 av. J.C.," *AC* 25 (1956), 340–344.

Pfohl, Gerhard. *Greek Poems on Stones*, vol. I. Leiden, 1967.

Plenio, W. "Die letzte Rede des Perikles." Unpub. diss., University of Kiel, 1954.

Pusey, N. M. "Alcibiades and τὸ φιλόπολι," *HSCP* 51 (1940), 215–231.

Quinn, T. J. "The Unpopularity of the Athenian Empire," *Historia* 13 (1964), 257–260.

Redard, Georges. *Recherches sur χρή, χρῆσθαι: Etude semantique*. Paris, 1953.

Robertson, Noel. "Tyche," in *The Oxford Classical Dictionary*[2] (1970), 1100–01.

Rokeah, David. *"Periousia chrematon:* Thucydides and Pericles," *RFIC* 91 (1963), 282f.

Romilly, Jacqueline de. "La Crainte dans l'oeuvre de Thucydide," *Classica et Mediaevalia* 17 (1956), 119–127.

—— *Histoire et raison chez Thucydide.* Paris, 1956.

—— "L'Optimisme de Thucydide et le jugement de l'historien sur Périclès," *REG* 78 (1965), 557–575.

—— "Le Pseudo-Xénophon et Thucydide: Etude sur quelques divergences de vues," *Rev. de Phil.* 36 (1962), 225–241.

—— *Thucydides and the Athenian Empire,* trans. P. Thody. Oxford, 1963.

—— "L'Utilité de l'histoire selon Thucydide," in *Histoire et historiens dans l'antiquité* (Entretien sur l'antiquité classique IV) (Vandoeuvres-Genève, 1956), 39–66.

Ros, Jan. *Die μεταβολή (Variatio) als Stilprinzip des Thukydides.* Vienna, 1938.

Ruhl, L. "Tyche," in W. H. Roscher, *Ausführliches Lexicon der griechischen und römischen Mythologie* (Leipzig, 1916–1924). V, 1309–57.

Schachermeyer, Fritz. *Religionspolitik und Religiosität bei Perikles.* Vienna, 1968.

Schaerer, René. ἐπιστήμη et τέχνη. *Etude sur les notions de connaissance et d'art d'Homère à Platon.* Lausanne, 1930.

Schäublin, Christoph. "Wieder einmal πρόφασις," *MH* 28 (1971), 133–144.

Schmid-Stählin. *Geschichte der griechischen Literatur.* Parts I (5 vols.) and II. Munich, 1929–1948.

Schüller, S. "About Thucydides' Use of αἰτία and πρόφασις," *Revue Belge* 34 (1956), 971–984.

Schulz, H. -J. "Zu Thukydides 3, 30, 4," *Hermes* (1957), 255–256.

Schwartz, Eduard. Review of F. Taeger, *Thukydides* (Stuttgart, 1925), in *Gnomon* 2 (1926), 65–82.

Sealey, R. "Thucydides, Herodotus, and the Causes of the War," *CQ* NS 7 (1957), 1–12.

Seaton, R. C. "On Thucydides IV.18, 4," *CR* 14 (1900), 223–224.

Smyth, H. W. *Greek Grammar.* Cambridge, 1959.

Snell, Bruno. *Die Ausdrücke für den Begriff des Wissens in der vorplatonischen Philosophie.* Berlin, 1924.

—— *The Discovery of the Mind,* trans. T. G. Rosenmeyer. Cambridge, Mass., 1953.

—— *Scenes from Greek Drama.* Berkeley and Los Angeles, 1964.

Stahl, H. -P. *Thukydides: Die Stellung des Menschen im geschichtlichen Prozess (Zetemata* 40). Munich, 1966.

Stanford, W. B. *Sophocles: Ajax.* London, 1963.

Ste.-Croix, G. E. M. "The Character of the Athenian Empire," *Historia* 3 (1954–55), 1–41.

Stenzel, Julius. Review of F. Taeger, *Thukydides* (Stuttgart, 1925), in *Göttingische gelehrte Anzeigen* 7–8 (1926), 193–206.

Sternbach, Leo. *Gnomologium Vaticanum e Codice Vaticano Graeco* 743. Berlin, 1963.

Strasburger, Herman. "Die Entdeckung der politischen Geschichte durch Thukydides," *Saeculum* 5 (1954), 395–428; repr. in Hans Herter, ed., *Thukydides*

Works Cited

(Wege der Forschung XCVIII. Darmstadt, 1968), 412–476.

——— *Die Wesensbestimmung der Geschichte durch die antike Geschichtsschreibung.* Wiesbaden, 1966.

Strauss, Leo. *The City and Man.* Chicago, 1963.

Strohm, Hans. *Tyche: Zur Schicksalsauffassung bei Pindar und den frühgriechischen Dichtern.* Stuttgart, 1944.

Syme, Sir Ronald. *Thucydides. Transactions of the British Academy,* vol. 48. Oxford: Oxford University Press, 1960.

Thucydidis Historiae. Ed. H. S. Jones. Critical apparatus corrected and amplified by J. E. Powell. 2 vols. Oxford, 1942. Repr. 1951, etc.

Thucydidis Historiae. After Hude ed. Otto Luschnat. Vol. I (Books I, II). Leipzig: Teubner, 1960.

Commentaries

Classen, Johannes. *Thukydides.* Berlin, 1879. Vol. II.

Classen, Johannes, and Julius Steup. *Thukydides.* 8 vols. Berlin. I (1919). II (1914). III (1892). IV (1900). V (1912). VI (1905). VII (1908). VIII (1922).

Dover, K. J. *Thucydides: Book VI.* Oxford: Oxford University Press, 1965.

——— *Thucydides: Book VII.* Oxford: Oxford University Press, 1965.

Gomme, A. W. *A Historical Commentary on Thucydides.* 3 vols. Oxford: Oxford University Press, 1956.

———, A. Andrewes, and K. J. Dover. *A Historical Commentary on Thucydides.* Oxford: Oxford University Press, 1970. Vol. IV.

Works Cited

Graves, C. E. *The Fifth Book of Thucydides*. London and New York, 1891.

Kakridis, Johannes. *Der thukydideische Epitaphios: ein stilistischer Kommentar (Zetemata 26)*. Munich, 1961.

Lamberton, W. A. *Thucydides: Books II and III*. New York, 1905.

Translations

Bétant, E.-A. *Histoire de la Guerre du Péloponèse de Thucydide*. Paris, 1869.

Crawley, R. *The Complete Writings of Thucydides: The Peloponnesian War*. New York: Random House, The Modern Library, 1951.

Hobbes, Thomas. *Thucydides: The Peloponnesian War*, ed. David Grene. 2 vols. Ann Arbor, 1959.

Jowett, Benjamin. *Thucydides Translated into English*. Oxford, 1881.

Regenbogen, Otto. *Thukydides Politische Reden*. Leipzig, 1949.

Smith, C. F. *Thucydides*. Cambridge, Mass.: Harvard University Press, and London: Heinemann, The Loeb Classical Library, 1951.

Warner, Rex. *Thucydides: History of the Peloponnesian War*. Baltimore: Penguin Books, The Penguin Classics, 1954.

Wilkins, H. M. *Speeches from Thucydides Translated into English*. London, 1873.

Tompkins, Daniel P. "Stylistic Characterization in Thucydides: Nicias and Alcibiades," *YCS* 22 (1972), 181–214.

Topitsch, Ernst. "ἀνθρωπεία φύσις und Ethik bei

Works Cited

Thukydides," *Wiener Studien* 61–62 (1943–1947), 50–67.

Traywick, J. G. "θεοί and ἀγαθὴ τύχη in Headings of Attic Inscriptions." Unpub. diss., Harvard University, 1968.

Vernant, J.-P. "Remarques sur les formes et les limites de la pensée technique chez les Grecs," *Revue d'Histoire des Sciences* 10 (1957), 205–225; repr. in *Mythe et pensée chez les Grecs* (Paris, 1971), II, 44–64.

Vlastos, Gregory. "ἰσονομία πολιτική," in *Isonomia: Studien zur Gleichheitsvorstellung im griechischen Denken,* ed. J. Mau and E. G. Schmidt (Berlin, 1964), 1–35.

Vretska, Helmuth. "Perikles und die Heerschaft des Würdigsten," *RM* NS 109 (1966), 108f.

Wasserman, F. M. "The Melian Dialogue," *TAPA* 78 (1947), 18–36.

———"The Speeches of King Archidamus in Thucydides," *CJ* 78 (1953), 193–200.

———"The Voice of Sparta in Thucydides," *CJ* 59 (1964), 289–297.

Weidauer, Klaus. *Thukydides und die Hippokratischen Schriften.* Heidelberg, 1954.

Weiss, Helene. *Kausalität und Zufall in der Philosophie des Aristoteles.* Basel, 1942.

West, M. L. *Hesiod: Theogony.* Oxford, 1966.

Westlake, H. D. *Individuals in Thucydides.* Cambridge, 1968.

———"Nicias in Thucydides," *CQ* 35 (1941), 58–65.

Wheeler, J. R. "The Participial Construction with τυγχάνειν and κυρεῖν," *HSCP* 2 (1891), 143–157.

Wiener, Norbert. *The Human Use of Human Beings: Cybernetics and Society.* New York, 1967.

Wilamowitz-Moellendorf, Ulrich von. *Euripides Herakles.* Bad Homburg vor der Höhe, 1959.

———*Der Glaube der Hellenen,* vol. II. Basel, 1956.

Wössner, Walter. *Die synonymische Unterscheidung bei Thukydides und den politischen Rednern der Griechen.* Würzburg, 1937.

Zahn, Rose. *Die erste Periklesrede (Thukydides I* 140–144): Interpretation und Versuch einer Einordnung in den Zusammenhang des Werkes. Borna-Leipzig, 1934.

Zimmerman, Arnd. "Tyche bei Platon." Unpub. diss., University of Bonn, 1966.

An important bibliographical source is the unpublished manuscript by William C. West, III, "A Bibliography of Scholarship on the Speeches in Thucydides, 1873–1970."

Index

DATE DUE